SHAKESPEARE'S STYLES

SHAKESPEARE'S STYLES

Essays in honour of
Kenneth Muir

Edited by
Philip Edwards, Inga-Stina Ewbank and G. K. Hunter

CAMBRIDGE UNIVERSITY PRESS

CAMBRIDGE

LONDON · NEW YORK · NEW ROCHELLE
MELBOURNE · SYDNEY

Published by the Press Syndicate of the University of Cambridge
The Pitt Building, Trumpington Street, Cambridge CB2 1RP
32 East 57th Street, New York, NY 10022, USA
296 Beaconsfield Parade, Middle Park, Melbourne 3206, Australia

First published 1980

Printed in Great Britain at the
Alden Press, Oxford

Library of Congress Cataloguing in Publication Data
Main entry under title:
Shakespeare's styles.
Bibliography: p.
Includes index.
1. Shakespeare, William, 1564–1616 – Style – Addresses,
essays, lectures. 2. Muir, Kenneth. I. Muir, Kenneth.
II. Edwards, Philip. III. Ewbank, Inga-Stina.
IV. Hunter, G.K.
PR3072.S4   822.3'3   79-51226
ISBN 0 521 22764 X

CONTENTS

Preface   *page* vii

Rhetoric and insincerity
    L. C. KNIGHTS   I

Some aspects of style in the *Henry VI* plays
    WOLFGANG CLEMEN   9

Poem and context in *Love's Labour's Lost*
    G. K. HUNTER   25

The declaration of love
    PHILIP EDWARDS   39

Juliet's Nurse: the uses of inconsequentiality
    STANLEY WELLS   51

Language most shows a man. . .? Language and speaker in
Macbeth
    NICHOLAS BROOKE   67

Poetic language and dramatic significance in Shakespeare
    R. A. FOAKES   79

Feliciter audax: Antony and Cleopatra, I,i,1–24
    G. R. HIBBARD   95

'My name is Marina': the language of recognition
    INGA-STINA EWBANK   III

Leontes and the spider: language and speaker in Shakespeare's Last
Plays
    ANNE BARTON   131

Shakespeare's 'bombast'
    E. A. J. HONIGMANN   151

The defence of paradox
GEOFFREY BULLOUGH   163

'True, gallant Raleigh': some off-stage conversations in Shakespeare's plays
A. C. SPRAGUE   183

Shakespeare's recollections of Marlowe
M. C. BRADBROOK   191

Caliban as a Red Man
G. WILSON KNIGHT   205

Shakespeare's Dark Lady: a question of identity
S. SCHOENBAUM   221

Checklist of writings by Kenneth Muir, 1937–1979   241

Index   245

PREFACE

More than thirty years ago, Kenneth Muir published an essay on 'The Future of Shakespeare' (*Penguin New Writing*, summer 1946), in which he outlined what he saw as the likely directions and concerns of Shakespeare scholarship and criticism in the next few decades. Now that the 'future' of that essay has become the past, we can see his predictions as uncannily accurate. Most of the books and articles which he then described as needed have now been written – many of them, indeed, by himself. (The Checklist at the end of this volume speaks for itself of the range of his activities in Shakespearian study.) But there are omissions; and when colleagues who have been associated with Professor Muir during his long, fruitful and happily continuing career wished to honour his achievement, it seemed best to do so by trying to remedy one such omission. Hence the focus of this collection of essays is the question of 'Shakespeare's styles'. It is strange that the era of 'close reading' and 'practical criticism' has almost passed without any volume appearing which concerned itself exclusively with this question.

There are obvious reasons for the presence of the plural in the title. Whether we think of how Shakespeare's ways with language changed and developed between the *Henry VI* plays and *The Tempest*, or of how each of his plays, almost without exception, employs a variety of modes of expression, it becomes necessary to speak of his 'styles' rather than his 'style'. But beyond that we wished by our title to indicate some of the difficulty that lies in the way of 'practical criticism' of Shakespeare; for such is the variety of responses which Shakespeare's writing offers us that no single characterisation of his style will suffice. This very variousness may, of course, be considered an advantage. It was hoped that the volume could offer its readers a conspectus of the various ways in which Shakespeare's stylistic techniques may be discussed, of the variety of levels on which those techniques may be seen to operate, and above all of the interrelationships between his poetic power and his dramatic purpose.

The primary plan for the volume was that each contributor should take one or two passages and base his critical observations on the stylistic features appearing there. Essays of this kind form the bulk of those printed here. Some contributors have, however, preferred a greater degree of generalisation and have ranged more widely. The editors have arranged the volume so that the more narrowly focussed essays on style come first: the list of contents thus develops towards a greater degree of distance between the stylistic evidence and the critical generalisation. The essays based on specific passages are placed by chronological order of the plays from which passages have been chosen (following the E. K. Chambers order). It seemed more important that each contributor should write on passages and problems which particularly interested him or her than that a complete chronological survey should be attempted. But we hope that the variety of passages chosen for comment, the range of deductions made and the diversity of critical methods used will give the reader a sense of scope in the critical vocabularies that can be employed as well as an enhanced appreciation of key passages in the plays.

The untimely deaths of Ernest Schanzer, Clifford Leech and Terence Spencer have deprived the volume of the contributions which we had looked forward to receiving from them. Illness forced Michel Grivelet to set aside work on his essay. We are all of us the poorer for these losses.

The essays printed use the Peter Alexander text of Shakespeare (*The Complete Works*, London and Glasgow, 1951) as the norm (with the alteration of final -'d to -ed, and -ed to -èd). If another text is drawn on for a particular purpose, that fact is noted.

Philip Edwards
Inga-Stina Ewbank
G. K. Hunter

Rhetoric and insincerity

L. C. KNIGHTS

What, dost thou turn away, and hide thy face?
75 I am no loathsome leper – look on me.
What, art thou like the adder waxen deaf?
Be poisonous too, and kill thy forlorn Queen.
Is all thy comfort shut in Gloucester's tomb?
Why, then Dame Margaret was ne'er thy joy.
80 Erect his statue and worship it,
And make my image but an alehouse sign.
Was I for this nigh wrecked upon the sea,
And twice by awkward wind from England's bank
Drove back again unto my native clime?
85 What boded this but well-forewarning wind
Did seem to say 'Seek not a scorpion's nest,
Nor set no footing on this unkind shore'?
What did I then but cursed the gentle gusts,
And he that loosed them forth their brazen caves;
90 And bid them blow towards England's blessèd shore,
Or turn our stern upon a dreadful rock?
Yet Æolus would not be a murderer,
But left that hateful office unto thee.
The pretty-vaulting sea refused to drown me,
95 Knowing that thou wouldst have me drowned on shore
With tears as salt as sea through thy unkindness;
The splitting rocks cowered in the sinking sands
And would not dash me with their raggèd sides,
Because thy flinty heart, more hard than they,
100 Might in thy palace perish Margaret.   (*2 Henry VI*, III,ii,74–100)

In 1932 I wrote an essay for *The Criterion* on 'Education and the Drama in the Age of Shakespeare', in which I tried to show that far more of Shakespeare's audience were likely to have had some formal education than was then assumed, and that the methods of school and university education – reinforced by the many books on rhetoric and the arts of

speech – were likely to have influenced the approach to dramatic poetry
made by many of the original auditors. Today my essay seems to belong
to the pre-history of modern Shakespearian scholarship. Rather large
works by T. W. Baldwin, Sister Miriam Joseph, B. L. Joseph and Brian
Vickers – to name no others – have established beyond doubt the
importance of rhetoric in Elizabethan poetics; and it is commonplace that
Shakespeare was well versed in, and made effective use of, the rhetorical
training of the schools. His early plays make abundant, indeed osten-
tatious, use of the well-known tropes and figures. And although his
vigorous self-delighting verbal imagination could leap from the serious to
the satirical, as in *Love's Labour's Lost*, even the greatest poetry of his
later plays can be shown to have a rhetorical base. As Vickers puts it:
'Shakespeare's poetic language was nourished on rhetoric.'[1]

We should be grateful to the scholars who have established this,
though, as they are themselves aware, the really interesting questions
remain on our hands: one concerning the ways in which the greater poets
went beyond their rhetorical base, another concerning the ways in which
a knowledge of the common forms helped – or helps – a reader or auditor
to appreciate the poetry more fully. As regards the first, Vickers, referring
to some of his predecessors, speaks well of 'the development which they
trace from a stiff, "external", use of rhetorical forms to a supple and
flexible absorption of them', and he quotes an admirably succinct statement from Hardin Craig: 'In Shakespeare and his later contemporaries
rhetoric is so naturally employed as almost to escape notice. There is no
longer any creaking of the machine...."the art itself is nature"' (pp.
44–5). True: but there is still a tendency to obscure an important
question. Rhetoric was primarily an art of persuasion: its teachers
assumed that the speaker or writer already knew what he wanted to say:
rhetoric helped him to present his 'material' clearly and effectively.
Vickers speaks of 'a definite range of emotional and psychological effects'
associated with the figures; and he refers to 'the classical–medieval–
Renaissance concept of literary composition as being a deliberate process,
involving a plan, a definite aim, and a distinct range of emotional effects
on the audience' (pp. 12, 57). There is testimony from the poets of course
that they sometimes find what they want to 'say' by concentrating on
what they want to 'do', i.e. by concentrating, as craftsmen, on technique.
But it is the emergent meaning, a living power that can't be caught in the
conceptual net of 'a plan, a definite aim', that distinguishes the poets
whom we continue to read for profit and delight. This may be obscured

by too strenuous an advocacy of the – admitted – importance of rhetoric in the history of English poetry.[2]

As for the ways in which a knowledge of rhetoric helped the more learned auditors at, say, the Globe, to respond intelligently to the plays they saw, no one has yet improved on what Gladys Willcock and Alice Walker said in the Introduction to their edition of Puttenham's *The Arte of English Poesie*:

Poets who took so much trouble to follow Art would not wish this Art to be ignored in the reading and would expect their listeners, and still more their readers, to respond with aural and mental agility. The 'schemes' are nothing but the organisation of patterning; this patterning contented the ear like rhyme and the identification of the patterns was a delight to the instructed mind. Such a response to poetry was never vague or half-awake.[3]

There are, however, other ways of approaching poetry – ways that distinguish between the dead and the living – that are neither vague nor half-awake. At all events, I don't think it is only my lack of a classical grounding, or a constitutional inability to remember the difference between *auxesis, epanalepsis* and *epizeuxis,* that makes me wonder whether – or to what extent – the modern reader needs to be familiar with the tropes and figures taught in Elizabethan school-rooms.

I intrude these doubts, though I think them important, merely in passing. What I mainly want to do is to suggest that one of the ways in which Shakespeare used his knowledge of rhetoric has been ignored. He discovered this addition to his dramatic resources early, and continued to use it, though with increasing subtlety. In the first tetralogy of English History Plays it is easy to pick out examples of very many 'figures' used in the way the schoolmasters said they should be used.

> Dead life, blind sight, poor mortal living ghost,
> Woe's scene, world's shame, grave's due by life usurped,
> Brief abstract and record of tedious days,
> Rest thy unrest on England's lawful earth,
> Unlawfully made drunk with innocent blood.

This, from *Richard III*, iv,iv,26–30, is part of a long formal scene in which the Duchess of York, Queen Elizabeth and Queen Margaret lament their woes and accuse the monster, Richard: through emphatic rhetorical patterning Shakespeare leaves the spectators in no doubt of the shape of the plot or, for that matter, of the nature of his moral. Significantly, the episode ends, as Richard approaches, with the virtually technical, 'be copious in exclaims'.[4]

This is rhetoric used 'straight'. But turn to the passage printed under my title and something different comes into view. Margaret is here protesting against the grief of Henry VI at the death of his uncle, the Duke of Gloucester, to the neglect of his 'forlorn Queen'. The passage I have extracted starts with three rhetorical questions (ll. 74–8), all neatly balanced. Lines 80–1 use identical structure to emphasise the contrast of 'his' and 'my'. In lines 82–91 there are three more rhetorical questions, with corresponding structure, or *parison* ('Was I for this. . .?'; 'What boded this. . .?'; 'What did I then. . .?'), thick with alliteration, initial or medial – 'Plosives for the wind, gutturals for the rocks, and sibilants for the winds and waves', as the New Arden editor says, but also for more complicated effects: all this concluding with the end-of-line contrasts, 'brazen caves', 'blessèd shore' and 'dreadful rock'. In lines 94–6 the emphatic repetition of 'sea. . .sea', 'drown. . .drowned', whether or not we label it *ploce,* adds to the obvious attempt at pathos. The last few lines quoted return to alliterative s's, with *paronomasia* in the clinching 'heart. . .hard', 'palace perish'. The speech goes on for another twenty lines or so, including a classical comparison of the approved sort, with Margaret–Dido 'witched' by tales of Henry–Aeneas told her in France by Suffolk–Ascanius. She breaks off with, 'Ay me, I can no more!', which is not surprising after nearly fifty lines, but the device was well known to the rhetoricians.

Margaret, then, is skilled in rhetoric. She is also insincere. How do we know? Well, in this case we have the plot to guide us. In *1 Henry VI* Suffolk had declared his love for Margaret, and on that account wooed her on his king's behalf, persuading Henry to break his previous engagement. In the present play Margaret is shown in collusion with Suffolk against Gloucester (i,iii; ii,i), and they both agree with the Cardinal that he must die. At the end of the scene from which I have quoted, when Suffolk is banished, their parting is that of lovers. But even without these clues I think we should feel in Margaret's rhetoric what Coleridge, referring to Lady Macbeth's welcome of Duncan, called an 'insincere overmuch'. It is the rhetoric that virtually tells us how to take the speech.

This use of rhetoric in the early History Plays is, I think, exceptional.[5] But in the light of the later plays it does seem an interesting anticipation of some of Shakespeare's ways of prompting the audience, without explicit comment, to see some kind of insincerity, whether in the sense of a deliberate attempt to deceive others, or in the sense of a half-conscious or unconscious attempt to deceive others, or oneself, about the true state of affairs. Kenneth Muir, at the end of an essay in which he makes some lively discriminations between Shakespeare's different uses of rhetoric, tells us that 'we should not fall into the error of contrasting rhetoric and sincerity'.[6] Indeed we shouldn't; everything depends on particular use in a particular context. What, in a rhetorical speech, warns us to suspect 'insincerity'?

Vickers remarks that 'Spenser's creation of specious rhetoricians is one of his finest achievements, and demonstrates the truth of Aristotle's argument that all good things can be abused'; and in his fine account of 'the Persuasions of Despair' (*The Faerie Queene*, Bk I, Canto 9) he rightly observes that the effect of Despair's highly figured speech to Red-Cross Knight, like that of the deliberate sophistry put in the mouth of Faustus or Falstaff, 'relies on our logical sense being stronger than that [of the speaker]'. We recognise, though until Una intervenes Red Cross does not, 'the professionalism of the rhetoric coating these flimsy arguments' (pp. 157–60). This is well said; but it is not only, or always, false logic that puts us on our guard, or helps us to distinguish what Vickers calls 'white rhetoric' from black. It is often the mere presence of a particular kind of rhetoric – lying somewhere between its 'straight' use, as in the more formal speeches of *Richard III*, and the total absorption of the devices in a powerful imaginative current – that prompts us to ask the question about the speaker's 'sincerity' that needs to be asked.

Shakespeare, to be sure, sometimes alerts us to the speciousness of some kinds of formal word-use by other verbal means. Thus the Dauphin's love-rhetoric supporting the politic alliance with Blanch in *King John* is promptly deflated by the Bastard when he exaggerates it and leads it to a different conclusion (II,i,496–509). In the opening scene of *Henry V* the tactic is less direct but no less effective. Canterbury gives a rhetorician's encomium of the reformed Henry, relying mainly on simple *anaphora* and *parison*, but with a marked shift of manner from that of the two bishops when, a moment before, they were really engaged: 'This [the bill against church revenues] would drink deep' – ''Twould drink the cup and all.' The laconic idiomatic expression is our cue for understanding much that follows: it's almost the equivalent of a wink. Such cues, however, are not always present, and we are left to our own intuitive – not uninformed – sense of tone and manner on which to base our judgements. The more interesting cases are of course the more difficult ones, where we are left in more doubt of dramatic function than in, say, Antony's funeral oration in *Julius Caesar*.

An example is the Duke's long speech to Claudio – unfortunately too long to quote in full – at the beginning of the third act of *Measure for Measure*.

> Be absolute for death; either death or life
> Shall thereby be the sweeter. Reason thus with life.
> If I do lose thee, I do lose a thing
> That none but fools would keep.

The speech is a formal 'persuasion' – 'Reason thus with life' – and T. W. Baldwin points out that Shakespeare faithfully follows the account in the *Rhetorica ad Herennium* of how to organise one's arguments – *propositio, ratio, rationis confirmatio. . .complexio*.[7] The speech is indeed rhetorically effective, but the 'confirmations' deserve rather more than a label. They are in fact an odd mixture of truths of very different full-truth status: some are irrelevant, some call out for a complementary 'but', one (about the expectant heirs) takes a limited class for the whole; there is also some quibbling and straight sophistry. Of course the Duke is using his argument to bring Claudio to a more resolved state of mind; and even out of context his speech is the powerful expression of an attitude to life that we need to assimilate, one indeed that in some moods we may find especially attractive, as it seems to have been to Eliot when he wrote 'Gerontion'. My point is that although rhetorical analysis does nothing to help us towards the necessary discriminations, the accomplished rhetoric *is* a way of suggesting that we taste rather carefully before we swallow the whole. It may not be unreasonable to suspect a tinge of dry irony in Claudio's 'I humbly thank you. / To sue to live, I find I seek to die.' At all events both speech and speaker demand something less than full assent, even before we come to Claudio's tremendous assertion of the instinctive recoil from death, 'Ay, but to die, and go we know not where. . .'.

T. W. Baldwin, after instancing this speech, follows with other examples that emphasise the importance of *confirmatio* (including *The Winter's Tale*, ii,i,172ff.: by this time we know what to think of Leontes's logic), and then notes 'one other instance where Shakespeare has pointed the technicalities of this type of speech', namely Gaunt's attempt to console his son who is going into banishment (*Richard II*, i,iii,275ff.). Sister Miriam Joseph adduces the same speeches of Duke Vincentio and Gaunt as 'examples of sustained and closely knit syllogistic reasoning', and adds to them Pandulph's lengthy explanation of why it would be right for the King of France to break his oath to King John (*King John*, iii,i,263ff.).[8] Baldwin and Sister Miriam Joseph are of course right in what they say, but what they do not say is equally important; for the fact remains that the appeal to, or the use of, formal rhetorical procedures is often – as I think it is in all these instances – the dramatist's tacit admonition to the audience that the persuasions are not, and are not intended by him to be, fully persuasive.

Such considerations could of course be pursued further, not only by collecting more examples. In some of his soliloquies Hamlet lapses into rhetoric (the phrase feels right when we contrast his other modes of utterance) when he tries only too hard to persuade himself of the appropriateness of a particular attitude. We are not simply moved to sympathetic participation by his rhetorical *pathos*: the dramatist has more subtle means at his disposal than the rhetorician. And there are characters whose habitual mode of speech we properly label rhetorical, whether or not, in defining it, we need the help of any *ars dicendi*. All dramatic poetry is a heightening of ordinary speech; but the modes I am referring to are heightened in relation to norms and expectations established within the play itself. Tackling big subjects with unseemly brevity, I would say that the characteristic speech of both Richard II and Othello, though in very different ways, is, for much of the time, rhetorical in this more general sense. It is framed, whether the speaker is supposed to know it or not, to express and seek endorsement for a particular – and vulnerable – posture. But to say that both Richard and Othello deceive themselves, and that, as in the more easily definable examples I have given, one of the ways in which we are made aware of this is the use of a particular mode of utterance invented for them by the dramatist – to say this is not to detract from the genuine pathos, the genuine tragedy: it is simply that a complex dramatic art demands from the audience a complex response. In 'Shakespeare and the Limits of Language' Anne Barton speaks of aspects of Shakespeare's later style that anticipate so much post-Chekhov drama: 'Words define the gap between individuals; they do not bridge it.'[9] This fine essay has different concerns from those I have pursued here, but the sentence I have extracted is pertinent. Sometimes the more rhetorically heightened the words, the greater the gap.

To sum up. We may agree that Shakespeare's poetry was 'nourished on rhetoric', provided we remember that, even more importantly, it was nourished by the language of common life. Although Shakespeare sometimes made fun of his rhetorical training he certainly used it, at first in rather obvious ways, then with increasing skill and subtlety. But through his early perception that rhetorical devices could be used not only to express but to disguise, to manipulate, or to 'put across' an attitude not wholly sincere, he learnt yet another way of alerting his audience to the importance of the unspoken. To become aware of this is to get some further insights into the infinitely varied resources of his art.

NOTES

1 *Classical Rhetoric in English Poetry* (London, 1970), p. 163.
2 The distinction between what a poet 'wants to say' and what he 'wants to do' is Valéry's ('Au sujet du *Cimetière Marin*'). I have quoted other remarks by poets to similar effect in 'Poetry as Discovery' (in *Reality and Creative Vision in German Lyrical Poetry*, ed. A. Closs (London, 1963)), and in my essay on Ben Jonson's poetry in *Explorations 3* (London, 1976).
3 Cambridge, 1936, p. lxxvi.
4 'Copious', a familiar term for cultivated abundance of words and examples; *exclamatio*, 'the figure which expresses grief or indignation by means of an address to some man or city or place or object' (*Rhetorica ad Herennium*, IV, xv, quoted by Vickers, *Classical Rhetoric*, p. 32).
5 In the second scene of *Richard III*, however, there is an interesting example of Shakespeare's feeling his way towards the expression of psychological truth by comparable means. When Lady Anne laments over the coffin of Henry VI she speaks in the approved rhetorical fashion: 'Cursèd be the hand that made these fatal holes! / Cursèd the heart that had the heart to do it!', etc. Richard's increasing influence over her is shown when the two are made to share between them various rhetorical figures (I,ii,68ff.), and the implausibility is to some extent lessened: when Anne engages in word-games with Richard she is lost.
6 Kenneth Muir, 'Shakespeare and Rhetoric', *Shakespeare-Jahrbuch*, 90 (1952), p. 68.
7 *William Shakspere's Small Latine & Lesse Greeke*, 2 vols (Urbana, 1944), vol. II, pp. 84ff.
8 *Shakespeare's Use of the Arts of Language* (New York, 1947), pp. 182ff.
9 *Shakespeare Survey 24* (1971), pp. 19–30.

Some aspects of style
in the *Henry VI* plays

WOLFGANG CLEMEN

Duchess. Ah, Gloucester, teach me to forget myself!
          For whilst I think I am thy married wife
          And thou a prince, Protector of this land,
30   Methinks I should not thus be led along,
          Mailed up in shame, with papers on my back,
          And followed with a rabble that rejoice
          To see my tears and hear my deep-fet groans.
          The ruthless flint doth cut my tender feet,
35   And when I start, the envious people laugh
          And bid me be advisèd how I tread.
          Ah, Humphrey, can I bear this shameful yoke?
          Trowest thou that e'er I'll look upon the world
          Or count them happy that enjoy the sun?
40   No; dark shall be my light and night my day;
          To think upon my pomp shall be my hell.
          Sometime I'll say I am Duke Humphrey's wife,
          And he a prince, and ruler of the land;
          Yet so he ruled, and such a prince he was,
45   As he stood by whilst I, his forlorn duchess,
          Was made a wonder and a pointing-stock
          To every idle rascal follower.
          But be thou mild, and blush not at my shame,
          Nor stir at nothing till the axe of death
50   Hang over thee, as sure it shortly will.
          For Suffolk – he that can do all in all
          With her that hateth thee and hates us all –
          And York, and impious Beaufort, that false priest,
          Have all limed bushes to betray thy wings,
55   And, fly thou how thou canst, they'll tangle thee.
          But fear not thou until thy foot be snared,
          Nor never seek prevention of thy foes.
                       (2 *Henry VI*, II,iv,27–57)

Led along in shame as a prisoner, barefoot 'in a white sheet, and a taper

burning in her hand' (as the stage-direction indicates), the Duchess of
Gloucester breaks out into this speech while Gloucester and his men,
having waited for her arrival in the street, stand by. The scene terminates
the personal tragedy of the Duchess, who has been convicted of treason,
thereby accelerating Duke Humphrey's fall. The speech has been described as one of the many set speeches in the *Henry VI* plays which carry
on the tradition of Senecan declamation, and it has been classified as a
'lamentation'.[1] But is it a typical lamentation, is it a set speech proper?
Perusing these plays we notice that there is no dividing line between 'set
speeches' and those lengthy speeches which arise out of various occasions
but do not conform to type. Our text is an example of the way in which
Shakespeare the dramatist, while carrying on the Senecan tradition of
long speeches, links them up with the action, with stage-business and
setting. Instead of giving us the conventional appurtenances of the
lament which had been established as a well-defined genre in pre-Shakespearian tragedy,[2] Shakespeare 'concretises' and localises the lament.
Rather than expressing her grief by means of abstract formulae, apos-
trophes, hyperboles and rhetorical questions, the Duchess conveys to us
her woeful state by describing the scene: her own physical appearance,
the painful walking with bare feet over 'the ruthless flint', the humiliation
of being stared at and ridiculed by 'a rabble that rejoice to see my tears
and hear my deep-fet groans'. This evocation of the outward scene
imparts to reader or audience a more poignant impression of suffering
than the mere rhetorical lament could have done, although the Duchess,
to be sure, does not reveal what is going on within her, but looks upon this
scene, in which she figures as chief protagonist, from outside. Shakespeare uses the speech to dramatise the whole scene, for the mocking
remarks made by the rabble suggest something like a dialogue. The
balanced metrical structure adds to the impression of objectivity (rather
than subjective expression of an inner state of mind) conveyed by the first
part of the speech.

We should also note that Shakespeare makes this speech grow out of
the dramatic action preceding it. The scene described by the Duchess is
twice prepared for, significant details being suggested by the same words
('the flinty streets', l. 8; 'flint', l. 34; 'the abject people gazing on thy face',
ll. 11, 20). The first line of the speech still carries on the dialogue with
Gloucester, taking up in scorn his phrase 'forget this grief'.

It is only after this 'spectacle' has been established in our minds – an
early example of Shakespeare's 'word-scenery'[3] – that Shakespeare has

the Duchess express her grief in a more abstract manner. And it is in this second part of the speech that the only rhetorical formulae (double paradox enforced by alliteration and rhyme) are to be found: 'No, dark shall be my light, and night my day.' The comparison between what has been and what is now, between the respect due to the Duchess on account of her position and the humiliating role which she now must play may also be traced back to one of the conventions of lament. It occurs at the beginning of the speech and is taken up with amplification and variation in line 42; it is again closely related to the outward scene which brings home to us, better than words can do, this contrast between past and present.[4] However, this contrast is seen by the Duchess primarily as a reversal of her social role, as a denial of her legitimate claim to quite a different treatment. It is this reversed social position rather than her suffering as a human individual which to her appears to be the greater cause for complaint.

The way in which the Duchess here points at herself, holding up her 'case' as an example of undeserved misery, is typical of the illustrative method of presentation which Shakespeare employs in these plays (the phrase 'pointing-stock' is revealing in this context). The transition to this renewed self-comparison is made by two questions (ll. 37f.). Questions also count among the obligatory accessories of set speeches. In Senecan drama they were mostly 'rhetorical questions'[5] addressed to a partner not present. Shakespeare, however, here as elsewhere, uses questions as a means to relate the speech more closely to the listener, the same effect being achieved by the repeated address to Gloucester (ll. 27, 37) and the frequent occurrence of 'thou', 'thee' and 'thy'. The isolation of the set speech, a characteristic feature of Senecan tragedy, by which the speech becomes a self-contained declamation, is rarely to be found in Shakespeare. Here the person to whom the speech is addressed is ever present.

The third part of the speech (ll. 48–57) has little to do with lamentation: in an ironical way the Duchess enjoins her husband (l. 48), expressing one of those many forebodings (ll. 49–50) which are scattered throughout these plays and which are characteristic of their mode of presentation.[6] Her warning is at once given its foundation in fact: the three chief figures of whose enmity Gloucester is as yet unaware – Suffolk, York, Beaufort – are mentioned and briefly characterised. Shakespeare thus achieves a 'survey of the situation' found in many of the long speeches, which also serves to pass information on to the audience.

The metaphors ('limed bushes', 'tangle thee', 'snared') belong to the powerful animal imagery, running through all three parts of *Henry VI*, suggesting brutal force, trapping of unsuspecting victims, etc.; it occurs not only in obvious similes and comparisons, but also in 'figures and images, often merely implicit and hardly recognised'.[7]

Is this speech typical of the play's style and language? The answer is: 'only partly'. For those features which are to be found in many other passages as well can rapidly be enumerated: syntactical and metrical units are usually coextensive. Run-on lines are rare. Reiteration of the same idea occurs frequently and along with this a certain copiousness of expression. All statements are rounded off, definite and clear; the whole speech can be subdivided into smaller sections, one theme being dealt with after another. But other stylistic features, even more characteristic of the *Henry VI* plays, are lacking. Shakespeare did not use a uniform language for all his long speeches in the Histories, but varied his style a good deal,[8] adapting it to the occasion and to the subject to a greater degree than can be said of the long speeches in Senecan drama and pre-Shakespearian tragedy.

As an example of another long speech in an entirely different style let us look at a speech of persuasion, a *suasoria*, in the second scene of Act II in *3 Henry VI*, of which I quote the first 24 lines:

Clifford. My gracious liege, this too much lenity
10   And harmful pity must be laid aside.
     To whom do lions cast their gentle looks?
     Not to the beast that would usurp their den.
     Whose hand is that the forest bear doth lick?
     Not his that spoils her young before her face.
15   Who scapes the lurking serpent's mortal sting?
     Not he that sets his foot upon her back.
     The smallest worm will turn, being trodden on,
     And doves will peck in safeguard of their brood.
     Ambitious York did level at thy crown,
20   Thou smiling while he knit his angry brows.
     He, but a Duke, would have his son a king.
     And raise his issue like a loving sire:
     Thou, being a king, blest with a goodly son,
     Didst yield consent to disinherit him,
25   Which argued thee a most unloving father.
     Unreasonable creatures feed their young;
     And though man's face be fearful to their eyes,
     Yet, in protection of their tender ones,
     Who hath not seen them – even with those wings
30   Which sometime they have used, with fearful flight –

Make war with him that climbed unto their nest,
Offering their own lives in their young's defence?

(*3 Henry VI*, II,ii,9–32)

Clifford tries to change King Henry's mind, urging him not to forfeit the young Prince's right to succession. To emphasise his point he makes no fewer than four comparisons with the animal world, the first three symmetrically arranged in equal pairs of two lines (a question each time followed by an answer) followed by a *sententia* and a proverb illustrating and, as it were, objectifying the same idea.[9] The fourth comparison from the animal world, inserted after the reiterated statement of the main argument (expressed by antithesis and demonstration), covers no fewer than seven lines, being a stylistic amplification of what has gone before. Rhetoric here appears in its original function, as 'the art of deliberative and persuasive public speaking',[10] and the extravagant display of rhetorical devices is therefore appropriate in this context. But Shakespeare makes us aware of this by an explicit justification of this 'oratory style'. King Henry's reaction to this speech:

Full well hath Clifford played the orator,   (*3 Henry VI*, II,ii,43)

places it in its proper perspective. Scattered throughout the early Histories we find quite a few such critical comments on rhetorically heightened speeches, beginning with the Pucelle's scoffing at Sir William Lucy's enumeration of great names in *1 Henry VI*, 'Here's a silly-stately style indeed!' (*1 Henry VI*, IV,vii,72), continuing with angry comments such as the Cardinal's lines addressed to Gloucester:

Nephew, what means this passionate discourse,
This peroration with such circumstance?   (*2 Henry VI*, I,i,99–100)

and with other references, indirect or direct, to the art of oratory.[11] Such passages betray Shakespeare's 'consciousness of language' and show us 'Shakespeare not only playing in language the same games as other men of his age but also watching the game', as Gladys Willcock put it more than forty years ago.[12] An examination of the Jack Cade scenes and the scene with Horner the Armourer supports the assumption that Shakespeare, while using heightened rhetorical language for his nobles, also at times held it up for critical comment and even parodied it.[13] The insertion of the prose-scenes with Cade and his 'rabblement' in *2 Henry VI* makes us conscious of the fact that the 'stately speeches and well sounding phrases clyming to the height of Seneca his style' (Sidney) by no means represent the only language spoken in the world.

Long speeches hold up the action and tend to develop into self-contained declamations, moving away from the scene and its characters. Such speeches pose a problem for the producer, who wonders what to do with all those characters standing and waiting (sometimes for a considerable length of time) while the speaker is delivering his oration. Shakespeare the dramatist must have felt this from the very beginning, for we can observe, throughout the historical plays, the development of several means of integrating these speeches into the dramatic action. One way was to turn them into theatrical performances in their own right, to make them create accompanying action. The speech of the Duchess, as we saw, evokes not only the lively scene in the street, but also the reactions of 'the rabble', although primarily addressed to Gloucester. Clifford, at the end of his speech ('Were it not pity that this goodly boy . . .', l. 34; 'look on the boy', l. 39) points to the young Prince standing by and puts words into his mouth which this youth might utter at some future time. Thus the eyes of the audience are directed not only to the character addressed but also to a third person. In many speeches of some length, a character is not only addressed, questioned, implored, attacked or taunted, but also asked to 'observe', 'look', 'see', 'gaze',[14] so that with him (or her) the audience are made to look around or to imagine in their 'mind's eye' the physical appearance of characters who are absent. Frequent allusions to the physiognomy, the appearance, the bearing of the characters suggest that Shakespeare is progressing towards a concept of his figures which does not allow them to remain static even when they deliver long speeches. Many speeches moreover reflect the reaction of the listener, his shock, his startled gesture, his hesitation, his assent,[15] and by means of indirect stage-directions a great many accompanying gestures are indicated, such as kneeling, shaking hands, taking leave, embracing or raising an arm, drawing a sword and the like. The use of direct reported speech, inserted into some of the long speeches (as into Clifford's *suasoria*) is another means of enlivening formality,[16] as is the transition from highly pitched rhetoric to a more straightforward language.[17] Some speeches, too, are interrupted by characters standing by,[18] while in others it is the speakers who interrupt themselves, thus for a short moment giving the impression of spontaneous utterance in the midst of an otherwise 'prefabricated' speech.[19] In some speeches the first line takes up the cue from the last speaker by repeating a phrase in a contrasting mood.[20] Moreover, most of the speeches, usually at the end or the beginning, link up with the political circumstances, the actual situation, thus carrying on the 'business of the play' and adding to the information passed on to the audience.

The most notable example of a long speech combined with dramatic action is the scene in which Margaret, after having dragged York onto a molehill, puts a paper crown on his head, taunting and mocking him in violent terms (*3 Henry VI*, I,iv).[21] York's reaction, his defenceless and mute standing in front of Margaret is – paradoxically enough – conveyed through the language of this vituperative speech. The rhetorical figures become a tool of ruthless attack, declamatory language being transformed into harsh provocation. Sensing the utter brutality of the spectacle we are apt to forget the rhetorical artistry. In this speech, too, we have an example of heightened declamation, which, however, at its climax over-turns itself to become an idiom of colloquial coarseness:

> And where's that valiant crook-back prodigy,
> Dicky your boy, that with his grumbling voice
> Was wont to cheer his dad in mutinies?   (*3 Henry VI*, I,iv,75–7)

Perusing the early Histories we find every now and then phrases and sometimes whole lines which by their very simplicity and terseness anticipate this element of Shakespeare's dramatic language in his later plays and counterbalance the artifice of rhetoric. F. P. Wilson's contention that 'even in Shakespeare's earliest manner the natural is ever present with the artificial'[22] holds true of the *Henry VI* plays, too. In putting blunt phrases of this kind into the mouth of Richard Gloucester, Shakespeare for the first time catches the individual accent of a character,[23] whereas in the rest of the trilogy we seek in vain for the complete individualisation of character through language which will be such a notable feature in the later plays.[24] Apart from this instance the style in the early Histories is determined by the occasion and the theme rather than by the character of the speaker.

The foregoing remarks suggest that at many points style and language merge into other elements of dramatic art. Style in the plays does not exist 'in itself', but as part of character and of the dramatic whole. Moreover, style being a highly complex phenomenon, many aspects would have to be taken into consideration if a balanced assessment of language and style in these plays were to be attempted. For this would have to include not only the figures of rhetoric but also grammar and syntax, vocabulary and sound, forms of address, tempo and versification. We would also have to consider to what extent versification and syntax are adapted to 'the speaking voice', a development to be noticed as early as in the *Henry VI* plays.[25]

However, bearing in mind the warning pronounced by Brian Vickers that 'it would take many years to study Shakespeare's stylistic development with the attention it deserves',[26] a short essay like this must be restricted to some fragmentary observations and cannot hope to do justice to the complex phenomenon of style in the early Histories. The commonplace that Shakespeare had many styles[27] also holds true of the *Henry VI* plays, in which we find straightforward language side by side with richly adorned speech, or brisk dialogue followed by formal and slowly moving declamation, and in the Second Part some notable prose-scenes, again not uniform in style, counterpoising the artificial rhetoric of many verse passages. Moreover, we are faced, in these plays, with considerable differences of quality in style, which some scholars attributed to multiple authorship or to later insertions of some passages by Shakespeare himself – a much disputed problem. The well-known speech of Young Clifford when discovering his dead father (*2 Henry VI*, v,ii,31)[28] shows a mastery of language and vision much surpassing the uninspired, flat passages in the adjoining scenes.

How could we – in view of this great diversity – describe the style of these plays in a way that would set it apart from that of later Histories? One first step would be to single out those features of style which do not occur again, or occur much less frequently, in later plays.

One might begin with the passages with an excessive and obtrusive use of rhetorical devices, the 'patterned speeches', the many parallelisms, repetitions and the piling up of similes and *sententiae*, the accumulation of questions and exclamations, the frequent instances of self-address and the many classical allusions of incidental rather than functional character, and the symmetrically structured exchanges of vituperative attack and counterattack. As has often been observed, this 'exploitation of all the devices for heightening, amplifying, and varying expression'[29] is a characteristic of Shakespeare's early style, and, one would have to add, this exploitation is particularly obvious and sometimes even obtrusive in the *Henry VI* plays. However, this must not mislead us into believing that Shakespeare used fewer rhetorical figures in his later work, for in fact, according to Sister Miriam Joseph's findings, he used more. Kenneth Muir, taking the matter up from this point, has well described the essential 'difference of emphasis': 'He came to use more metaphors and fewer similes, and he abandoned some of the more obtrusive figures. There is less obvious alliteration. He no longer begins successive lines with the same word. He compromises more with colloquial speech. But to say he abandoned rhetoric is a misuse of terms.'[30] In a previous article Muir had summarised the stages of development in Shakespeare's use of rhetoric, and because of its relevance to the subject treated in this volume this passage ought to be quoted here, too: 'Shakespeare began by using the arts of rhetoric formally and deliberately and. . .as he matured he came to use them with greater freedom and individuality, until at last he seemed to use them instinctively.'[31]

However, when the language in the *Henry VI* plays is being discussed, rhetoric, though only one aspect of Shakespeare's style, usually receives most attention. But there are quite a few other features which we ought to look at, trying to coordinate them with observations already made. Therefore I should like to offer, as a conclusion to this essay, a few tentative suggestions as to how to relate certain striking features of style to attitudes and principles underlying the dramatic intention of these plays.[32]

A desire for clarification appears to be at the root of many stylistic phenomena. It accounts for the twofold and threefold expression of an idea, and this cannot be attributed merely to Shakespeare's indulgence in rhetorical devices or to his 'immaturity', for it suits the underlying intention of these plays and finds an equivalent in the formalised action which tends to double incidents and roles. The reiterated expression of an idea is related to the unambiguous formulation of all subject matter. For we seldom come across passages which leave us wondering, 'What is meant here?' Shakespeare's later manner of making his characters express themselves by innuendo, by subtle hints, so that we have to look below the surface in interpreting their utterances, is not yet evident in these early plays.

Much of the clarification which we can trace on several levels of expression may be related to the didactic purpose of these Histories, which are designed to teach a political lesson and point a moral in a manner intelligible to everybody. The need for clarification also accounts for those numerous passages which – always with a wealth of names (and often too many names!) – recapitulate the preceding events, review the situation, inform us about the claims, the intentions, the plans of all the quarrelling parties and their representatives. Clarification is particularly important in view of the 'intractable mass of events'[33] which the chronicles presented to Shakespeare, for 'chronicle history is the most recalcitrant to free artistic fashioning. . .The reign of Henry VI, in any case, was too long, its events too rambling and fortuitous to be easily digested into drama.'[34] Hence the need for repeated information and hence, too, the preference for the reiterative mode of presentation.[35]

The wish to illustrate, to demonstrate, to exemplify (rather than to create characters or events) is also a major incentive in the shaping of scenes as well as language. The characters view their own doings and the events of the drama from a distance, from outside, stepping aside, as it were, and thus becoming their own spectators, acting as their own chorus. They use similes, comparisons and maxims in order to point out the meaning and the moral of what is happening to them and around them. We are continually aware of their 'pointing forefinger', the drama-tist's forefinger in fact, that is to bring home to us the truths which are at stake. The frequent insertion of *sententiae* and proverbs serves as a means of objectifying and, as it were, depersonalising such utterances.

When, for instance, King Henry mourns over Gloucester's arrest which has just taken place, he first draws a comparison from the slaugh-terhouse ('And as a butcher takes away the calf. . .') and utilises it for what he wants to demonstrate:

> Even so, remorseless, have they borne him hence;

but then adds another simile ('And as the dam. . .') to illustrate his own predicament:[36]

> Even so myself bewails good Gloucester's case
> With sad unhelpful tears, and with dimmed eyes.
>
> (*2 Henry VI*, III,i,217–18)

Even in moments of extreme agony, facing his own murderer, a character may step aside to describe this situation from the outside, ritualising, as it were, his imminent murder. Thus Young Rutland face-to-face with Clifford, who is going to kill him in a few minutes, finds images for this terrible confrontation:

> So looks the pent-up lion o'er the wretch
> That trembles under his devouring paws;
> And so he walks, insulting o'er his prey.
> And so he comes, to rend his limbs asunder.
>
> (*3 Henry VI*, I,iii,12–15)

The most famous example of this 'demonstrating mode' is the scene with King Henry sitting on the molehill (*3 Henry VI*, II,v), commenting on his own role and on the 'piteous spectacle' (l. 73) of 'the son that has killed his father' and 'the father that has killed his son'. But this 'piece of stylised ritual writing' (Tillyard) has been commented on so much that a mere mention must be sufficient in this context.

Illustration is very often linked with inculcation. The emphasis and the zeal with which this is done may partly account for the doubling and tripling of pertinent nouns and epithets, for the reinforcement of crucial pronouncements through rhyme, assonance, anaphora, and various other repetitive and tautological devices. When, for instance, 'tyranny' is referred to, three epithets are needed to characterise it:

> And lofty proud encroaching tyranny. . .   (*2 Henry VI*, IV,i,96)

A few lines later, when Suffolk contemptuously speaks about the commons, he also strings together three epithets to characterise them:

> these paltry, servile, abject drudges!   (l. 105)

When King Henry, dismissing Gloucester, puts himself under God's protection, this is expressed in four terms:

> and God shall be my hope,
> My stay, my guide, and lantern to my feet.
> > (*2 Henry VI*, II,iii,24–5)

When Queen Margaret describes King Henry's ruin to the new King Edward she does it in this manner:

> his state usurped,
> His realm a slaughter-house, his subjects slain,
> His statutes cancelled, and his treasure spent.
> > (*3 Henry VI*, V,iv,77–9)

When Warwick in the last act of *3 Henry VI* concludes his 'dying-speech', he epitomises his conventional final meditation in two chiming lines of rhetorical artifice:

> Why, what is pomp, rule, reign, but earth and dust?
> And live we how we can, yet die we must.   (*3 Henry VI*, V,ii,27–8)

And when Salisbury, towards the end of the Second Part, wants to demonstrate the invalidity of a 'sinful oath', he adduces no less than five examples, formulated as a question:

> Who can be bound by any solemn vow
> To do a murderous deed, to rob a man,
> To force a spotless virgin's chastity,
> To reave the orphan of his patrimony,
> To wring the widow from her customed right?
> > (*2 Henry VI*, V,i,184–8)

These examples are different in kind, and repetition, parallelism, and accumulation may serve various ends in these plays. But one function surely is to hammer certain truths into our heads, to make things which are obvious even more obvious. Fullness and circumstantiality, especially in the elaboration of long-drawn-out similes as, for instance, in Queen Margaret's famous *adhortatio* on the field of Tewkesbury (*3 Henry VI*, I,iv), are part of this striving for explicit clarity. On the other hand, the definiteness of expression finds its metrical equivalent in the balanced end-stopped line.[37]

Explicitness rather than implicitness is a pervading mark of style. Everything is said, nothing is held back, except in some cases of quite overt hypocrisy; there is no room for ambiguities, for subtle hints, for wordless moments in which the limits of expression through language might be reached. But again we must ask ourselves whether Shakespeare really wished his characters to give utterance to their inner conflicts, to 'express' themselves.

Self-description rather than self-expression is the basis of speech in these plays, and even this description, though sometimes related to strong emotions externalising them, as it were, rarely allows us to look into the minds of the characters, but mostly serves to sketch out future actions. Even in the moment of dying the characters describe in orderly speech and unconcerned manner their physical conditions, their situation as to friends and enemies, their past doings and their intentions.[38] At other times they may give descriptions of their own qualities[39] or an account of their present plight.[40]

Language in those early Histories is a kind of prop on which these two-dimensional characters lean in order to assert their title, their claim, their power or their hatred, and all this is voiced *forte* or *fortissimo*, low-pitched or quiet scenes being rare. This constant pursuit of corroboration and affirmation on the part of the characters has been well described as 'the seeking of maximal self-assertion at every moment' which is 'impatient of indirection'.[41] Language thus may be transformed into outward gesture. The numerous asseverations and protestations, outnumbering by far those in the later Histories, are an appropriate manifestation of this constant self-assertion. But the language spoken by these figures does not allow us to catch a glimpse of their inner lives, does not betray their motivations; in short, with very few exceptions it tells us very little of their character. From the complex nature of man Shakespeare has selected only a small sector, so that these strutting figures are, after all, not real persons but embodiments of limited functions for which they are the mouthpiece. And we should hesitate to attribute this to a lack of ability only, and should consider the question of whether this limited range was not designed to fit the conception of these morality plays. That the dramatis personae so often speak 'out of character' would then be the natural outcome of the plays' intention and design. The many passages written in a ceremonious, formal, sometimes almost 'heraldic' manner, and contributing to the impression of an impersonal, not yet individualised style, should perhaps also be seen in this light. Pope's complaint that Shakespeare 'generally used to stiffen his style with high words and metaphors for the speeches of his Kings and great men: he mistook it for a mark of greatness'[42] may be partly justified if we limit it to the early Histories. But it loses some of its force when we see this feature together with the frequency of choric utterance as being in keeping with the didactic mode of these plays, which have aptly been called 'a prolonged morality with England as its central character'.[43] Much of what is said thus resembles the caption to be found under a painting or the legend under an emblem.

The lack of human relationships in the encounters between the characters may well account for such features of style as are especially notable in the many scenes of confrontation, in which the dialogue is built on an exchange of reciprocal vituperation, of violent accusation and angry retort, the general pattern being 'one of give and take'.[44] The characters do not speak with each other so much as at each other, they have no intention of sounding the thoughts of their partners, or of understanding them. Dialogue as a means of bringing people more closely together or of replying to a point which has been made by the other party is as yet unknown, the encounter of Suffolk and the Queen (*2 Henry VI*, III,ii) being a rare exception. Unrelated and in irreconcilable opposition to one another the nobles confront each other, power pitted against power. The sharply alternating challenges and retorts, which are embodied in symmetrically structured lines, employ the figures of speech, especially the echoes and correspondences, in a reverse sense: to express hostility and separation, but not interrelationship.[45] This technique of dialogue ('a repetitive push and pull, back and forth, over and over again')[46] reminds us of the battle of words, the combat of wit in the Comedies, but takes on a more sinister aspect, as the clash of words prepares for the clash of swords. In a full-length study the examination of the vituperative language in these plays could make up a whole chapter, for one could point out several techniques of using demeaning and insulting terms,[47] of which we find in these plays far more than, for instance, in *Richard III* or *Henry IV*.

If the clash of power is the mainspring of some elements of the language, the expression of will is another. On almost every page we find vows and oaths, promises and threats, and we find, too, many forms of 'will', 'shall', etc. Here the method applied by D. M. Burton in *Shakespeare's Grammatical Style*[48] would be helpful. For even a rapid perusal of the text reveals a great number of conditional clauses expressing affirmation and protestation. Not to the same degree as with Marlowe but still in a great measure, the lords of these plays express with their fierce and pompous language more of what they would like to do, of what they aim at, than of what they are actually achieving. Language constantly makes gestures towards the future with promises and keen intent, and this attitude may to some degree be a heritage from Marlowe.

But what is the effect of the language of the *Henry VI* plays on us, on the audience, on the reader? To put this question implies a change of approach, for it has less to do with stylistic analysis than with the assessment of the reaction of audience or reader. Although any answer given to this question is bound to be subjective, it may be worth while to attempt one. For when we read or watch these plays it appears that we begin to doubt whether we can accept, and believe in, this deliberately moulded convincingness and distinctness. What in the speeches of the characters began as a skilful use of time-honoured classical devices of rhetoric, apparently promoting clarity, in fact turns into something different when we question our over-all impression. For as we look more closely, the extraordinary clarity of utterance and character in this somewhat two-dimensional world serves in the end only to accentuate the nightmare absurdity of it all. This intolerable sequence of a century of senseless war in which the successive characters comment in an apparently convincing manner makes us all the more aware of the ultimate futility of it all. The magnification, the sharp light in which these stalking, depersonalised figures appear before our eyes make even more acute the final blurring of moral values. In the end, the issue is not clarified but confused. We do not know which side is right, for they are all wrong. Shakespeare, having built up this monumental array of seemingly uncontroversial figures, endowing them with a maximum of eloquence, self-assurance and distinctness, seems to have ended his work with a question mark.

NOTES

1   Hardin Craig, 'Shakespeare and the History Play', in *John Quincy Adams Memorial Studies* (Washington, 1948). For a detailed examination of the set speeches in the Histories I am indebted to Bernhard Schmid, 'Form und Gehalt der grossen Rede in Shakespeares Historien' (Ph.D. dissertation, University of Munich, 1955). For the set speeches in general see M. B. Kennedy, *The Oration in Shakespeare* (Chapel Hill, 1942). For their treatment of Shakespeare's early Histories I am indebted to the following books: M. M. Reese, *The Cease of Majesty* (London, 1961); David Riggs, *Shakespeare's Heroical Histories* (Cambridge, Mass., 1971); Robert Ornstein, *A Kingdom for a Stage* (Cambridge, Mass., 1972); but most of all to Robert Y. Turner, *Shakespeare's Apprenticeship* (Chicago, 1974).

2   See Part Three of my *English Tragedy before Shakespeare* (London, 1961).

3   Rudolf Stamm, *Shakespeare's Word-Scenery* (Zürich, 1954).

4   See J. P. Brockbank's remarks on this scene in 'The Frame of Disorder', *Stratford-upon-Avon Studies 3: Early Shakespeare* (London, 1961).

5   See H. V. Canter, *Rhetorical Elements in the Tragedies of Seneca* (Urbana, 1925), pp. 140ff.

6   See the Introduction to *3 Henry VI*, New Arden edition (London, 1964), by A. S. Cairncross, p. lv.

7   The phrase is Cairncross's. These aspects of the imagery in *Henry VI* were underrated in my early book. See Cairncross's justified criticism in his Introduction to *2 Henry VI*, New Arden edition (London, 1957), p. liii.

8   See, besides Craig and Schmid, Horst Oppel, 'Die erste Meisterszene: Der Tod Beauforts', in *Shakespeare. Studien zum Werk und zur Welt des Dichters* (Heidelberg, 1963).

9   See F. P. Wilson, *The Proverbial Wisdom of Shakespeare* (Modern Humanities Research Association, 1961); Horst Weinstock, *Die Funktion elisabethanischer Sprichwörter und Pseudosprichwörter bei Shakespeare* (Heidelberg, 1966).

10   Gladys D. Willcock, *Language and Poetry in Shakespeare's Early Plays* (Annual Shakespeare Lecture of the British Academy, 1954).

11   'The King / Prettily, methought, did play the orator' (*1 Henry VI*, iv,i,175); 'For Warwick is a subtle orator' (*3 Henry VI*, iii,i,33); 'But you, my lord, were glad to be employed, / To show how quaint an orator you are' (*2 Henry VI*, iii,ii,273); Richard Gloucester: 'I'll play the orator as well as Nestor' (*3 Henry VI*, iii,ii,188). See, too, *2 Henry VI*, i,i,155; iii,i,79; *1 Henry VI*, iii,iii,40,78.

12   G. D. Willcock, *Shakespeare as a Critic of Language* (Shakespeare Association, London, 1934).

13   See C. Leech, *Shakespeare, The Chronicles* (British Council Series, London, 1962), p. 17. See the illuminating remarks on the language of Jack Cade by Jürgen Schäfer, *Shakespeares Stil. Germanisches und romanisches Vokabular* (Frankfurt, 1973), p. 78. See also Turner, *Shakespeare's Apprenticeship*, p. 140.

14   See, for instance, the speech of the Duchess at the beginning of *2 Henry VI*, i,ii; the Queen's speech in *2 Henry VI*, iii,i,4ff.; iii,ii,50,74,159; iii,iii,24.

15   As, e.g., in *2 Henry VI*, iii,ii,50,73.

16   As in *2 Henry VI*, iii,i,222; iii,ii,85; *3 Henry VI*, ii,ii,37; v,vi,75.

17   As in *2 Henry VI*, iii,ii,119.

18   As in *1 Henry VI*, iii,i,41; *2 Henry VI*, iv,vii,74.

19   As in *2 Henry VI*, iii,ii,52,352.

20   As in *2 Henry VI*, iii,ii,72; *3 Henry VI*, i,i,230.

21 See the comment on this scene by Turner, *Shakespeare's Apprenticeship*, pp. 53f.
22 *Shakespeare and the Diction of Common Life* (Annual Shakespeare Lecture of the British Academy, London, 1941).
23 See especially *3 Henry VI*, III,ii, and Act V.
24 See Charlotte Ehrl, *Sprachstil und Charakter bei Shakespeare* (Schriftenreihe der Deutschen Shakespeare-Gesellschaft, Heidelberg, 1957).
25 Introduction by John Dover Wilson to *3 Henry VI* in the New Cambridge Shakespeare (Cambridge, 1952).
26 'Shakespeare's Use of Rhetoric', in *A New Companion to Shakespeare Studies*, ed. Kenneth Muir and S. Schoenbaum (Cambridge, 1971).
27 'Shakespeare has not one style, but many'; Oliver Elton, *Style in Shakespeare* (Annual Shakespeare Lecture of the British Academy, London, 1936).
28 Some critics believe it to be a later insertion; see Kenneth Muir, 'Image and Symbol in Shakespeare's Histories', *Shakespeare the Professional* (London, 1973), p. 74.
29 Willcock, *Language and Poetry in Shakespeare's Early Plays*.
30 Muir, 'Shakespeare the Dramatist', *Filološki Pregled* (Beograd, 1964).
31 'Shakespeare and Rhetoric', *Shakespeare-Jahrbuch*, 90 (1952).
32 For valuable suggestions on how to relate stylistic features to recurring attitudes I am much indebted to Turner, *Shakespeare's Apprenticeship*, and to Sigurd Burckhardt, 'I am but Shadow of Myself. Ceremony and Design in *I Henry VI*, *Modern Language Quarterly*, XXVIII (1967).
33 B. Ifor Evans, *The Language of Shakespeare's Plays* (London, 1952), p. 31.
34 Cairncross, Introduction to *2 Henry VI*, New Arden edition, p. l.
35 Cairncross: Shakespeare 'knew the value and effect of the schoolmaster's damnable iteration as a means of inculcating a fact or projecting a character' (Introduction to *3 Henry VI*, New Arden edition).
36 See Turner, *Shakespeare's Apprenticeship*, p. 112.
37 Burckhardt: 'The lines of verse behave like the characters, each striving to stand in self-sufficient and self-assertive orotundity', in 'I am but Shadow of Myself', p. 142.
38 See the dying speeches by Mortimer (*1 Henry VI*, II,v,3–16), Clifford (*3 Henry VI*, II,vi,1–30), and Warwick (*3 Henry VI*, V,ii,5–28).
39 See King Henry in *3 Henry VI*, IV,viii,38–46.
40 See Warwick in *3 Henry VI*, II,iii,1; King Henry in *3 Henry VI*, III,i,12ff.
41 Burckhardt, 'I am but Shadow of Myself'.
42 Quoted by Joseph Spence, in *Anecdotes, Observations and Characters*, ed. S. W. Singer (1820). See James Sutherland, 'How the Characters Talk', in *Shakespeare's World*, ed. J. Sutherland (London, 1964).
43 Reese, *The Cease of Majesty*.
44 Turner, *Shakespeare's Apprenticeship*.
45 See R. Y. Turner, 'Characterisation in Shakespeare's Early History Plays', *English Literary History*, 3 (1964).
46 Madeleine Doran, *Shakespeare's Dramatic Language* (Madison, 1976).
47 See H. O. Thieme, 'Studien zur Zornesszene in Shakespeares Historien' (Ph.D. dissertation, University of Marburg, 1972).
48 Dolores M. Burton, *Shakespeare's Grammatical Style* (London, 1973).

Poem and context in
Love's Labour's Lost

G. K. HUNTER

100 If Love make me forsworn, how shall I swear to love?
O never faith could hold, if not to beauty vowed;
Though to myself forsworn, to thee I'll constant prove;
Those thoughts, to me like oaks, to thee like osiers bowed.
Study his bias leaves and makes his book thine eyes,
105 Where all those pleasures live that art can comprehend.
If knowledge be the mark, to know thee shall suffice;
Well learned is that tongue that well can thee commend;
All ignorant that soul that sees thee without wonder;
Which is to me some praise, that I thy parts admire.
110 Thine eye Jove's lightning seems, thy voice his dreadful thunder,
Which, not to anger bent, is music and sweet fire.
    Celestial as thou art, O, do not love that wrong,
      To sing heaven's praise with such an earthly tongue.
          (*The Passionate Pilgrim; Love's Labour's Lost*, IV,ii,100–13)

Did not the heavenly rhetoric of thine eye,
'Gainst whom the world could not hold argument,
Persuade my heart to this false perjury?
Vows for thee broke deserve not punishment.
60 A woman I forswore; but I will prove,
Thou being a goddess, I forswore not thee:
My vow was earthly, thou a heavenly love;
Thy grace being gained cures all disgrace in me.
My vow was breath, and breath a vapour is;
65 Then, thou fair sun, that on this earth dost shine,
Exhale this vapour vow; in thee it is:
If broken, then it is no fault of mine.
    If by me broke, what fool is not so wise
    To break an oath, to win a paradise?
          (*The Passionate Pilgrim; Love's Labour's Lost*, IV,iii,56–69)

Berowne. Here stand I, lady – dart thy skill at me,
      Bruise me with scorn, confound me with a flout,
      Thrust thy sharp wit quite through my ignorance,
      Cut me to pieces with thy keen conceit;

400   And I will wish thee never more to dance,
           Nor never more in Russian habit wait.
           O, never will I trust to speeches penned,
           Nor to the motion of a school-boy's tongue,
           Nor never come in vizard to my friend,
405   Nor woo in rhyme, like a blind harper's song.
           Taffeta phrases, silken terms precise,
           Three-piled hyperboles, spruce affectation,
           Figures pedantical – these summer flies
           Have blown me full of maggot ostentation.
410   I do forswear them; and I here protest,
           By this white glove – how white the hand, God knows! –
           Henceforth my wooing mind shall be expressed
           In russet yeas, and honest kersey noes.
           And, to begin, wench – so God help me, law! –
415   My love to thee is sound, sans crack or flaw.
Rosaline. Sans 'sans', I pray you.
Berowne.   Yet I have a trick
           Of the old rage; bear with me, I am sick;
           I'll leave it by degrees.   (*Love's Labour's Lost*, v,ii,396–418)

The statement that the language of a successful play exists to create what its audience can accept as 'a sense of reality' is so basic a truth that it is also a tautology, for 'reality' is largely to be defined as the word we use to signify our sense of 'artistic' achievement. But not entirely so: the word at the same time carries another and less blanketing significance. We know what a critic means when he says that the language of *Hobson's Choice* is more 'real' than that of *Love's Labour's Lost*, even though we allow that both have equal though different 'realities' (in our first sense of the word). The two meanings are, of course, interconnected. The tissue of the commonest language of real life remains a norm against which all dramatists fashion their own 'reality' of expression, whether by close mimicry or by patent selection and distortion. In either case the art-language of the play exercises its power through the tension it sets up between what is said on the stage and what we in the auditorium would be likely to say. It exists between two equally implausible opposites. Too close a connection between the language of the play and that of real life limits the dramatist's power to the mere arrangement (and rearrangement) of the events in real life to which the language normally pertains – in a process that may remind us of what Coleridge called 'Fancy'. Too distant a relation on the other hand detaches what people say on the stage from the expression of such acts in our own lives and turns the events into contexts for recitation.

The choice of poetry or prose as the principal medium for plays predetermines the act of balance that will be required and the dangers to be avoided. One practitioner has to teach his prose to rise, another must condition his poetry to sink; but in both cases the movement must be made to seem 'natural', a function first of the experience and only subsequently of the language. For the poetic dramatist the problem is how to evoke the ordinary level, for poetry is, in relation to ordinary speech-life, always the extraordinary. This is an old issue, much debated by the first apologists for 'the natural', in the English Restoration. But the answers offered then and since (from Rymer to Yeats) have been so befuddled by polemic that the problem may be worth posing once again. A satisfactory answer would seem to depend on compromise rather than holism. Certainly the most successful poetic drama known to us (Shakespeare's) moves continually between the evocation of casual speech and the projection of elaborate rhetoric. Shakespeare offers the listener a series of levels of linguistic artifice which operate by continual cross-criticism to build up a whole world in which every part is related linguistically to every other part. We find ourselves assenting to an evocation of 'ordinary' and 'extraordinary' which derives in part from the language of the outside world but much more from our sense of linguistic hierarchy created by the work itself.

An obvious way of beginning to think about such a range of languages is to make the usual assumption that low or prosaic language signifies the real external world, so that fanciful or impassioned poetry is to that extent unreal – the poetic impulse (in other terms) representing the spiritual where the prosaic shows us material life. This is certainly one of the ways in which Shakespeare presents the spectrum of languages in his plays. His explicit references to poets and poetry harp on the role of the poet as a feigner or liar, and stress truth of experience rather than eloquence as the proper expression of good conduct in the real world. But to assume that the prosaic is always the touchstone of true perception in the plays would be a gross distortion. Touchstone himself may be realistically cynical about the flummery of romantic love, and we can see why he is so, but *As You Like It* does not rest its values on his reality. The mutual criticism that the different levels of the play establish is open ended, but not so open that some valuations are not preferred to others; Rosalind's is seen as better than either Touchstone's or Jaques's. The discovery that Shakespeare's most moving characters are often 'poets' (Richard II, Othello, Hamlet, Macbeth) is no doubt critically immature; but awareness that it is the eloquence of their verse that gives them their power over us seems to be accurate and inescapable. If Othello's poetry is seen at first sight to be 'unreal' when set against Iago's prose, the play soon requires us to revalue this shallow 'reality' in the light of an intense poetic vision more true and no less real. I ask how this comes to happen.

It is usually assumed that good or great poetry operates upon us by commanding our assent to or identification with the sentiments proposed. If we are moved by

> But she is in her grave, and, oh,
> The difference to me.

or

> Thou wast not born for death, immortal bird,

we are assumed not to be simply admiring the artifice of versification but finding that the good or great verse offers us immediate access to good and great feelings. These assumptions are, of course, nourished on the large body of non-dramatic, usually lyric, verse closest to what is commonly but tendentiously called 'pure poetry'. Once poetry is embodied in drama and serves the cross-critical functions I have noted above, mediation might seem to have become the rule of our response. Then we have to reconcile these opposite, prosaic and poetic, low and high, 'realities'. Clearly the whole story cannot be told in terms of identification with the speakers of great poetry or the assumption that their eloquence is the mirror of their human centrality, any more than it can be told in terms of our identification with the anti-poetic stance of the 'realists'. The plays are full of speeches that we easily recognise as Great Poetry. But we recognise this most easily when we read them as if in an anthology; when they are functioning fully inside plays, the standards of Great Poetry seem inadequate, though not untrue. The distinction we make automatically, but it is hard to describe. One detail that seems relevant concerns the different relationships set up between the 'I' of the poem and the 'I' of the reader. In Shakespeare's sonnets, for example, the common I-locutions in the first lines ('Weary with toil I haste me to my bed', 'Shall I compare thee to a summer's day', 'Being your slave, what should I do but tend', etc.) invite us to become that 'I', and tell us that the emotional pattern of the poem is to be taken for granted, the perspective fixed from that point of view. The room that these sonnets provide for the reader to re-invent the poem exists at the level of the proper relation of detail, the patterns between 'I' and 'you', not at all in terms of the question, How is it that he has come to be writing a poem? The 'I' of a character in a play, on the other hand, is open all the time to the question Why: Why is it that he is saying this? What does his language tell us about the kind of man he is or will become?

These questions about 'I' are raised in a particularly teasing way by the sonnets cited at the head of this essay. As published in William Jaggard's catchpenny anthology *The Passionate Pilgrim* of 1599 these poems appear in a procession of miscellaneous erotic lyrics and are depersonalised by the unsupportive quality of the context. In the original editions the poems follow one another only as the pages follow one another (one poem to each recto page). In modern editions numbers are usually used to represent this mechanical relationship. The first of our poems is thus called '5'. What the number (or page position) means, of course, is that the poem appears after '4' ('Sweet Cytherea, sitting by a brook') and before '6' ('Scarce had the sun dried up the dewy morn') and relates to them only as 'another of the same', as some anthologies actually say. As a member of the vaguely conceived class 'erotic lyric', the poem is expected to fulfil certain conditions: it is expected to be a largely anonymous exercise in one of the appropriate styles, which we respond to in terms of its expertise in exploiting the conventions and bringing them alive within the sealed-up moment of the individual poem. In these terms, both these poems can be thought of as highly successful. In both, the persona 'I' sets up the easily accessible fiction of an address to a cruel mistress, whose power is such that the individual lover's shame at self-betrayal is over-come by the higher ethic of his worship. The poet, we conceive, wittily exploits the conventional paradox of faith (to oneself) against faith (to another). We enjoy, and take it that we are meant to enjoy, the balancing feats of 'forsworn. . .swear' or 'grace. . .disgrace' as instances of the poet-entertainer's virtuosity. And beyond this we are not encouraged to go. The question whether the poet and the lover are the same may indeed be raised; but the context gives us no means of answering it. We may say, if we wish, that the poet is only pretending to be the lover, so that he may entertain us. What we cannot say is that the poet preserves an ironic distance from the lover. Each poem offers us one voice, not two.

Let us now consider the same sonnets (in more or less the same texts) as they appear in *Love's Labour's Lost*. They are, of course, two of the four poems that the four Navarrese noblemen write to their ladies. The contexts in which our two specimen poems appear differ slightly from one another, but require no great distinction. The first poem (Berowne's) is discovered to us when it is misdelivered to Jaquenetta and read aloud by Nathaniel. The second (Longaville's) is read aloud by its author as an expression of his passion and his hope. The second reading is overheard and commented on by the scornful Berowne as the first is overheard and criticised by the supercilious Holofernes. In both cases the context of the play allows us to see that the poems make direct reference to actions and expectations that the play has established as part of its world. The 'I' is identified in the most simple way in the second case. Longaville is both lover and poet; as lover he expresses dissatisfaction with his effort as poet:

> I fear these stubborn lines lack power to move.
> O sweet Maria, empress of my love!
> These numbers will I tear, and write in prose.   (IV,iii,51–3)

Poetry is seen as a poor substitute for action or even exclamation ('O sweet Maria'). But even beyond Longaville's distrust of his versing lies Berowne's distrust of lovers, given critical advantage by his privileged position in this scene and in the play. Berowne's judgement takes us closest to the judgement of the play and so (in the only meaningful sense of the words) to the judgement of the author. Our application of contextual knowledge to the Berowne poem is not quite so simple. We do not see him read his own poem; but we do hear his comment on his own insufficiency as a poet, and this creates an ironic distance similar to that set up by Longaville. He enters in Act IV, scene iii 'with a paper'; we gather that this paper contains sonnet number two, as he comments on both poems:

I do love; and it hath taught me to rhyme, and to be melancholy; and here is part of my rhyme, and here my melancholy. Well, she hath one o' my sonnets already; the clown bore it, the fool sent it, and the lady hath it: sweet clown, sweeter fool, sweetest lady! (IV,iii,11–15)

Earlier, when he had handed over the first sonnet for delivery, he had made a very similar comment on the absurdity of love and therefore of its expressions:

> Well, I will love, write, sigh, pray, sue, and groan:
> Some men must love my lady, and some Joan.   (III,i,194–5)

Berowne does not sharply differentiate writing from other absurd and shameful manifestations of the self-betrayal that constitutes falling in love: the intent to write is, he implies, as foolish as the writing itself. Longaville fears that his sonnet is (like himself) unworthy of his lady;

characteristically, Berowne has no such fear; his melancholy is not self-distrust but self-scorn. Consequently his sonnet is heard, when we hear it, as the natural expression of the self-ridiculed emotions that he has already told us that he feels:

> What! I love, I sue, I seek a wife –
> . . .   .
> Nay, to be perjured, which is worst of all;
> And, among three, to love the worst of all,
> . . .   .
> And I to sigh for her! to watch for her!
> To pray for her! Go to; it is a plague.   (III,i,179ff.)

The structure of the play does not allow another character to 'place' Berowne's poem for us (as he 'places' Longaville's) and so he has to come forward himself and expresses its absurdity.

Berowne's condemnation of his sonnet concentrates on the foolishness of the motive that drives him to write, and this allows us to be still capable of feeling detached or uncommitted about its literary merit. The gap between the poem and what the ostensible author says about the poem is not, of course, one that is clearly shown to us. All that is presented is the possibility that another mode of judgement might eventually appear. That Shakespeare is anxious not to foreclose judgement on the poem seems to be indicated by the part given to Holofernes in the manipulation of our response. Holofernes is presented as the opposite of Berowne. As a 'professional' literary critic he is not concerned with context or even content. His vulgar curiosity about the contents of the letter undergoes a comic transformation when he discovers that it impinges on the area of his 'special competence':

Under pardon, sir, what are the contents? or rather as Horace says in his – What, my soul, verses?

Not only in his critique of Berowne's poem but in his display of literary talent in his own poem, or rather exercise in 'affecting the letter', in his subsequent immensely self-satisfied description of his creative processes and in his comments on Mantuan and Ovid, he sees poetry only as technique, judged good or bad by the arbitrary standards of self-importance. The effect of Holofernes's irrelevant judgements is to leave the poem clearly unjudged, and to throw our attention back from literary to dramatic standards, from poem to poetry, from expression to the intention and character of the dramatised author – Berowne. The paradoxes which, when we read the poem in *The Passionate Pilgrim,* seem to be the

conventions of the Petrarchan mode, are now seen to express the paradoxical mind of the stated author. The poem is now a commentary on the
story which is expressed more fully and more humanly in the course of
the play. Berowne is perceived to be writing about his own swearing and
intended forswearing and the process by which he will use the casuistry of
vows to justify his change of heart. As the context is perceived to be
comic, so the sonnet is sucked into the comic mode and becomes one
more example of the lengths to which the 'learned. . .tongue' will go in its
efforts to prove that what it desires is also what is right to be desired.
Poetry is validated as fiction.

What has happened to the standards of judgement that seemed appropriate to the same poem when it appeared in *The Passionate Pilgrim*? Are
the thoughts about good and bad verse that we judge by in the context of
an anthology now totally irrelevant? It may be argued that the poems in
Love's Labour's Lost are not good enough in any context to pose such an
all-or-nothing kind of question. They are certainly not the greatest
sonnets ever written. But let us suppose that more admired Shakespeare
sonnets – say 'If the dull substance of my flesh were thought' (44) or
'Where art thou, Muse, that thou forget'st so long' (100) – were among
the poems presented by the Navarrese lords to their ladies; would we not
assimilate these also to the comic and derisory context? Certainly it would
not be too difficult then to observe the comic reassessment of the 'muse'
in the latter poem, the discovery of darkness and worthlessness in what
had earlier seemed the higher pursuit. And in the former poem the
impediment that physical distance imposes on the substance of love
would probably be read as a comic reversal of the earlier assumption that
thought would operate to conquer flesh, as in Longaville's 'The mind
shall banquet, though the body pine' (1,i,25). Had we known these poems
only in the context of *Love's Labour's Lost* we would, I suspect, regard
them as parodic in their essential nature and not simply by virtue of the
context to which they were assimilated. For the comparisons we have
made would suggest that it is the latter, the context, that is dominant,
limiting our mode of aesthetic judgement to what the play makes possible. It is probably true that a poem as patently bad as Holofernes's

The preyful Princess pierced and pricked a pretty pleasing pricket

cannot seem other than bad, whatever the context. Had this been
Berowne's sonnet, the basic congruity between character and language
would seem to have been lost. But within a narrower range of effects,

from neutral to excellent, the point would seem to hold – poetic suffi-
ciency is absorbed into its dramatic context and takes the particular
colour that the context allows. But one must not push this perception too
far. The energy of the poem does not simply drain away into the context
of the play; it remains obvious enough to challenge us, as it were, to
remember its anthology potential.

These observations would seem pertinent to *Love's Labour's Lost* not
only in the dramatisation of the lovers' sonnets, but throughout its
length. For *Love's Labour's Lost* is of all Shakespeare's plays the one
which most consistently and openly expresses moral or psychological
norms in terms of stylistic ones. This is most obvious in the cases of the
marginal eccentrics – Armado, Holofernes, Dull, Jaquenetta, etc. These
are characters whose competence to organise or even understand their
experience is open to general doubt; but this incompetence is expressed
primarily in terms of the language they use rather than the deeds they do,
shown as constantly derived from the desire to make an effect rather than
achieve an end, and so either too high or too low, too luxuriant or too
starved for the simple business of connecting inner desires and outer
conditions. The weight of our theatrical expectation is thrown on to what
they will say rather than what they may do:

> Our court, you know, is haunted
> With a refinèd traveller of Spain,
> A man in all the world's new fashion planted,
> That hath a mint of phrases in his brain;
> One who the music of his own vain tongue
> Doth ravish like enchanting harmony.   (I,i,160ff.)

After this preparation, it is properly Armado's style rather than Armado's
person that is brought on to the scene, and that so quickly that we are not
allowed to forget the expectations that have been formed. Berowne is
clearly meant to speak for all of us when he says, in response to the King's
reading of Armado's letter: 'This is not so well as I looked for, but the
best that ever I heard' (I,i,260–1). But judgement is not allowed to rest
there. The King's response to Berowne, 'Ay, the best for the worst',
reveals how quickly even for these eccentrics, stylistic criticism modu-
lates into moral judgement. But the movement between one and the other
is never allowed to be simple or secure. When, at the end of Act I, we
learn of Armado's love for Jaquenetta, our first response is in terms of the
linguistic gap between the two characters; but before the end of the play

even Armado's language comes to seem a way of expressing his human spirit. The human context has pushed rhetoric towards speech, as poems towards poetry.

These are, however, peripheral concerns of the play. If we wish to consider *Love's Labour's Lost* as a structure of alternative linguistic levels our concern must centre on the story of the four noblemen and their vow to use words to pursue learning and not at all to pursue women. As privileged by noble birth, education and social position we would expect these gentlemen to display the easy command of the high style that indicates effortless and unselfconscious superiority in the social structure that language implies. And so they do. But the play is organised not only to display but also to frustrate this simple linguistic superiority, since the vow outlaws the natural expression of their superior natures in 'talk with a woman'. The complexity of this treatment can easily be seen in a comparison with a contemporary play equally concerned with socio-linguistic levels – Ben Jonson's *Poetaster*. In *Poetaster* we meet a linguistic lunatic fringe comparable with that in *Love's Labour's Lost*. In Tucca, Ovid, Chloe, Hermogenes, etc., we find excesses of pedantry, courtliness, rhetorical force and melting romanticism presented as parallel to the social instability that explains their characters. But the central issue in *Poetaster* – the 'purging' of Crispinus's linguistic affectations in the Roman Academy set up by Virgil, Horace, Maecenas and Augustus – repeats rather than varies the peripheral matter. Jonson, unlike Shakespeare, shows us a clear central norm, against which all the other speech-modes must be judged – a mode depending chiefly on discrimination and rejection:

> There is no bountie to be shew'd to such,
> As haue no reall goodnesse: Bountie is
> A spice of vertue: and what vertuous act
> Can take effect on them, that haue no power
> Of equall habitude to apprehend it,
> But liue in worship of that idoll, vice,
> As if there were no vertue, but in shade
> Of strong imagination, meerely enforc't?
> This shewes, their knowledge is meere ignorance;
> Their farre-fetcht dignitie of soule, a phansy;
> And all their square pretext of grauitie
> A meere vaine glorie: hence, away with 'hem.   (IV,vi,62–73)

This self-consciously simple, grave and declarative eloquence presents itself as the transparent register of true social understanding. Jonson gives us little or no sense that socially approved men may find a gap between self-expression and social truth – a gap in which words offer the pleasures of exploration and of alternative existences, without threatening to become either narrowly normative or broadly deliquescent. It is over this precise gap, however, that the noblemen of Navarre are required to lift their various structures of art, allowed to display eloquence, but never free of the teasing perception that all modes of speech are modes of disguise, the more dazzling the more unstable. And it is just this situation that is the test of their nobility and their intelligence. Berowne moves through the instabilities of language with a tightrope-walker's elegance. But we should not think of this movement as leading naturally to a Jonsonian stability. Shakespeare uses the instability of language to express the quality of balance rather than the search for stasis.

The final passage I have quoted is, of course, the great expression of this linguistic *sprezzatura*, by which a gentleman is seen to stand above the styles he uses, savouring them, tempted by them, but finally balancing them against one another. The speech is, technically speaking, a palinode: Berowne forswears the Masque of Muscovites and other comparable obliquities. But the speech culminates in a stylistic renunciation which is larger than any particular event. The expensive and highly wrought clothings of the court – taffeta, silk, three-piled velvet – are seen as both deforming and unsubstantial. The maggots in the fly-blown clothes pushing up the nap of the material remind us of the puffed and quilted bombast or ostentation of clothes which enhance and conceal the poverty of the natural form. These are the products of the 'summer flies' who buzz and multiply when living is easy, but 'evaporate and fall' when the winter comes. Somewhere behind the wording lies, I assume, the fable of the grasshopper and the ant. The ant does not sing but is provident for winter. The grasshopper, the fly and the courtier dressed up in his bombastic language are all condemned as fit only for a protected 'unreal' environment. Ben Jonson again offers a parallel, in his related condemnation of clothes and language:

The excesse of Feasts, and apparell, are the notes of a sick State; and the wantonnesse of language, of a sick mind.[1]

But again Shakespeare goes beyond Jonson in his effort to show something more than condemnation. There is an alternative to courtly affectation, Berowne implies, in plain and honest talk, as honest as the clothes of peasants. Shakespeare, if not Berowne, invites us to wonder how honest that is. We may seem to have returned to our initial point that low or prosaic styles seem to be 'real' where high or complex styles are affectations. But Shakespeare, we notice, keeps the image of style as clothes on both sides of the comparison. A gentleman dressed in 'russet yeas and honest kersey noes' might be thought to be no less (and no more) affected than a gentleman in silk or a university professor in dungarees. Certainly Berowne's first attempt at his new language is not encouraging:

> Wench – so God help me, law! –
> My love to thee is sound, sans crack or flaw.

The play is quick to draw to our attention the persistence of affectation into the new mode. Berowne assures Rosaline that this is a mere remainder which practice will soon remove. I do not suppose that we are meant to be so sure. The very word *affection* (or *affectation*) should raise the question. In many modern texts line 407 reads 'spruce affectation'. But the early texts read 'spruce affection'. There was no difference of meaning between the two forms. There was, however, a spectrum of meanings available to Shakespeare in the verb *affect* and its derivatives: 'to be fond of', 'to be drawn to', 'to assume the character of', 'to profess, take upon one' and so, as the *OED* says, 'by imperceptible gradation', 'to counterfeit or pretend'. Berowne calls the lords 'affection's men-at-arms', or the knights of love (IV,iii,286). 'I do affect the very ground. . . where her shoe. . .doth tread', says Armado (I,ii,158ff.), meaning 'I am in love with it.' What the play asks is whether one can ever *profess* such affection without moving towards affectation (in the modern sense). Poise, balance and fully civilised humanity demand some degree of self-awareness and even self-regard so that the stylish presentation of the self can express properly the complex relation between the affector and the thing affected, the inner life and the outer world. In most of Shakespeare's comedies the male lovers are given an amused tolerance of their own noble absurdity as lovers; but they are not required to 'place' their follies for us, in relation to their other qualities. The beloved ladies do that for them (and us) by their characteristic combination of intellectual mockery and emotional dependence. But the ladies do not have this function in *Love's Labour's Lost*; their business is to assert one side of the dialectic and one side only – that the lords' gestures of affection have been pure affectation, their poetry of love mere poems. The answer to this point of view is not clearly stated in the play, and probably cannot be made too categorically without destroying the effect sought for; but if we respond to the gaiety and inventiveness of the verbal styles adopted by

the lords, and particularly by their _raisonneur_, Berowne, we may allow
that the boundary line between affection and affectation cannot be drawn
so neatly. But it is not simply in the attractiveness of these personalities
that the ladies are answered; the whole play moves in a direction which
keeps open (at the very least) the possibility that stylishness is a necessity
rather than a self-indulgence. The surface seems to say the opposite: the
play seems to promise a future in which the ladies will be satisfied, in
which affection will be freed from affectation and language will become a
simple and direct expression of meaning. Not surprisingly, Shakespeare
never shows us this future, and perhaps he means us to see that he is
promising it with his tongue in his cheek.

The promise to move forward to simple language is returned to again
when Berowne tells the Princess, 'Honest plain words best pierce the ear
of grief' (v,ii,741). But the speech these words introduce is anything but
plain. Its argument, indeed, runs counter to the possibility of speaking
plainly about love. Love, says Berowne, is dependent on things outside
the mind and is therefore essentially an unstable commodity:

> skipping and vain;
> Formed by the eye and therefore, like the eye,
> Full of strange shapes, of habits, and of forms,
> Varying in subjects as the eye doth roll
> To every varied object in his glance.   (v,ii,749–53)

We respond to the sophistries of this speech as an index to the attractive
energy of the mind that framed them. The end proposed (love) seems to
imply, of necessity, an exhibition of the traits that make the individual
lovable – power, fun, flexibility, self-awareness as well as committedness
– and so to justify their appearance. But the Princess will have none of it.
Letters, presumably containing the poems discussed above, have been
received but have been discounted 'As bombast and as lining to the time'.
As preparation for a future language without playfulness or self-regard,
Berowne is ordered to practise his wit in a hospice, where there will be no
self-pleasing responses to his jokes, for

> A jest's prosperity lies in the ear
> Of him that hears it, never in the tongue
> Of him that makes it.   (v,ii,849–51)

This is a death-sentence to dramatic poetry, in which words exist to
express selves. It is no surprise that the play now quickly evaporates into
the de-dramatised impersonality of the final songs, with a promise (but
no more than a promise) of human resolution in the future.

The ending decrees the abolition of style in order to assert the primacy of experience. This powerful gesture has to be seen, of course, in relation to the whole play. For the play might seem to have lost balance by allowing too easily that the dazzle of poetic delight is sufficient to be counted truth, or even that it is a true index of the moral worth of its speakers. Shakespeare has been able to indulge himself (and us) in the fun of rhetoric only because he has preserved an un-Jonsonian gap between poetic power and social truth, poems and poetry. In fact he has allowed us to be constantly aware not only of the stylist's command but also of his tendency to solipsism, the extent to which language as a window into other lives can become a mirror in which we make faces at ourselves, turning talk into style and communication into self-expression. The extremity of the final rejection reminds us that stylistic self-correction is hardly adequate to carry the weight of moral approval that the play requires before it can come to rest. I have spoken above of the tension between poem and context, which is also the tension between language as the mirror of self and language as the servant of society. I have suggested that the 'poems' are placed in our attention by the contexts in which they appear. What needs to be stressed further is that they do not thereby lose their potential as mere poems: the 'I' of the lover can easily reappear as the 'I' of the poet. However savagely the play finally forecloses its options we should not forget that it is this freedom of potential status that gives the poetry its extraordinary hold on our attention.

NOTE

1 *Discoveries:* 'de corruptela morum', ll. 956–8 in vol. VIII (1947), p. 593, of *Ben Jonson,* ed. C. H. Herford and P. and E. Simpson, 11 vols. (Oxford, 1925–52).

The declaration of love

PHILIP EDWARDS

I

Romeo.	Ah, Juliet, if the measure of thy joy	1
	Be heaped like mine, and that thy skill be more	2
	To blazon it, then sweeten with thy breath	3
	This neighbour air, and let rich music's tongue	4
	Unfold the imagined happiness that both	5
	Receive in either by this dear encounter.	6
Juliet.	Conceit, more rich in matter than in words,	7
	Brags of his substance, not of ornament.	8
	They are but beggars that can count their worth;	9
	But my true love is grown to such excess,	10
	I cannot sum up sum of half my wealth.	11

(*Romeo and Juliet*, II,vi,24–34)

This essay examines Shakespeare's use of a very ordinary idea: that in expressing love words may be inadequate or treacherous. There are several occasions in the plays when there is a rather formal declaration of love, or a demand for it as in the passage from *Romeo and Juliet* above, and almost always on these occasions one or other of the partners shows a distrust of language. The need to make or receive a verbal profession of love seems as constant as the doubt about its value. Shakespeare exploits and varies the commonplace notion that there is a gap between words and feelings with a good deal of subtlety, and to attend closely to what he is doing in each play is to come closer not only to the individuality of the characters but to the quality of the play itself. And in the long run we sense the scepticism of a great master of language about the reliability of his own verbal stock-in-trade as the true voice of feeling.

Act II, scene vi of *Romeo and Juliet* is the short scene in which the two

lovers come to Friar Lawrence's cell for their secret wedding. Juliet
enters 'somewhat fast, and embraceth Romeo', as the first quarto puts it.
Romeo greets her with the words quoted above. His speech is a ceremonious demand for a formal statement of their shared happiness, and it
seems important to him that she should thus certify the extent of her love
for him. The word 'blazon' (l. 3) is not dominated by the heraldic sense,
as the *OED* makes clear; it interacts with the verb 'blaze' to have a
meaning something like 'proclaim in fitting words'. It has to do with
public, even defiant utterance, and it has to do with description – as in
the 'eternal blazon' which the Ghost in *Hamlet* is prohibited from
making. The 'imagined happiness' (l. 5) is tricky for us, wrongly suggesting that which is only in the mind, or foreseen, rather than that which is
real and present. The easiest paraphrase is 'the happiness within', or 'the
happiness in our thoughts'. The idea of an interior region where things
are truly experienced and registered but not expressed in words is very
important in what we are examining. So too is the image of a quantity of
love heaped up like wheat (ll. 1–2) in that interior storehouse, reflecting
the richness of giving and receiving spoken of in Luke 6.8.

   The interior experience or possession is what Juliet calls 'conceit' (l. 7):
that which one has a conception or inner knowledge of. It is 'more rich'
(l. 7) both in quantity and in value. That is to say, what is within is bigger
than the words available to express it, and the substance is weight-for-
weight more valuable than the words. We are taken aback, surely, when
conceit 'brags of his substance' (l. 8) because the last thing we expect in
this context is the notion of boastful assertion. We could accept a word
meaning 'is proud of', but it is hard to make 'brag' mean only that.
Schmidt in his *Shakespeare-Lexicon* remarks that Shakespeare uses the
word with an apparently favourable meaning only twice, here and earlier
in this same play (concerning Romeo; 1,v,65–6):

> Verona brags of him
> To be a virtuous and well-governed youth.

The best we can do for 'brag' is to let it mean 'speaks proudly of', and it
leaves us with a puzzle because conceit's pride ought properly to be silent
pride. Juliet refuses to meet Romeo's request that she should 'unfold the
imagined happiness' in words. That inner awarenesss which she calls
'conceit' knows and values its true possessions, but scorns words, which
are ornamental decoration. Once conceit brags of its substance it seems to
have strayed into the treacherous world of words. There are always

difficulties in using speech to express the virtues of inarticulacy; but
'brags' seems to me an unfortunate word.

In the next three lines (9–11) Juliet's argument changes course. She
has claimed that what matters is what one has: speech is only decoration.
In saying 'They are but beggars that can count their worth' she turns
towards the cliché later used by Antony, 'There's beggary in the love that
can be reckoned'; that is, not that language is irrelevant or inessential, but
that it is inadequate. Now this cliché is the commonest figure of speech
for expressing a great emotion – 'words fail me' – and is constantly used
for effect by experienced orators. By quite a slight alteration of course,
Juliet softens her refusal of Romeo's demand. What she has so far said is a
gentle rebuke for believing in the value of spoken declarations. But then,
essentially, she makes the declaration: 'my true love is grown to such
excess, / I cannot sum up sum of half my wealth.'

There is a history to Romeo's demand which helps to explain Juliet's
intricate answer. In the balcony-scene (II,ii) Juliet comes out unaware of
Romeo's presence and tells the night of her love, speaking of 'that dear
perfection which he owes', and ending 'Romeo, doff thy name; . . .Take
all myself' (ll. 47–9). In speaking to herself she has spoken the truth;
there is no question of the deceitfulness of language. She says later, 'Thou
overheardst, ere I was ware, / My true love's passion' (l. 104). When
language is social communication, things are different.

> Fain would I dwell on form, fain, fain deny
> What I have spoke.   (ll. 88–9)

She has, unwittingly, broken through that language which is given us to
disguise our thoughts and confessed her love to him. Her desire is that he
should do the same. 'Dost thou love me?' she asks; and of course the
emphasis falls 'Dost *thou* love *me*?' But at once her anxiety about the
treachery of language shows itself.

> I know thou wilt say ay,
> And I will take thy word; yet, if thou swear'st,
> Thou mayst prove false; at lovers' perjuries
> They say Jove laughs. O gentle Romeo,
> If thou dost love, pronounce it faithfully.   (ll. 90–4)

Everyone observes in this wonderful scene the contrast between the
directness and straightforward simplicity of Juliet's language and the
showiness of Romeo's conceits. He is only bantering when he constantly
turns aside her direct questions with elaborate evasions, but, playful or

not, his tendency to project the situation on a screen by verbalising it
connects with his ceremonious demand in II,vi that Juliet should 'blazon'
their love. Juliet craves for something as simple and informal as her own
unguarded admission. It is unfortunate that Romeo, charged to 'pro-
nounce it faithfully', begins with an elaborate protestation.

> Romeo. Lady, by yonder blessèd moon I vow,
>   That tips with silver all these fruit-tree tops –
> Juliet. O swear not by the moon, th' inconstant moon,
>   That monthly changes in her circled orb,
>   Lest that thy love prove likewise variable.
> Romeo. What shall I swear by?
> Juliet.   Do not swear at all;
>   Or, if thou wilt, swear by thy gracious self,
>   Which is the god of my idolatry,
>   And I'll believe thee.
> Romeo.   If my heart's dear love –
> Juliet. Well, do not swear. Although I joy in thee,
>   I have no joy of this contract tonight:
>   It is too rash, too unadvised, too sudden.   (ll. 107–18)

It is scarcely possible to think of a 'contract' without the words in which it
is expressed; it is a mutual exchange of vows of love. And this it is which
Juliet suddenly shirks. It is surely the feeling that there is something
wrong with the words that makes Juliet feel that the agreement is wrong.
The beautiful image which follows, of the bud of love ripening to a flower
'when next we meet', suggests perhaps a maturing of language too, so that
next time love and the avowal of love would fuse into one.

Romeo, however, is unwilling to relinquish this moment of verbal
contract, this pronunciation which will seal their love:

> Romeo. O, wilt thou leave me so unsatisfied?
> Juliet. What satisfaction canst thou have to-night?
> Romeo. Th' exchange of thy love's faithful vow for mine.   (ll. 125–7)

The laugh which this exchange properly gets in the theatre enhances
rather than obscures his earnestness. Juliet is willing to repeat her vow at
this; she yearns as much as he does for the troth-plight which she
distrusts.

> My bounty is as boundless as the sea,
> My love as deep: the more I give to thee,
> The more I have, for both are infinite.   (ll. 133–5)

But the Nurse interrupts before Romeo has another chance of declaring
his love. When Juliet comes back she has turned from the assurance of

words to the assurance of deeds, the marriage ceremony. Next time they meet, as we have already seen, Romeo immediately returns to the declaration of love. The grand manner in which he puts the demand must surely make Juliet shrink just a little from being drawn into that arena of protestation which made her unhappy for a moment on the previous occasion. Her sensitivity that one whose affection she does not question might coarsen their love by a misuse of language leads her to reject as inessential the kind of pronouncement which Romeo would like. She is able, however, to turn her comment on the poverty of language into a pretty enough, if commonplace, avowal of love. She has good sense enough to compromise; knowing that if language could tarnish love, silence might do worse.

II

Polixenes.	I have put you out.	1
	But to your protestation; let me hear	2
	What you profess.	3
Florizel.	Do, and be witness to't.	4
Polixenes.	And this my neighbour too?	5
Florizel.	And he, and more	6
	Than he, and men – the earth, the heavens, and all:	7
	That, were I crowned the most imperial monarch,	8
	Thereof most worthy, were I the fairest youth	9
	That ever made eye swerve, had force and knowledge	10
	More than was ever man's, I would not prize them	11
	Without her love; for her employ them all;	12
	Commend them and condemn them to her service	13
	Or to their own perdition.	14
Polixenes.	Fairly offered.	15
Camillo.	This shows a sound affection.	16
Shepherd.	But, my daughter,	17
	Say you the like to him?	18
Perdita.	I cannot speak	19
	So well, nothing so well; no, nor mean better.	20
	By th' pattern of mine own thoughts I cut out	21
	The purity of his.	22

(*The Winter's Tale*, IV,iv,359–75)

Florizel makes a public declaration of love, and Camillo is confident that the spoken words are a guarantee of Florizel's feelings. Perdita, like Juliet, won't participate, and her refusal carries a tacit rebuke. The immediate import of her speech (ll. 19–22) is of course depreciation of herself and praise of Florizel: his eloquence is far beyond hers and she cannot surpass his love. The implication of her words goes quite another way. Their true burden is that Florizel's speech, by itself, is nothing. 'I cannot speak so well. . .nor mean better.' There is a clear inference that although speech has meaning, people have meanings too; the meanings of the heart do not depend on speech and can exist without it. In 'nor mean better' Perdita puns on the two senses; i.e. 'I could not have better intentions than his speech imports'. Her final sentence (ll. 21–2) goes a good deal further. She has already implied, in 'nor mean better', that she can 'mean' as well as he though without the power of eloquence. She goes on to imply that she does not need and does not accept his words as the true voucher of his affection.

> By th' pattern of mine own thoughts I cut out
> The purity of his.

It is an extraordinary remark. Though Florizel spoke well he might have 'meant' ill. Perdita's interior awareness of her emotions (Juliet's 'conceit') provides a pattern for her to judge his by. But that is not quite what she says. The image is presumably from tailoring or dressmaking (or glove-making). So we should say more strictly that the shape of her own feelings enables her to make out the shape of his. The idea is strongly conveyed of heart speaking to heart, the one instinctively interpreting the meaning of the other without the intervention of words. Something else besides his words communicates his love and his faith to her. His meaning is excellent; she could not better it; indeed, their hearts' meanings are as identical as a garment-maker's pattern and the material which is cut from it. But neither the quality of her love nor her recognition of Florizel's has anything to do with a formal declaration in words, such as Florizel rather pretentiously makes.

III

Goneril.	Sir, I love you more than word can wield the matter;	1
	Dearer than eyesight, space, and liberty;	2
	Beyond what can be valued, rich or rare;	3
	No less than life, with grace, health, beauty, honour;	4
	As much as child e'er loved, or father found;	5
	A love that makes breath poor, and speech unable:	6
	Beyond all manner of so much I love you.	7
Cordelia [aside].	What shall Cordelia speak? Love, and be silent.	8

· · ·   · · ·   · · ·   · · ·   · · ·

Lear.	What can you say, to draw	9
	A third more opulent than your sisters? Speak.	10

Cordelia.	Nothing, my lord.	11
Lear.	Nothing!	12
Cordelia.	Nothing.	13
Lear.	Nothing will come of nothing. Speak again.	14
Cordelia.	Unhappy that I am, I cannot heave	15
	My heart into my mouth. I love your Majesty	16
	According to my bond; no more nor less.	17

(*King Lear*, 1,i,54–61; 84–92)

Once again, though in such different circumstances, a heroine is called upon for a declaration of love and once again she refuses. How can anyone who has really deep feelings be so voluble about them? In two of her sentences, 'I am sure my love's / More ponderous than my tongue' (not quoted above) and 'I cannot heave / My heart into my mouth' (ll. 15–16), Cordelia repeats the image of weightiness within and implies the common contrast of feeling heart and glib tongue. But there is a real problem here, which Anne Barton wrote perceptively about in 'Shakespeare and the Limits of Language'.[1]

The irony lies in the fact that [Cordelia's] broken statements only echo what her sisters have so fulsomely been saying: 'I love you more than word can wield the matter.' In Cordelia's case, the declaration of the inadequacy of language happens to express a true state of feeling. Her love for her father does indeed make her breath poor and speech unable; it is not a mere rhetorical flourish. But how can one tell the difference between sincerity and pretence, especially when both employ the same disclaimers? Cordelia's sisters have usurped, falsely, her own genuine excuse. . .Their professions have contaminated the truth of her own situation.

As spectators and listeners we are asked to distinguish between sincere and insincere people, both of whom protest that words cannot utter the weight or depth of their feelings. The difficulty goes deeper. Is there any trick in the words which enables us to distinguish sincerity from hypocrisy in declarations of love *generally*? When Goneril says, 'Beyond what can be valued, rich or rare' (l. 3), what denotes her falseness? Nothing in the words at all. It is more moving than Juliet's 'I cannot sum up sum of half my wealth.'

Here is Ferdinand's reply, in *The Tempest*, to Miranda's question, 'Do you love me?'

> O heaven, O earth, bear witness to this sound,
> And crown what I profess with kind event,
> If I speak true! If hollowly, invert
> What best is boded me to mischief! I,
> Beyond all limit of what else i' th' world,
> Do love, prize, honour you.

Miranda.   I am a fool
To weep at what I am glad of.   (iii,i,68–74)

Some might vote that Goneril does it better. Given almost any protestation of love by a 'good' character in Shakespeare one could transfer it without indecorum to a hypocrite. Only the situation teaches us how it should be read. Our inability to discriminate, speech for speech, between the sincere and the insincere is striking support for Juliet and Perdita in their instinctive unwillingness to put faith in formal protestations even from those who they know genuinely love them. Elaborate speeches are suspect, and so too are statements of inability to make elaborate speeches. The ease with which Juliet slips from despising language to using scorn for language as a rhetorical device is indicative of the problem. What ways are open through this inscrutability of language? There is no escape from words, and, as we have seen, the need for assurance in words is keen in those who know their unreliability. Although in her essay Anne Barton rightly says of Cordelia, 'Actions are the only test. Words have lost all significance', we have to reflect that both speeches and silence are actions, inalienable members of the world of deeds. Cordelia's refusal to 'blazon' her love is the direct cause of the tragic events in *Lear*. She deceives the king by her silence, or at least the chilliness of her response, as Goneril and Regan deceive him by the warmth of theirs. Unexceptionable feelings and conduct may be compromised by the words or the silence misguidedly chosen to accompany them, and it is not only in *King Lear* that we feel this. While Cordelia speaks too little, Troilus speaks too much. In my last extract I look at the problem of the relation between words and deeds in *Troilus and Cressida*.

IV

Cressida.	. . . To fear the worst oft cures the worst.	1
Troilus.	O, let my lady apprehend no fear. In all Cupid's pageant	2
	there is presented no monster.	3
Cressida.	Nor nothing monstrous neither?	4
Troilus.	Nothing, but our undertakings when we vow to weep seas,	5
	live in fire, eat rocks, tame tigers; thinking it harder for	6
	our mistress to devise imposition enough than for us to undergo	7
	any difficulty imposed. This is the monstruosity in love,	8
	lady, that the will is infinite, and the execution confined;	9
	that the desire is boundless, and the act a slave to limit.	10
Cressida.	They say all lovers swear more performance than they	11
	are able, and yet reserve an ability that they never perform;	12
	vowing more than the perfection of ten, and discharging less	13
	than the tenth part of one. They that have the voice of lions	14
	and the act of hares, are they not monsters?	15

Troilus.	Are there such? Such are not we. Praise us as we are	16
	tasted, allow us as we prove; our head shall go bare till	17
	merit crown it. No perfection in reversion shall have a	18
	praise in present. We will not name desert before his birth;	19
	and, being born, his addition shall be humble. Few words to	20
	fair faith: Troilus shall be such to Cressid as what envy	21
	can say worst shall be a mock for his truth; and what truth	22
	can speak truest not truer than Troilus.	23
Cressida.	Will you walk in, my lord?	24

(*Troilus and Cressida*, III,ii,70–95)

Pandarus has just left Troilus and Cressida together for the first time. At the beginning of the scene, Troilus's expectation expressed itself in verse as he spoke of lily beds and love's thrice-repurèd nectar. But these first exchanges are in the cooler element of prose. Troilus's first long speech (ll. 5–10) covers a lot of ground. In the first two lines he is jocular: the only thing monstrous in love is the absurdity of lovers' undertakings. It is really protestations in well-worn conventions that he is talking about, the sort of thing Juliet was worried that Romeo might go in for. Troilus puts it lightly, accepting the extravagance – '*our* undertakings' (l. 5). With the following clause, however, 'thinking it harder' (l. 6), he becomes more serious, for the subject is now not verbal protestations but the real ambition to perform – not *saying* we'll perform impossible missions but believing that we could. The movement is slight but important, because in the renowned sentence which follows (ll. 8–10) the monstruosity in love has quite shifted from what it started as. From banter about outrageous promises, we have moved to a protest about the nature of man. From laughable exaggeration we go to the infinite capacity of the imagination and the pettiness of material possibilities. Monstruosity began as a humorous conception of the grotesqueness of what infatuated lovers promise; it ends by being the bad bargain of living. The grotesqueness has shifted from the human imagination to the limitations of earthly achievement. The nobility of the final idea is, however, qualified by its bad start. The vision of infinite will and boundless desire struggling to get free of mortal constraints has begun in the verbal boasting of lovers and remains theatrical. 'Weep seas, live in fire, eat rocks, tame tigers'; is this the boundless desire of man?

In reply (ll. 11–15), Cressida ignores entirely Troilus's philosophic ending and returns to the *terra firma* of the beginning of the speech, agreeing with what Troilus did not quite say. 'All lovers swear more performance than they are able' (ll. 11–12) charges men with a deceitfulness very different from the heroic protestations of well-meaning men which was what was in Troilus's mind. She continues with the remarkable further charge that lovers do not deceive in words only but also in their deeds. They 'reserve an ability that they never perform' (l. 12). Their vows are excessive and their behaviour is a cheat. This view of men is consistent with that which she so succinctly expressed in her famous first soliloquy (I,ii,274–87): 'Women are angels, wooing: / Things won are done.' So for her, monstruosity in love is not essentially a matter of language, nor of the discrepancy between the life of the mind and the limits of action, but of masculine unreliability in promising adoration but being casual and inattentive in actual affection: 'the voice of lions and the act of hares' (ll. 14–15).

It is against this low view of the characteristics of men that Troilus now speaks (ll. 16–23), not attempting to raise again the divorce between desire and act but concentrating on the relation between words and deeds. *He* will be judged by his acts, not by his statements or promises, which he calls 'perfection in reversion' (l. 18). The kernel of his speech is the disavowal of language: 'Few words to fair faith' (ll. 20–21). He concludes with a contorted sentence (ll. 21–3) which attempts to show his silent faith surrounded by and unmoved by the words of others. Envy will be able to do no more than mock at his unassailable constancy; and on the other side there can be no exaggeration or overpraising since words can't improve on perfection. Troilus's constancy would be absolute so that detraction could not reach it nor praise falsify it. Cressida listens to this and says (her finest moment?): 'Will you walk in, my lord?'

It is amusing that in the very act of disowning rhetoric ('Few words to fair faith') Troilus should fall into bragging. It is not at all as with Juliet and Goneril that the shortcomings of language are used to stress the extent of his love. He truly believes that his conduct is set apart from the world of words. But in both these speeches to Cressida he becomes elevated by an idea of himself that has everything to do with the power of words. In the first, he sees himself tragically caught in the trap of life; in the second he is the model of constant lovers. Towards the end of the play, Troilus tears up the letter which Cressida has sent him from the Grecian camp: 'Words, words, mere words, no matter from the heart.'

> My love with words and errors still she feeds,
> But edifies another with her deeds.   (V,iii,111–12)

There is no doubting Troilus's constancy, but in talking of *feeding love*

with words he names his own ailment. In the very first scene he demanded
from himself, via Apollo, a verbal projection of his love:

> Tell me, Apollo, for thy Daphne's love,
> What Cressid is, what Pandar, and what we?
> Her bed is India; there she lies, a pearl.   (i,i,97–9)

By words and images he inflates the glory and romance of his relationship
and when he talks of his own affection this inflation shows a self-absorp-
tion that is not appealing:

> I stalk about her door
> Like a strange soul upon the Stygian banks
> Staying for waftage. O be thou [Pandarus] my Charon,
> And give me swift transportance to these fields
> Where I may wallow in the lily beds
> Proposed for the deserver!   (iii,ii,8–13)

In particular, he tends to dramatise the purity, intensity, and immuta-
bility of his devotion, and in two speeches the self-regard is remarkable.
The first closely follows the passage we have been discussing, and in it he
questions whether any woman could match his own constancy. He wishes

> that persuasion could but thus convince me
> That my integrity and truth to you
> Might be affronted with the match and weight
> Of such a winnowed purity in love.
> How were I then uplifted! but, alas,
> I am as true as truth's simplicity,
> And simpler than the infancy of truth.   (iii,ii,160–6)

The second passage comes just after they have been told that Cressida is
to be sent to the Greeks.

> Cressid, I love thee in so strained a purity
> That the blest gods, as angry with my fancy,
> More bright in zeal than the devotion which
> Cold lips blow to their deities, take thee from me.   (iv,iv,23–6)

The trouble with Troilus is less that he over-values Cressida, as he
over-values Helen, than that she is scarcely there at all. As in a cruder way
his 'anticipation' speech (iii,ii,17–28) dwelt entirely on the kind and
amount of pleasure which he himself was about to receive, so love as a
mutual exchange is quite obscured by the 'lily beds' of words regarding
the quality of his own devotion in which he rests or wallows. Even in a
speech forswearing wordy proclamation he proclaimed his steadfastness;

and in this last speech quoted, at the moment of disaster he interprets the catastrophe as vengeance by the gods, jealous of his loving so beautifully.

In an extreme way Troilus exhibits what Juliet feared in Romeo and what so many of Shakespeare's male lovers show, a tendency to cheapen a sincere affection in the effort to affirm it in words. Juliet's nervousness that words might tamper with love seems justified. Juliet, Perdita, Cordelia – and Cressida too – are front-line troops in a campaign to deflate a rotundity of language which seems to characterise even the best people when they try to voice their feelings of love. In their declarations the best become confused with the worst; their language is indistinguishable. To suit word to feeling and action is Shakespeare's concern too: he spends his whole life trying to find language which will give the sense of authenticity to emotions. One cannot help feeling that the challenge to lovers to make words and faith match represents in some measure the great ventriloquist's acknowledgement of how pliable and meretricious language is, creating falsehood and uncreating truth with equal ease.

NOTE

1 *Shakespeare Survey 24* (Cambridge, 1971), pp. 19–30 (24–5).

Juliet's Nurse: the uses of inconsequentiality

STANLEY WELLS

	Lady Capulet.	Thou knowest my daughter's of a pretty age.
	Nurse.	Faith, I can tell her age unto an hour.
	Lady Capulet.	She's not fourteen.
	Nurse.	I'll lay fourteen of my teeth –
		And yet, to my teen be it spoken, I have but four –
15		She's not fourteen. How long is it now
		To Lammas-tide?
	Lady Capulet.	A fortnight and odd days.
	Nurse.	Even or odd, of all days in the year,
		Come Lammas Eve at night shall she be fourteen.
		Susan and she – God rest all Christian souls! –
20		Were of an age. Well, Susan is with God;
		She was too good for me. But, as I said,
		On Lammas Eve at night shall she be fourteen;
		That shall she, marry; I remember it well.
		'Tis since the earthquake now eleven years;
25		And she was weaned – I never shall forget it –
		Of all the days of the year, upon that day;
		For I had then laid wormwood to my dug,
		Sitting in the sun under the dove-house wall.
		My lord and you were then at Mantua.
30		Nay, I do bear a brain. But, as I said,
		When it did taste the wormwood on the nipple
		Of my dug, and felt it bitter, pretty fool,
		To see it tetchy, and fall out with the dug!
		Shake, quoth the dovehouse. 'Twas no need, I trow,
35		To bid me trudge.
		And since that time it is eleven years;
		For then she could stand high-lone; nay, by th'rood,
		She could have run and waddled all about;
		For even the day before, she broke her brow;
40		And then my husband – God be with his soul!
		'A was a merry man – took up the child.
		'Yea,' quoth he, 'dost thou fall upon thy face?
		Thou wilt fall backward when thou hast more wit,

```
                              Wilt thou not, Jule?' And, by my holidam,
45                            The pretty wretch left crying, and said 'Ay'.
                              To see, now, how a jest shall come about!
                              I warrant, an I should live a thousand years,
                              I never should forget it: 'Wilt thou not, Jule?' quoth he;
                              And, pretty fool, it stinted, and said 'Ay'.
50   Lady Capulet.  Enough of this; I pray thee hold thy peace.
     Nurse.         Yes, madam. Yet I cannot choose but laugh
                              To think it should leave crying and say 'Ay'.
                              And yet, I warrant, it had upon it brow
                              A bump as big as a young cock'rel's stone –
55                            A perilous knock; and it cried bitterly.
                              'Yea,' quoth my husband, 'fall'st upon thy face?
                              Thou wilt fall backward when thou comest to age;
                              Wilt thou not, Jule?' It stinted, and said 'Ay'.
     Juliet.        And stint thou too, I pray thee, nurse, say I.
```

(Romeo and Juliet, I,iii,11–59)

The style of the Nurse's speeches in Act I, scene iii of *Romeo and Juliet* makes a vivid impact on both readers and spectators. It is described by Nicholas Brooke as 'something altogether new, both in this play and, in fact, in Shakespeare's output'. He finds its 'nearest antecedent', not in verse, but in 'the prose of I,i'. While 'it goes far beyond that', nevertheless 'its characteristic is that it is close to prose, or rather to prosaic speech, developing its own rhythmic momentum'.[1] By the time that Shakespeare wrote *Romeo and Juliet* he had written much dialogue that approximates to prosaic speech rather than to literary prose; and I should like to begin this essay by examining some of the characteristics of the Nurse's utterance which may account for the claim that it represents 'something altogether new'.

It is easy to point to aspects of the style which create the illusion of spontaneity. There are colloquial expressions such as 'Come Lammas Eve at night', 'Shake, quoth the dovehouse' (so personal as to be obscure in meaning), 'stand high-lone', and 'broke her brow'. The diction is familiar, even vulgar: 'dug', 'tetchy', 'trudge', 'waddled'. There are emphatic or asseverative expressions, including 'Well', 'as I said', 'marry', 'Nay', 'I trow', 'by th'rood', 'by my holidam', 'I warrant'. Some of these words and phrases, and others, are repeated or slightly varied in a manner that would be avoided by a literary artist but which helps to bind the speech together and to give the impression that they are idiosyncratic to the speaker: 'God rest all Christian souls!'. . .'God be with his soul!': is this sententiousness or piety? – the performer may decide; 'I remember it well. . .I never shall forget it. . .I never should forget it'; 'pretty fool. . . pretty wretch. . .pretty fool'; and 'To see it. . .To see, now. . .'.

These devices might equally well be discerned in the racy prose dialogue of Act I, scene i, or in individually longer prose speeches, such as Launce's principal soliloquies in *The Two Gentlemen of Verona* (II,iii; IV,iv). More individual to the Nurse is the structure and argument of the speech (or, in effect, its denial of structure and argument): the sequence of ideas and images, and the aim to which they are applied. Coleridge referred to them in an 'Essay on Method in Thought'[2] as an example of Shakespeare's exhibitions of 'the difference between the products of a well disciplined and those of an uncultivated understanding'. He remarks that 'the absence of Method, what characterises the uneducated, is occasioned by a habitual submission of the understanding to mere events and images as such, and independent of any power in the mind to classify or appropriate them'. One very obvious symptom of the 'absence of Method' in the Nurse's disquisition is the frequency with which she interrupts herself. Sometimes this is because she follows an associative train of thought irrespective of its relevance to her listeners:

> I'll lay fourteen of my teeth –
> And yet, to my teen be it spoken, I have but four –
> She's not fourteen.

Is her self-interruption here a conscious playing with 'four' and 'teen', or rather the subconscious struggle to clear her mind of verbal entanglements? Again, the performer may choose.

Part of the comedy of the Nurse's utterance lies in the fact that what she interrupts has in itself no logical sequence. The information that she has to convey in her main speech is entirely contained in its second line:

> Come Lammas Eve at night shall she be fourteen.

This fact might well be pointed by stage business, Lady Capulet endeavouring to resume the conversation after this statement. But the Nurse's well of recollection has been tapped, and the flow cannot be quenched. Coleridge parallels this speech of the Nurse with one of Mistress Quickly. In answer to Falstaff's question 'What is the gross sum that I owe thee?', she replies

Marry, if thou wert an honest man, thyself and the money too. Thou didst swear to me upon a parcel-gilt goblet, sitting in my Dolphin chamber, at the round table, by a sea-coal fire, upon Wednesday in Wheeson week, when the Prince broke thy head for liking his father to a singing-man of Windsor – thou didst swear to me then, as I was washing thy

wound, to marry me and make me my lady thy wife. Canst thou deny it? Did not goodwife
Keech, the butcher's wife, come in then and call me gossip Quickly? Coming in to borrow
a mess of vinegar, telling us she had a good dish of prawns, whereby thou didst desire to
eat some, whereby I told thee they were ill for a green wound? (*2 Henry IV*, II,i,81–94)

Here, Coleridge remarks that 'the connexions and sequence which the
habit of Method can alone give have in this instance a substitute in the
fusion of passion'. The Nurse lacks Mistress Quickly's vituperative
passion of self-righteous indignation, but her recollections, too, are
grounded in emotion, provoked by the memory that she had had a
daughter of the same age as Juliet. The very fact that Susan's relationship
with the Nurse is not explicitly stated is itself an aspect of Shakespeare's
dramatic style here. It tells us obliquely of the Nurse's intimacy with the
family in which she lives, an intimacy which the performers can use by
suggesting a sympathetic, if bored, acceptance that once the Nurse has
embarked on this tack, she must be indulged. And it engages the audience
by requiring them to make the inference. The death of an infant has an
inevitable poignancy, and one which must link the Nurse to the Capulets
since Juliet has thriven on the milk which should have reared Susan. And
we may recall that the shadow of infant mortality has already darkened
the play, in Capulet's 'Earth hath swallowèd all my hopes but she'
(I,ii,14).

The Nurse's recollection that Juliet and Susan 'Were of an age' is
interrupted by the pious commonplace 'God rest all Christian souls!',
leading us to infer that Susan is dead, and is followed by two more clichés:
'Susan is with God; / She was too good for me.' The ordinariness of these
expressions is surely part of their point; they come naturally from the
mouth of a simple-minded woman. To say, as G. I. Duthie does in the
New Cambridge edition,[3] 'She knows she has faults. When she declares
that little Susan was too good for her, she is speaking partly jocularly but
partly, for a second, seriously, with self-knowledge', is surely to ignore
the stereotyped quality of the assertion.

After her digression, the Nurse's pulling herself up with 'But, as I
said', and coming full circle with

On Lammas Eve at night shall she be fourteen,

marks another point at which she might have concluded. But her recollections have a self-generating momentum, and as she goes on, she
becomes increasingly self-absorbed. Coleridge's 'Method' implies consideration for the listener (or reader), an ordering of statements requiring

the application of fundamental brainwork such as is associated with literary artistry or conscious rhetoric, and is thus outward-looking; the 'absence of Method', on the other hand, implies a delving into the subconscious which produces the kind of monologue that achieves communication rather by accident than by design. The Nurse makes no pretence that her ramblings are relevant to the situation. They are a form of self-indulgence which is also a form of both self-investigation and (when conducted in public) self-revelation, so the response of listeners is a measure of their response to the speaker's character. The Nurse's listeners allow her to continue; whether they do so with complete indulgence or with some degree of indifference, and with attempts to interrupt, is open to interpretation. The Nurse's repetitions of 'But, as I said' may be regarded as a method of staving off interruption, or they may be less outward-looking, her own method of attempting to exert some control over her discourse.

After concluding the first paragraph of her speech, she marks time for a moment with 'That shall she, marry; I remember it well' before embarking on another paragraph whose beginning also is to reappear as its ending. And from the recollection of one landmark – Lammas Eve as the time of the infant's birth – she passes to another – the day of 'the earthquake' as that on which Juliet was weaned. That Shakespeare was here considerately making a topical allusion in order to help scholars of the future to know when he wrote his play is improbable. An 'earthquake' is chosen as the kind of event which would be significant in the lives of all who experienced it, an episode certain to engrave itself upon the collective memory. It serves again to link the masters with their servants. The coincidence of Juliet's being weaned on the day of the earthquake is stressed in the phrase 'Of all the days of the year', and seems to confer importance upon the event; but always, as these facts emerge, they are linked and given significance by being shown as part of the life-experience of the woman who recollects them. It is her memory in which they dwell – 'I remember it well', 'I never shall forget it'; and it is her body with which they are associated.

So far we have had only statements; now, as she becomes more immersed in her topic, she becomes anecdotal. The absence of intellectual logic in what she says is apparent in the false connective 'For' – 'For I had then laid wormwood to my dug' – but the sudden sequence of nouns in this and the succeeding line – 'wormwood. . .dug. . .sun. . . dovehouse' and 'wall' – helps to create a vivid picture of peaceful normality which gains in credibility by its association with a violently abnormal event. Yet another association obtrudes – 'My lord and you were then at Mantua' – and the pressure of recollection becomes so great that the Nurse returns to the present in wonderment at her own mental powers – 'Nay, I do bear a brain.'[4]

She resumes her anecdote, losing herself again in memories which allow no acknowledgement that the baby of whom she speaks is the girl who stands beside her. Her style is not expository but exclamatory, deepening the suggestion that she is re-living the experience:

> pretty fool,
> To see it tetchy, and fall out with the dug!

This exclamation is followed by another, elliptical and slightly obscure,[5] which recalls the earthquake's shocking disruption of normality – 'Shake, quoth the dovehouse.' Again she is jolted back to the present as she recalls her hasty flight and rounds off the second paragraph with a return to the statement with which it began: 'And since that time it is eleven years.'

The final part of the speech again begins with a false connective, and has no logical link with what precedes it, nor even any obvious associative one, unless it is that the Nurse's memory of her need to 'trudge'[6] leads from her own legs to Juliet's, and thus to the recollection that Juliet was able to *stand* by herself. The second anecdote features another newly introduced character, the Nurse's husband; the touch of sadness that he is dead is offset by her memory of him as 'a merry man'. For the first time now she quotes direct speech, in her husband's somewhat bawdy, familiar remark to the child 'Jule'. The Nurse's own, self-absorbed delight in her recollections is evident in her repetition of the anecdote. Whether she has carried her stage audience along with her is again a matter for interpretation. Lady Capulet's interruption,

> Enough of this. I pray thee, hold thy peace

appears to demonstrate impatience, yet it can be played against its sense, in full enjoyment of the comedy of the tale. Coleridge referred to the Nurse's 'childlike fondness of repetition in her childish age – and that happy, humble ducking under, yet resurgence against the check –

> Yes, madam! *Yet* I cannot choose but laugh.'[7]

And she adds the circumstantial and bawdy detail of the 'bump as big as a

young cock'rel's stone' before winding herself to a standstill with her
fourth telling of the tale.

I have written of the speech so far as if it were composed in prose, not
verse. I have referred to the 'prose' characteristics of its diction and
structure, and to the fact that it quotes a passage of (supposedly) prose
speech. Although in modern editions we read the speech as verse, it is a
curious fact that it was printed as prose in all the early editions: the bad
quarto (1597), the good quarto (1599), and the First Folio (1623). It is less
surprising that verse should appear as prose in the memorially recon-
structed bad quarto than that most of the Nurse's speeches in this scene
are set in italic type in both quartos. There is evidence that in Q2 the first
thirty-four lines of the scene are reprinted directly from Q1,[8] and it is
likely that this fact influenced the Q2 compositor to go on setting these
speeches as prose even though they were presumably written out as verse
in the holograph from which he is believed to have set the remainder of
the scene. Not until Capell's edition (1768) were the Nurse's speeches
arranged as verse. In the meantime Thomas Otway had adapted and
amplified them, while retaining their substance, in unmistakable prose in
his *Caius Marius* (1679). Garrick, naturally, set them as prose in his
adaptation of 1748, followed, in spite of Capell, in John Bell's acting
edition (1774). At least two nineteenth-century editors – Staunton
(1857) and Keightley (1865) – did the same, and so does Frank A.
Marshall in the *Henry Irving Shakespeare* (8 vols, 1888–90), with a note
condemning 'the modern editors who have tried to make verse of what
was surely never intended for it', and asking: 'Why should Shakespeare
be made to violate every rule of rhythm and metre, for the sake of trying
to strain this conventional prose into blank verse?' (vol. 1, p. 240). Irving's
acting edition of 1882, however, prints the expurgated remnants as
verse.[9] G. B. Harrison reverted to prose in his Penguin edition (1937),
and even Dover Wilson wrote that 'editors have never been able to make
anything but very rough verse out of these speeches and it is quite
possible that Shakespeare intended them to be rhythmical (i.e. easily
memorized) prose'.[10] But this statement is impressionistic rather than
accurate. G. Walton Williams (p. 107) analyses the scene carefully and
shows that the earlier section of the Nurse's long speech 'is marked by
irregular verse': the nineteen lines include one four-syllable line (35),
three hypermetrical lines with unaccented final syllables (18, 22, 31); and
five hypermetrical lines with accented final syllables (23, 25, 26, 28, and

32); these are not violent irregularities, and several of them may be explained as contractions in pronunciation; the remainder of the scene, Williams finds, is 'in smooth verse' with minor exceptions. Minor rhythmic irregularities may be expected in verse which is so clearly intended as this is to represent 'prosaic speech'; as Kenneth Muir says, 'Shakespeare obtains some subtle effects by the verse rhythm underlying the apparently colloquial speech.'[11] Little more than a glance is needed to show that in both the inauthentically and the authentically derived sections, the ends of lines are almost invariably also the ends of sense-units: the only enjambment in the main speech is at lines 31–2 ('the nipple / Of my dug. . .'). There can be no question that Shakespeare was fully conscious that he was writing verse, nor, to my mind, that he was going further than ever before in the experiment of combining the diction, rhythms, and even the mental processes normally associated with prose utterance within the over-all rhythms of blank verse. The speeches would be remarkable enough as an exhibition of the 'quick forge and working-house of thought' if they had indeed been in prose; it is the fact that in them prose rhythms are counterpointed against a verse structure that makes them 'something altogether new, both in this play and. . .in Shakespeare's output'.

I should like now to draw back from a close focus on the speech itself to a broader consideration of its function in the play as an aspect of Shakespeare's dramatic style. *Romeo and Juliet* is often dated 1594–5, a fact that it has in common with *Love's Labour's Lost, The Two Gentlemen of Verona, The Comedy of Errors, The Taming of the Shrew, A Midsummer Night's Dream, The Merchant of Venice, Richard II, King John,* and *Titus Andronicus.* Obviously the composition of these plays must have been spread over a period of several years, but it is fair to regard *Romeo and Juliet* as one of a group of early plays in which Shakespeare shows an experimental interest in verbal style. *King John* and *Richard II*, along with the earlier *1* and *3 Henry VI*, but like no other plays in the canon, are written entirely in verse. In them Shakespeare seems to be deliberately limiting his stylistic range, seeking intensity rather than diversity. In other plays he seems rather to be seeking a wide range of stylistic variation. Part of the effectiveness of the Nurse's speech derives from the fact that, though it occurs no later than the opening of the third scene, it has been preceded by passages written in very different styles, including the sonnet form of the Prologue; the colloquial prose of the opening dialogue of the servants; Prince Escalus's dignified blank verse; the more lyrical blank verse of Benvolio's description of the lovesick Romeo; Romeo's own rhapsodic verse, which includes rhyming couplets and has some of the qualities associated with metaphysical poetry; the comic prose of Capulet's servant; and sonnet-type sestets from both Benvolio and Romeo.

This rich stylistic diversity has helped to establish verbal style as a guide to character, and has encouraged us to respond to verbal effects. We know that this is to be a play in which plot is not all-important, and this is essential, since in terms of plot the whole of Act I, scene iii could exist without the Nurse. Her big speech is a set-speech in more senses than one. It is an extended show-piece for the performer, and also for the Nurse herself. This is, we may well suspect, an oft-told tale. Do we not feel, as soon as she says 'I can tell her age unto an hour', that she is about to give us every detail? And may we not feel, too, that her on-stage audience has heard it all many times before? This seems to me to be suggested by the line, completing a verse couplet, with which Juliet almost succeeds in bringing the Nurse's recollections to an end. 'And stint thou too, I pray thee, nurse, say I.' What is the tone? Is Juliet embarrassed or bored? indulgent or irritable? imploratory or imperative? Again, there is room for variety of interpretation.

If the Nurse's speech is irrelevant to the plot, we may ask how Shakespeare came to write it, and why he was disposed to lavish so much of his artistry on it. Is it merely an exuberant exercise of virtuosity, a set-piece for the author as well as for the actor and the character? Is it an inartistic irrelevance, a fanciful embroidery of the situation unnecessarily pursuing a hint suggested by the source? There is, indeed, some basis for it in Arthur Brooke's *Tragicall Historye of Romeus and Juliet*,[12] which may provide pointers to the style in which the scene should be played as well as help to explain the style in which it is written. One vexed question relates to the Nurse's age. Brooke clearly thought of her as old: he calls her 'an auncient dame' (l. 344), an 'olde dame' (l. 345), an 'auncient nurse' (l. 689). Yet 'in her youth' she 'had nurst' Juliet 'with her mylke' (l. 345). Brooke's Juliet is sixteen, more than two years older than Shakespeare's; but this still leaves some awkwardness about the Nurse's having been able to suckle the infant Juliet, and have a child of the same age herself, and yet now being 'auncient'. In a narrative poem, the point may pass unnoticed; on the stage it is more obtrusive. Thus St John Ervine, reviewing Edith Evans's legendary performance in 1935, remarked that though the character was 'superbly played' she was 'made to totter as if her legs had been racked with rheumatism for half a century'.[13] Terence Spencer attempts to reconcile the discrepancy, suggesting that she is not 'to be imagined as an aged crone but as, perhaps, in her early fifties'.[14] But perhaps the performer is best advised to ignore logic and to play for effect.

One function of the Nurse's repetitiveness is to lay great stress on Juliet's age, which has created a different problem. Shakespeare makes her younger than either Brooke or Painter (who says that she is eighteen). Geoffrey Bullough suggests that this is intended 'to emphasise the charm of her girlish directness, the pathos of her passion and resolution'. Charles Armitage Brown (quoted in the New Variorum edition) had a more practical suggestion: 'Juliet's extreme youth was, at the time, an apology to the audience for the boy who played so arduous a part.' Whatever the truth of this, actresses playing the role have frequently chosen not to include among its ardours the effort to look fourteen. Theophilus Cibber (1744) offers what might have been classed as an emendation if it had not occurred in a mere acting edition: Lady Capulet says: 'She's but fifteen', and the Nurse replies 'She's not fourteen' (but Cibber spoils the impression of thoughtfulness by then having her say 'come Lammas-Eve at night shall she be fifteen'). In Garrick's acting text (followed by Bell) Juliet is 'not yet eighteen' (with appropriate alterations to the number of the Nurse's remaining teeth and to other figures); Benson, like Garrick, relieved his leading lady from the strain of attempting to look no more than a fortnight under eighteen.

These are considerations that relate to the style of acting the Nurse's role. Shakespeare also derived hints from Brooke for the style in which he wrote it. Brooke's 'prating noorse', too, is repetitive and anecdotal; she makes a 'tedious long discoorse'. The crucial lines are worth quoting:

> And how she gave her sucke in youth she leaveth not to tell.
> A prety babe (quod she), it was when it was yong,
> Lord how it could full pretely have prated with it tong,
> A thousand times and more I laid her on my lappe,
> And clapt her on the buttocke soft and kist where I did clappe.
> And gladder then was I of such a kisse forsooth,
> Then I had been to have a kisse of some olde lechers mouth.
> And thus of Juliets youth began this prating noorse,
> And of her present state to make a tedious long discoorse.   (ll. 652–60)

Here, as in Shakespeare, we have prosaic speech cast into the form of verse. Shakespeare's diction is related to Brooke's ('prety babe', 'quod she', 'it' for 'she', 'thousand'). So also are the mode and tone of the Nurse's discourse. The comic earthiness of 'clapt her on the buttocke soft and kist where I did clappe' is reflected in the Nurse's unabashed acknowledgement of the physical details of breast-feeding and in the bawdy implications of the anecdote about her husband. Needless to say, this was not to the taste of the Victorians. Bowdler (1818) omitted the whole of the anecdote about falling backwards; he retained the breast-feeding while altering 'dug' to 'teat'. Lacy's acting edition of about 1855 outdoes Bowdler in purification, omitting even the breast-feeding, reducing the major speech to only eleven lines (compared with Bowdler's twenty-two), and entirely omitting the following speech. Henry Irving's acting edition of 1882 is even more brutal, and results in nonsense. Mary Anderson, at the Lyceum four years later, allowed Mrs Stirling her anecdote, but Forbes-Robertson, in 1895, omitted the bawdy, while curiously retaining the lead-in to it, as if to encourage the audience to recall (or imagine) it if they will:

> 'Yea,' quoth he, 'dost thou fall upon thy face?
> Thou wilt –'
> *Lady Capulet.* Enough of this.

To show that Shakespeare found some suggestions in his source for both the content and manner of the episode is not, of course, to provide artistic justification for it. But if it is irrelevant to the plot, it is far from irrelevant to the greater entity which is the play. Terence Spencer has remarked that the 'momentous and breathtaking four days' to which the play's action is confined 'are given a context in the passage of time much larger and longer', and that 'Old Capulet and the Nurse, in particular, carry the mind outside the framework of the play to events and emotions which nevertheless put Juliet and her Romeo in perspective'.[15] The Nurse's ramblings do indeed give us a sense of the past; and they do so in a particularly poignant context. The stage situation shows us a girl poised on the brink of womanhood. We have not met her before, and one function of the Nurse's speeches is to engage our sympathetic interest in the play's heroine. As the Nurse talks, her memories not only throw our minds back to the infancy of this girl, they also recall a prediction made at that time of how Juliet would react when she had 'more wit' and came 'to age'. The child who is talked about as an innocent infant is now before us, the subject of marriage plans. She retains the vulnerable innocence of the baby that 'stinted and said "Ay"', as we see in her reaction to the question 'How stands your dispositions to be married?' 'It is an honour that I dream not of', says Juliet. This is in naïve contrast to the sexuality of 'Thou wilt fall backward when thou hast more wit', and it partakes of the infantile naïveté of Juliet's earlier response: 'Ay.' Thus the Nurse's delving into the past recalls an anecdote which looked forward to beyond, but only just beyond, the present in which she speaks. The temporal complexities of the situation are subtle and ironical.

One function of the episode is, of course, to establish the Nurse's personality, and in this it has succeeded so notably as to have become a classic instance of Shakespeare's genius for character portrayal. Nicholas Brooke finds that her utterance here 'offers a very telling contrast to the hollow courtliness of I.ii: earthy, sentimental, warm-blooded, bawdy, repetitious. At all levels delightful, and most refreshing in its unselfconsciousness' (p. 93). And G. I. Duthie goes further in sketching a personality on the basis of what she says here: 'despite all her crudities, we can never forget the essential good-heartedness of this old woman who, vulgar and earthy as she is, looks back on past days and compresses precious memories into words which, while brief, suggest a loving and happy married life, with sorrow philosophically endured' (p. xxxvi). These comments testify to her credibility; but this is not enough. Coleridge, replying to suggestions 'that her character is the mere fruit of observation', spoke of it rather as a 'character of admirable generalisation'.[16] He betrays an implicit concern that the dramatic character should relate, at least, to recognisable characteristics of certain types of human beings. 'Let any man conjure up in his mind all the qualities and peculiarities that can possibly belong to a nurse, and he will find them in Shakespeare's picture of the old woman: nothing is omitted.' Some of these qualities are admirable, some not; so he finds in her 'all the garrulity of old age, and all its fondness. . .the arrogance of ignorance' and 'the pride of meanness at being connected with a great family', and 'the grossness, too, which that situation never removes' (p. 145). These observations are, of course, elicited by the Nurse's behaviour in all the scenes in which she appears, but it is significant that most of her qualities can be discerned in her initial speeches. The appeal that she exerts is as a 'character' in the sense that we speak of someone as 'a great character': one, that is, who is so self-consistent, so roundedly and immutably himself, so much of a fixed point in a landscape, that we can delight in his idiosyncrasies without needing to declare judgement on him. So Shakespeare, we feel, gives us the Nurse in her totality on her first appearance;

she is herself a landmark, a constant against which the changes and developments in other characters can be measured. And here we come to those aspects of Shakespeare's portrayal of the Nurse which make her not just credible as an individual and recognisably representative of a class, but of essential importance to the play in which she is found. The 'fondness' for Juliet which she clearly conveys draws us to Juliet as well as to the Nurse. And her limitations, suggested here, will later be tragically relevant to Juliet. Nicholas Brooke follows his expression of pleasure in the Nurse's character by saying that: 'It is also, humanly speaking, shallow enough in its own way, and this will be sharply exposed later; but here, the judgement is withheld.' Judgement comes, of course, when (only a few days later in the play's time-scheme) Juliet, a bride, is shown to have passed far beyond any understanding that the Nurse can offer. Then she becomes in Juliet's eyes 'Ancient damnation! O most wicked fiend!' (III,v,236). To this extent she is seen as a foil for Juliet, a rounded, developed but static character that serves as a measure of the speed and extent of Juliet's spiritual and emotional development. These opening speeches lay the groundwork of this relationship.

I have written of the Nurse's speeches in relation to their verbal style, and also to what we may call Shakespeare's theatrical and dramatic styles. Many aspects of the speeches can be admired; the one that seems most original, and most important for Shakespeare's later development, is their exploitation of inconsequentiality. By a carefully controlled representation of utterance which is characterised by an absence of linguistic control, Shakespeare creates interstices which can be filled with nuance. This is a splendidly theatrical mode, because it leaves something to the performer, who, by means of gesture, movement, facial play and subtlety of intonation, may create an appropriate physical realisation of all that the speech implies.

And such realisations may be very different from one another. As long ago as 1902, a theatre critic remarked that 'By tradition of the stage this is a comic character, the confidential retainer, rustling with silks and rattling with keys, interfering in everything, prone to take offence at imaginary slights, tyrannising over those she nominally serves, and all the time English to the finger-tips. Mrs Stirling [who played with Ellen Terry in Henry Irving's production, and with Mary Anderson] was a perfect embodiment of that type. Miss [Tita] Brand [who played in the Ben Greet production under review] gives us a very different person.

Here is an Italian crone, just such a figure as may be met by the dozen in the streets of Rome or Naples; a southern face, with parchment skin and hairy growth, and the four teeth to which the owner confesses much in evidence. . ..'[17] Such openness to interpretation is surely a mark of the truly theatrical conception.

As well as leaving something to the actor, the role no less importantly leaves something to the audience. Allusions, oblique references, incompleted logical connections, implications, half-concealed trains of thought require the audience's intelligent collaboration to be wholly meaningful. The audience is, as it were, drawn into the speaker's mind, engaged with a lively intensity which can be much greater than response to a harangue composed with complete 'Method'.

Whether Shakespeare derived the style of the Nurse's speech from sources in literature and life we cannot say.[18] Arthur Brooke contributed suggestions for their effect, but no model for their method. I suspect it is relevant that, at about the time the play was composed, Thomas Nashe was demonstrating his capacity in what he calls the 'extemporal vein'. What is clear is that, having, as it were, learnt the trick, Shakespeare, as we should expect, went on to develop and vary it. The Nurse's inconsequentiality arises from the fact that her mental processes are too feeble to create an adequate syntactical structure; or – to look at it from her creator's point of view – in the Nurse Shakespeare employs broken syntax and inconsequentiality to suggest a mind that is naturally lacking in intellectual control. He does something similar, though in prose, with Mistress Quickly, as we have already seen. The Nurse's speech patterns are related to those of Justice Shallow, in whom they suggest the effects of senility. All these characters give the impression of complete spontaneity. Lacking the power to order their thoughts and control their expression, they display no disjunction between the impulse to speak and the terms in which their thoughts are formulated. This gives them a kind of innocence. Pompey, in *Measure for Measure*, may seem rather to be using these tricks of language to pull the wool over his interlocutors' eyes than to be incapable of greater coherence:

As I say, this Mistress Elbow, being, as I say, with child, and being great-bellied, and longing, as I said, for prunes; and having but two in the dish, as I said, Master Froth here, this very man, having eaten the rest, as I said, and, as I say, paying for them very honestly; for, as you know, Master Froth, I could not give you three pence again.   (II,i,94–100)

These are speakers of prose. In verse, Shakespeare learnt that inconsequentiality could be a powerful means of portraying mental anguish, the overthrowing of a noble mind. Hamlet's soliloquies – like the Nurse's speech – encompass familiar diction, exclamations, repetitions, self-interruptions, and broken syntax within a verse structure:

> Why, she would hang on him
> As if increase of appetite had grown
> By what it fed on; and yet, within a month –
> Let me not think on't. Frailty, thy name is woman! –
> A little month, or ere those shoes were old
> With which she followed my poor father's body,
> Like Niobe, all tears – why she, even she –
> O God! a beast that wants discourse of reason
> Would have mourned longer – married with my uncle,
> My father's brother; but no more like my father
> Than I to Hercules.   (I,ii,143–53)

In *King Lear*, too, the breakdown of linguistic control is used to high emotional effect:

> No, you unnatural hags,
> I will have such revenges on you both
> That all the world shall – I will do such things –
> What they are yet I know not; but they shall be
> The terrors of the earth.   (II,iv,277–81)

And the same play exhibits at its most powerful Shakespeare's technique of counterpointing speech rhythms with a verse structure:

> And my poor fool is hanged! No, no, no life!
> Why should a dog, a horse, a rat have life,
> And thou no breath at all? Thou'lt come no more,
> Never, never, never, never, never.
> Pray you undo this button. Thank you, sir.
> Do you see this? Look on her. Look, her lips.
> Look there, look there!   (v,iii,305–11)

It seems to me that the Nurse's speeches in Act I, scene iii of *Romeo and Juliet* show Shakespeare to be suddenly the master of a technique that enabled him greatly to extend the expressive resources of dramatic language.

NOTES

1 *Shakespeare's Early Tragedies* (London, 1968), p. 92.
2 In *The Friend*, 1818; *Coleridge on Shakespeare*, ed. Terence Hawkes, Penguin Shakespeare Library (Harmondsworth, 1969), pp. 87–8.
3 1955, p. xxxvi.

4 There is ample evidence that this phrase, recorded as a proverb (M. P. Tilley, *A Dictionary of the Proverbs in England in the Sixteenth and Seventeenth Centuries* (Ann Arbor, 1950); B 596) is self-gratulatory, meaning, as Isaac Reed glossed it, 'I have a perfect remembrance or recollection'; though the opposite meaning may easily suggest itself to a modern reader, resulting in George Skillan's note, in French's Acting Edition (London, 1947), 'then suddenly realising that she is getting somewhat away from her subject and admitting it'. T. J. B. Spencer seems to concede some doubt in his New Penguin (Harmondsworth, 1967) gloss: '(perhaps) I have a good memory still'.

5 Barbara Everett, in her subtle essay '*Romeo and Juliet*: The Nurse's Story' (*Critical Quarterly*, summer 1972, pp. 129–39), writes that ' "Shake, quoth the dovehouse!" has not been quite helpfully enough glossed, presumably because few Shakespeare editors are sufficiently acquainted with what might be said to a very small child about an earthquake. It does not simply mean, as has been suggested, "the dovehouse shook"; it allows the unfluttered dovecote to satirise the earthquake, as in a comical baby mock-heroic – to be aloof and detached from what is happening to it' (p. 135).

6 I take it that the Nurse is saying that she was so shaken by the earthquake that she 'trudged' without having to be told to do so. Barbara Everett's comments on the passage (p. 136) seem rather to imply that the Nurse is saying that Juliet, in her tetchiness, had no call to send the Nurse packing, that the dovehouse was unimpressed equally by the fury of the earthquake and by the infant's crossness, and (possibly) that the Nurse was no more impressed by either. This seems to me to be an equally acceptable interpretation.

7 *Coleridge on Shakespeare*, p. 135.

8 See *William Shakespeare: The Most Excellent and Lamentable Tragedie of Romeo and Juliet, A Critical Edition*, by G. Walton Williams (Durham, N.C., 1964), p. xii.

9 It is of only incidental interest that the published screen script of Metro-Goldwyn-Mayer's film starring Norma Shearer and Leslie Howard prints *all* the verse as prose, with the explanation that this helped the actors 'to speak their lines as Hamlet wished his players to speak theirs, "trippingly on the tongue" ' (*A Motion Picture Version of Shakespeare's 'Romeo and Juliet'* (New York, 1936), p. 249).

10 'The New Way with Shakespeare's Text', *Shakespeare Survey 8* (Cambridge, 1955), p. 98.

11 *Shakespeare's Tragic Sequence* (London, 1972), p. 40.

12 References are to the reprint in Geoffrey Bullough's *Narrative and Dramatic Sources of Shakespeare*, 8 vols. (London, 1957–75), vol. 1 (1957), pp. 284–363.

13 *The Observer*, 3 November 1935.

14 New Penguin edition (1967), p. 184.

15 *Ibid.* pp. 33–4.

16 *Coleridge on Shakespeare*, p. 145.

17 W. Hughes Hallett, reviewing Ben Greet's production at Ealing, in *The Pilot*, 17 May 1902, p. 528.

18 Jonas Barish cites the Nurse as the earliest specific illustration of his claim that Shakespeare 'virtually invented linguistic satire on the English stage' (*Ben Jonson and the Language of Prose Comedy* (Cambridge, Mass., 1967), p. 284).

Language most shows a man. . .?
Language and speaker in *Macbeth*

NICHOLAS BROOKE

Lady Macbeth.	The raven himself is hoarse,
	That croaks the fatal entrance of Duncan
40	Under my battlements. Come, you Spirits
	That tend on mortal thoughts, unsex me here,
	And fill me, from the crown to the toe, top-full
	Of direst cruelty! make thick my blood,
	Stop up th' access and passage to remorse;
45	That no compunctious visitings of Nature
	Shake my fell purpose, nor keep peace between
	Th' effect and it! Come to my woman's breasts,
	And take my milk for gall, you murth'ring ministers,
	Wherever in your sightless substances
50	You wait on Nature's mischief! Come, thick Night,
	And pall thee in the dunnest smoke of Hell,
	That my keen knife see not the wound it makes,
	Nor Heaven peep through the blanket of the dark,
	To cry, 'Hold, hold!' (*Macbeth*, I,v,38–54)[1]

Macbeth.	O! full of scorpions is my mind, dear wife!
	Thou know'st that Banquo, and his Fleance, lives.
Lady Macbeth.	But in them Nature's copy's not eterne.
Macbeth.	There's comfort yet; they are assailable:
40	Then be thou jocund. Ere the bat hath flown
	His cloistered flight; ere to black Hecate's summons
	The shard-born beetle, with his drowsy hums,
	Hath rung Night's yawning peal, there shall be done
	A deed of dreadful note.
Lady Macbeth.	What's to be done?
45 *Macbeth.*	Be innocent of the knowledge, dearest chuck,
	Till thou applaud the deed. Come, seeling Night,
	Scarf up the tender eye of pitiful Day,
	And, with thy bloody and invisible hand,
	Cancel, and tear to pieces, that great bond
50	Which keeps me pale! – Light thickens; and the crow
	Makes wing to th' rooky wood;

Good things of Day begin to droop and drowse,
Whiles Night's black agents to their preys do rouse.
Thou marvell'st at my words: but hold thee still;
55   Things bad begun make strong themselves by ill.
                                        (*Macbeth*, III,ii,36–55)

Ben Jonson's 'discovery' was made of men and matters;[2] as a dramatist he reversed the process and created his men (and, less often, women) in language. They speak verse, of course, but their poetry is characteristically an extension of their idiosyncratic speech, as with Mammon or Subtle, or commonly enough of the role they are for the moment playing, as with Dol or Face, or Volpone. There is almost no problem in Jonson's plays of characters speaking a language which is rather a property of the play than of themselves. Nor is there with some of Shakespeare's most obvious 'character' roles, such as Juliet's Nurse or Shylock: their very distinctive speech intensifies into its own verse, but that verse remains peculiarly their own and finds no reflection in other utterances (except by direct parody). That is, however, a fairly rare distinction in Shakespeare's work. Minor members of the cast are always liable to break out into language of which, it is clearly understood, they can have no personal experience whatever – the Welsh captain, for instance, in *Richard II*, or Vernon in *1 Henry IV*:

All plumed like estridges that with the wind
Bated, like eagles having lately bathed,
Glittering in golden coats like images.   (IV,i,98–100)[3]

They *are* images: images of the show which Henry is putting on; and, because it is not simply show, images of a glorious honour which is one coordinate of the play; but they are only in the faintest degree images of Vernon, whose utterance is elsewhere plain and undistinguished – we remember the language and not the man.

But at least in those cases it can be said that the language is not in necessary contradiction of the man: Vernon is an educated soldier who may rise to fine sights like a tourist in Venice, and the Welsh captain is, after all, Welsh. Shakespeare sometimes went further:

The west yet glimmers with some streaks of day;
Now spurs the lated traveller apace,
To gain the timely inn.   (*Macbeth*, III,iii,5–7)

There has been wild speculation on the identity of the third murderer in *Macbeth*, but none about the first, who speaks these lines. They belong absolutely to the play and are absolutely alien to the speaker. This is a small instance, and there are very likely others as extreme in other plays. Clarence's murderers in *Richard III* start in prose and progress to an accusing verse which responds more to the rituals of the play than to their personal attitudes:

> Who made thee then a bloody minister
> When gallant-springing brave Plantagenet,
> That princely novice, was struck dead by thee? (1,iv,217–19)

In its context that is rather an extension than a flat contradiction of the murderer's utterance; the position for Banquo's murderer is a more extreme violation of Jonson's principle.

It is still a large step from what can loosely be called 'choric' speeches by minor characters to the major soliloquies of the principals, for they are certainly men and women and unquestionably shown by their speech. But the mode of showing, and the degree, still varies substantially. Richard III's opening soliloquy is well known to be composed out of two much older conventions, that of the Presenter (or Chorus), and that of the self-declaration of the Vice; it becomes more than either in the knowing self-projection of Richard into both roles, yet it still serves both functions as well. Hamlet's soliloquies are usually discussed as direct self-revelations and that seems appropriate: he speaks a variety of languages, and when he waxes most poetical it is always recognisable as self-dramatisation. All his languages do echo elsewhere in the play, from speakers as diverse as Horatio, Polonius, Claudius, and the ghost: the inner and outer bearings of man and world are significantly equivalent, and just as the man has no easily recognisable integrity, so also the play has no single language by which it can be identified (though its gnomic quotability is no mere chance). *Othello* is a somewhat different case, for what Wilson Knight dubbed the 'Othello music' does substantially characterise the play. But it is spoken by Othello alone (excepting Iago's parodies, and the choric dialogue on the storm in Act II, scene i), and that generates the well-worn critical problem that only Othello can articulate his own valediction; he alone has the language worthy of it – or, he is 'cheering himself up'. That is not a problem in *Antony and Cleopatra*, for although the play's characteristic magnificence is distinctively embodied in hero and heroine, their language is also heard in various other mouths: in Philo's opening speech (1,i,1–13), Enobarbus's 'barge she sat in' (11,ii,191–240), and even from Caesar when he reminisces on Antony in

the Alps (I,iv,55–71). It adumbrates an imperial theme in the largest
terms, yet it is always used by or about the man and woman: the principle
that it 'shows' them is not violated. The fact that an actor's language has
dramatic dimensions remote from his individual character is very clear
here, yet it is not conspicuously a problem.

Macbeth is a different matter, almost an opposite case. We know the
first murderer speaks for the play, not for himself; so, really, do Duncan
and Banquo in Act I, scene vi:

> *Duncan.* This castle hath a pleasant seat; the air
> Nimbly and sweetly recommends itself
> Unto our gentle senses.
> *Banquo.*   This guest of summer,
> The temple-haunting martlet, does approve,
> By his loved mansionry, that the heaven's breath
> Smells wooingly here.   (ll. 1–6)

The benignity may fit Duncan; it is not especially characteristic of
Banquo (nor especially inappropriate either). Rosse and the Old Man in
Act II, scene iv function like the Welsh Captain, but with a language so
like Macbeth's own that the distinction of man from words is even more
striking:

> by th' clock 'tis day,
> And yet dark night strangles the travelling lamp.
> Is't night's predominance, or the day's shame,
> That darkness does the face of earth entomb,
> When living light should kiss it?   (ll. 6–10)

The characteristics amplify as they get on to Duncan's horses:

> Beauteous and swift, the minions of their race,
> Turned wild in nature, broke their stalls, flung out,
> Contending 'gainst obedience, as they would make
> War with mankind.   (ll. 15–18)

That is not said about Macbeth, but it might perfectly be said by him.
He sees strange sights, but they are not distinctively his. The cliché that
in verse drama it tells you nothing about a man that he speaks in verse
becomes far more difficult here: Bradley claimed that Macbeth was an
exceptionally imaginative man, and if we credit all his words to his
consciousness then he certainly was. But we do not so credit all his words,
and frequently do not know whether to do so or not. An obvious case is
his speech after the murder is revealed:

> Had I but died an hour before this chance,
> I had lived a blessèd time.   (II,iii,91–2)

The words so perfectly extend his private musings before the event that it is quite ambiguous whether they are here a private utterance or a public speech. Kenneth Muir, in his note on these lines in the New Arden edition, adds his own view that Macbeth was unconscious of the truth of his words, but he quotes Middleton Murry to the opposite effect: 'Macbeth must needs be conscious of the import of the words that come from him.' The choice is vitally important for an actor, since it involves the difference between aside and address to others on stage. I am positive that Murry is wrong, not positive that Muir is right. The ambiguity remains, and the actor has no need to eliminate it. But this is certain, that Macbeth may speak words beyond his consciousness; which means that his language may show us things other than the man.

That ambiguity is conspicuous in his longest soliloquy before the murder (I,vii,1–28). At one level he pursues a train of thought about the consequences of his murder, through guilty reflections on his roles as subject and host, to a final reflection on his own ambition which leads logically to his statement to Lady Macbeth when she enters:

> We will proceed no further in this business. (I,vii,31)

But in elaborating his soliloquy he had illustrated his thoughts with similes that develop an extraordinary range of visionary images – of angels, naked new-born babe, Heaven's cherubin – which constitutes one of the most striking, and yet characteristic, passages of poetry in the play. 'In the play': it is ambiguous whether it is specifically characteristic of Macbeth himself. *His* imagination can foresee consequences, and can see horrid 'sights' (at least as conjured by the weird sisters), but it is by no means clear that he 'sees' the baroque vision his words so marvellously create for us.

It is that ambiguity which makes Macbeth's soliloquies so peculiarly difficult for the actor; and not Macbeth's only: Lady Macbeth frequently uses a very similar language, and the actress has the same problems to contend with. They are made more acute by the more positive form of statement to which she is prone:

> I have given suck, and know
> How tender 'tis to love the babe that milks me. (I,vii,54–5)

The long row over those words makes it hard to tell how odd they would seem if Bradley had never published his appendix, nor L. C. Knights his riposte. In theory it should be impossible to go behind the direct assertion of a dramatic character and question its veracity. Macbeth does not retort 'when did you ever give suck?'; so there it is, she did. Or did she? Muir quotes an early-nineteenth-century comment: 'Whether this be true or not does not appear; but the lady says it, and she must say it, in order to give emphasis to her speech.' Exactly: and it is impenetrably ambiguous whether she means it, let alone whether it is true or not. But as an imaginative fact that babe is certainly very vivid to us in ways that are no part of Lady Macbeth's consciousness: it takes its place, with Macbeth's naked new-born babe, and all the other babes of the play that Cleanth Brooks enumerated,[4] in a dimension well beyond the reach of the characters.

I do not believe that that example need be any special problem to the actress; but Lady Macbeth's earlier soliloquy – quoted at the head of this chapter – unquestionably is. The actress's problem is whether to make this a literal invocation of the Spirits, in which case she must enact some appropriate ritual on the stage, or to project it as at least partly meta-phoric, an extreme form of auto-suggestion. Kenneth Muir argues deci-sively for the first and believes that it was Mrs Siddons's interpretation, quoting this: '[She] having impiously delivered herself up to the excite-ments of hell. . .is abandoned to the guidance of the demons she has invoked.'[5] But I am not certain this is quite literal: the demons may well turn out to be more actual than she imagines – as conscience does in the sleep-walking scene. If she does literally enact a ritual, it becomes odd that no other such ritual ever occurs, just as a literal belief in her child makes the solitary reference to it odd. Muir comments that 'we need not necessarily assume that Shakespeare himself believed in demoniacal possession' (p. lxx); I agree, but would add that we need not necessarily believe that Lady Macbeth did either. If, on the other hand, the speech is allowed a primarily metaphoric force, then its extraordinary language tends to divide its reference (never, of course, precisely) between a relatively simple level corresponding to her consciousness, and a far more obscure level in which her words reverberate with images we do not specifically understand to be hers.

Lady Macbeth's speech therefore resembles Macbeth's of fifty lines later in its double focus – on herself, and far outside herself. It resembles it also in structure – she began, before the messenger's entry, with a direct discussion of Macbeth's tricky conscience:

> what thou wouldst highly,
> That wouldst thou holily; wouldst not play false,
> And yet wouldst wrongly win;   (I,v,20–2)

a syntactic tangle which is closely echoed in Macbeth's

> If it were done, when 'tis done, then 'twere well
> It were done quickly.   (I,vii,1–2)

From there, as Macbeth's images amplify through deep damnation to the
naked new-born babe and Heaven's cherubin, so hers expand from the
raven to 'Come, you Spirits' and 'make thick my blood', into 'Come,
thick Night', and so reach their climax in Hell and Heaven. The one
actual verbal echo is of the striking use of 'sightless', meaning both 'blind'
and 'invisible' – 'sightless substances' and 'sightless couriers of the air'.
Finally, Lady Macbeth's thought-train (as distinct from the image-train)
finishes in plain language, though whether it is absolutely complete or
broken off by interruption is not perfectly clear. She ends 'To cry, "Hold,
hold!"', and Macbeth enters, while he ends 'which o'erleaps itself / And
falls on th'other', and Lady Macbeth enters. In both speeches the
extraordinary imagery is left behind, and the thought-trains extend
beyond it, so that the effect is as though the thought-trains represent the
consciousness of the speakers while the image-train in its specific form
has been raised above and beyond their consciousnesses. Only, of course,
in its specific form: they are understood to use metaphor, and to be able to
see 'sights', but not necessarily to be absolutely aware of these specific
sights.

We, on the other hand, are very vividly aware of them, of the likeness
between them, and of the likeness to other utterances by them and by
other people in the play – Duncan and Banquo in Act I, scene vi; Rosse
and the Old Man in Act II, scene iv; the murderer in Act III, scene iii;
and so on. The situation resembles that of a traditional mode of painting
where human figures are represented in rapt contemplation in which they
might well see visions, but do not seem to be seeing the specific angels,
devils, or other images which are painted all around them. Pictorially that
is a common enough convention; dramatically it may often be partially
realised, but in such a fully developed form *Macbeth* is unique, as it is
generally unique in the extent of specific visualising it demands of its
audience. The effect is achieved by an ambiguity of reference: Macbeth
and Lady Macbeth do 'see', and they do use metaphor, but yet the
extraordinary visual detail of their language strikes us as not actually
theirs, as in fact a property of the play which exists outside them. Not
merely outside them, but almost in opposition to them, as of something
which it would be better for them if they *did* see: 'nothing is, but what is

not' (I,iii,142) has more meanings than Macbeth assigns to it, and 'what is not' is the force that ultimately destroys him.

There is a general echo of the structure of Lady Macbeth's speech in Macbeth's soliloquy in Act I, scene vii, but there is a very much closer one much later on in Act III, scene ii. He begins by referring to Banquo and Fleance, and against the background of that thought (and of Lady Macbeth's refusal to acknowledge it) develops an invocation that follows hers in form, word, and image so closely that in the theatre we need no training to have at least the feeling we have heard something like it before:

> Come, seeling Night,
> Scarf up the tender eye of pitiful Day,
> And, with thy bloody and invisible hand,
> Cancel, and tear to pieces, that great bond
> Which keeps me pale! – Light thickens; and the crow
> Makes wing to th' rooky wood;
> Good things of Day begin to droop and drowse,
> Whiles Night's black agents to their preys do rouse.   (III,ii,46–53)

The connection is by no means confined to the opening phrase: 'scarf' recalls the 'blanket' of the dark; 'tender eye of pitiful day', the 'compunctious visitings of Nature'; 'invisible', 'sightless'; 'Light thickens', 'thick Night'; 'crow', 'raven'; and, of course, the opposition of Night and Day is the foundation of the amplifying oppositions of both speeches. Again, as in the earlier speeches, Macbeth here concludes his thought in plain language beyond the image-train:

> Thou marvell'st at my words: but hold thee still;
> Things bad begun make strong themselves by ill.   (III,ii,54–5)

On the other hand, the speech does differ from the earlier ones in one striking respect: they were both soliloquies in which one was interrupted by the entry of the other; this is given in Lady Macbeth's presence, even ostensibly delivered to her (but that, again, is ambiguous), and so far from being broken off, it ends in conclusive couplets. The one is partly a function of the other, for as much as the couplets declare a firm ending, they also mask the absence of an ending – what Macbeth is talking about remains unstated, though it is as obviously the murder of Banquo as in both the earlier speeches it was the murder of Duncan.

Macbeth's speech, not identical with his wife's but remarkably close to it, creates the same problem of a language that extends beyond the speaker: the same language, though a different speaker. That might conclude my case but for the fact that, such is the intricacy of the play, the speaker is not absolutely different. Macbeth did not hear his wife's soliloquy, but it has always been a feature of the play how closely their minds interact: they are unique in Shakespeare as a central study of an intimate marriage (in this too the opposite of *Othello*). It is some while before either is explicit about their intent to murder Duncan, but they know immediately that it is in each other's mind. This has, in the past, caused speculation about a missing scene or scenes in which they should explain their thoughts to each other; that is absurd, because there is nothing even faintly unusual about this degree of understanding between any couple who live together (which is not to say that couples don't often find it remarkable, or that it is not used as part of the structure of supernatural hints in the play). Act III, scene ii marks a final crisis in their psychological relationship: earlier, Lady Macbeth achieved down-rightness, while Macbeth was lost in a maze of conscience; here, their roles are exactly reversed. At the beginning of the scene, both separately comment on their fear:

> *Lady Macbeth.*   Nought's had, all's spent,
> Where our desire is got without content:
> 'Tis safer to be that which we destroy,
> Than by destruction dwell in doubtful joy.   (ll. 4–7)

> *Macbeth.*   Better be with the dead,
> Whom we, to gain our peace, have sent to peace,
> Than on the torture of the mind to lie
> In restless ecstasy.   (ll. 19–22)

Earlier the understanding, however corrupt, was perfect; here there is perfect misunderstanding. Lady Macbeth is dwelling in fruitless regret on their first murder, while Macbeth is anticipating the second. The seemingly echoic ambiguity of language, which sustained their intimacy before, betrays it here, as they gradually discover:

> *Macbeth.*   Thou know'st that Banquo, and his Fleance, lives.
> *Lady Macbeth.* But in them Nature's copy's not eterne.   (ll. 37–8)

She means, presumably, that their line will not last for ever; he takes her to mean 'they are assailable', and her withdrawal from that understanding forces him at last to acknowledge the distance:

> *Lady Macbeth.*   What's to be done?
> *Macbeth.*   Be innocent of the knowledge, dearest chuck,
> Till thou applaud the deed.   (ll. 44–6)

The endearments become stronger as the intimacy recedes.

The psychological perception of the scene is very powerful indeed: no wonder this play seemed to Bradley outstanding in his study of character. But it seemed equally outstanding to the imagist critics between the wars, and it proved strangely difficult here to reconcile the two critical traditions. The reason, I suggest, is the peculiar disjunction which I have been tracing between speaker and image. The similarity of language between Macbeth and his Lady does not of itself demonstrate its independence of their consciousnesses; it *also* expresses their intimacy, and extends the duality of the play between character and image. It is even possible that it can be felt as hinting some parapsychological communication as part of the chain of possibly supernatural phenomena which the play erects without ever committing us to clear belief. That is no more than a hint, or a temptation to our speculation, but it takes its place well with the carefully varied range of illusions which are actually presented: the dagger, which only Macbeth sees (and knows to be not there); Banquo's ghost, which Macbeth and audience see; the weird sisters, who are seen by Banquo as well as Macbeth and us; or, in the other direction, the rational explanations which dissolve the illusions of the last act (Birnam Wood and Macduff's birth). Just as the 'sights' of the play have a range, so have the words in their degree of visual immediacy: Duncan and Banquo invite us directly to see what is not actually visible (Act I, scene vi goes well beyond the normal need of scene-setting); Rosse and the Old Man affirm that the horses actually had been seen, but not that they are on stage; Lady Macbeth declares that her babe had been at her breast. The extraordinary images in which Macbeth and Lady Macbeth equally speak are one stage further removed from actuality, but they are not less vivid; because we do not respond to them as confined within the speakers' consciousness, they become part of the total extraordinary visual construct of the play. Perhaps it is no more odd to find it a construct independent of, and even contrary to the speakers, than it is that the visual illusions in the staging are so independent of the actual structure of the theatre; for that, too, reaches actual contradiction when we realise that two-thirds of this play written for a daylight theatre is understood to be set in darkness.

That creates special difficulties for the modern theatre where darkness is the natural condition; the peculiarly sharp distinction of language from speaker creates special problems for actor and actress. In all these respects *Macbeth* is not so much typical of Shakespeare, as a uniquely extreme concentration of devices that he uses more sparingly elsewhere.

That is why I contrasted it with *Othello* and *Antony and Cleopatra*, where there is no such dislocation between character and setting, or the hero's language and the play's. The language of *Macbeth* does indeed show us a man and a woman; but it also shows us sights far beyond them, and even alien to them, and thus creates the extraordinary paradox that it is at once Shakespeare's most and his least naturalistic play, a baroque drama where the figures have a peculiar reality, though their context is peculiarly fantastic.

NOTES

1 The text used here and throughout the essay for all quotations from *Macbeth* is that of the New Arden *Macbeth*, edited by Kenneth Muir (London, 1951).

2 The title page of *Timber: or, Discoveries*, as first printed in the 1640 Folio of Jonson's works, describes it as 'Made upon Men and Matter: As they have flowed out of his daily Readings, or had their refluxe to his peculiar Notion of the Times'. The title of my essay refers to Jonson's statement '*Language* most shewes a man: speake that I may see thee': *Discoveries*, ll. 2031–2 in vol. VIII (1947), p. 625, of *Ben Jonson*, ed. C. H. Herford and P. and E. Simpson, 11 vols. (Oxford, 1925–52).

3 New Arden *1 Henry IV*, edited by A. R. Humphreys (London, 1960).

4 In *The Well-Wrought Urn* (New York, 1947), pp. 22–49.

5 New Arden *Macbeth*, Introduction, p. lxx.

Poetic language and dramatic significance in Shakespeare

R. A. FOAKES

Macbeth.	O, full of scorpions is my mind, dear wife!
	Thou know'st that Banquo, and his Fleance, lives.
Lady Macbeth.	But in them nature's copy's not eterne.
Macbeth.	There's comfort yet; they are assailable.
40	Then be thou jocund. Ere the bat hath flown
	His cloistered flight; ere to black Hecate's summons
	The shard-borne beetle with his drowsy hums
	Hath rung night's yawning peal, there shall be done
	A deed of dreadful note.
Lady Macbeth.	What's to be done?
45 *Macbeth.*	Be innocent of the knowledge, dearest chuck,
	Till thou applaud the deed. Come, seeling night,
	Scarf up the tender eye of pitiful day,
	And with thy bloody and invisible hand
	Cancel and tear to pieces that great bond
50	Which keeps me pale. Light thickens, and the crow
	Makes wing to th' rooky wood;
	Good things of day begin to droop and drowse,
	Whiles night's black agents to their preys do rouse.
	Thou marvell'st at my words; but hold thee still:
55	Things bad begun make strong themselves by ill.
	So, prithee go with me. (*Macbeth*, iii,ii,36–56)

It would not be difficult to compile an anthology of entertaining notes in which editors and others have chased elusive meanings through thickets of curious possibilities, without finally telling us a great deal about a troublesome passage in Shakespeare. One such would be the note the editor of the first Arden *Macbeth*, Henry Cuningham, attached in 1912 to the word 'rooky' in the line 'The crow makes wing to the rooky wood', and which runs as follows:

This somewhat obscure epithet, however spelt (and it should be spelt rouky), does NOT mean 'murky' or 'dusky' (Roderick, quoted by Edwards *Canons of Criticism*, 1765); NOR 'damp', 'misty', 'steamy with exhalations' (Steevens, also Craig); NOR 'misty', 'gloomy' (Clar. Edd.); NOR 'where its fellows are already assembled' (Mitford), and has NOTHING to do with the dialectic word 'roke' meaning 'mist', 'steam', etc.. . .the meaning here. . .I THINK, is simply the 'rouking' or perching wood, i.e., where the rook (or crow) perches for the night.

It is to start with a splendidly aggressive note, dismissing with its 'NOT' and 'NOR' in capitals all previous commentators, in the confidence that this latest editor has got it right, and the true definition is simple. Now we might find his conclusion somewhat more lame and impotent than perhaps he supposed it was, since it is not clear why his 'I THINK' should be trusted more than another's, and we would find very odd his assumption that there is a single correct meaning lurking to be identified. But this was written some time before ambiguity was recognised as an ever-present feature of Shakespeare's mature verse, not that the recognition solved the problem of 'rooky'. William Empson had a satisfying time exploring its associations in *Seven Types of Ambiguity*:

I believe it is that the peaceful solitary *crow*, moving towards bed and the other crows, is made unnaturally like Macbeth and a murderer who is coming against them; this is suggested by the next lines, which do not say whether the *crow* is one of the *good things of day* or one of *night's black agents* (it is, at any rate, *black*), by the eerie way that *light* itself is *thickening*, as a man turns against men, a *crow* against *crows*, perhaps by the portentous way a *crow's* voice will carry at such a time, and by the sharpness of its wings against the even glow of a sky after sundown; but mainly, I think, by the use of the two words *rook* and *crow*.

   Rooks live in a crowd and are mainly vegetarian; *crow* may be either another name for a *rook*, especially when seen alone, or it may mean the solitary Carrion crow. This subdued pun is made to imply here that Macbeth, looking out of the window, is trying to see himself as a murderer, and can only see himself as in the position of the *crow*; that his *day* of power, now, is closing; that he has to distinguish himself from the other *rooks* by a difference of name, *rook-crow*, like the kingly title, only; that he is anxious, at bottom, to be at one with the other *rooks*, not to murder them; that he can no longer, or that he may yet, be united with the rookery; and that he is murdering Banquo in a forlorn attempt to obtain peace of mind.

   Personally I am pleased and given faith by this analysis, because it has made something which seemed to me magical into something that seems to me sensible.[1]

The most striking feature of this account is Empson's visualisation of the passage; he thinks of real birds and real woods, and imagines Macbeth looking out of the window at this point and actually seeing a crow with which he identifies himself. This domestication of the line pleased him because it converted the magical into the sensible; in the end his aim, though not his reading of the line which is characteristically open and suggestive, was much like that of Cuningham, namely to beat the passage somehow into sense.

The editor's task in annotating such a line is a difficult one, since he has not the space in which to develop a speculation in the Empson manner, and he may be forgiven for being more peremptory; so in the later Arden edition (1951), Kenneth Muir chose to give his reader a ring of confidence rather than open up possibilities, firmly noting of the word 'crow', 'i.e. the rook; the carrion crow was not gregarious', and of 'rooky', 'i.e. black and filled with rooks'. He went on to list the various meanings Cuningham had rejected, added Cuningham's own definition, and prefaced the lot by the general comment: 'There have, however, been many attempts to save Shakespeare from writing this excellent line, which is regarded as tautological.' Like Cuningham he led his reader to think 'crow' means 'rook' here, although the distinction between these birds is the starting point of Empson's explanation of the line. The editor's job is to help, not confuse, his readers, and any annotation he provides for passages like this one is likely to be reductive, to transform magic into sense.

It is comforting to have explanations, and a necessary way of subduing Shakespeare's plays to the limitations of our own minds. Yet the very lists of alternative meanings of 'rooky' provided by the two editors, and Empson's comments on 'crow' and 'rook', register a penumbra of more or less ghostly significances which may be at work when we read the scene, and only Empson glimpses a man doing something at this point, looking out of the window. It could be staged this way, but Macbeth has no need of a window, which would be a distraction. In this speech he is invoking the powers of darkness, and his words relate, so to speak, to events in his imagination, not in the real world, to imaginary crows and rooky woods, not real ones. This line is a particularly 'difficult' passage in a sequence of speeches by Macbeth which are crowded with images whose sense is obscure or ambiguous. The commentator can explain the implications of 'Come, seeling night' in relation to falconry, and explore some of the connotations of 'sealing' (binding to secrecy? stamping with its approval and authority? echoing and inverting the New Testament use of the word to mean pledged irrevocably to the service of God, as in 'grieve not the holy Spirit of God, whereby ye are sealed unto the day of redemption'?[2] and so on), and they can have fun with the 'shard-borne' or 'shard-born' beetle. Pages of commentary would not exhaust possibilities of interpreting the sense of these lines. If we return, however, to the man or actor

Empson momentarily thought of, and ask what is happening in the theatre at this point, the explanations of the text may begin to seem almost an irrelevance.

In the swift passage of the scene on the stage the audience has no time to register ambiguities or nuances, or perhaps even any 'sense' at all in the form of an extractable meaning. Macbeth has three audiences in this scene: the 'black agents' he imagines he is communing with, Lady Macbeth, and the theatre audience. The theatre audience knows more than Lady Macbeth, who is kept in ignorance of the plot to kill Banquo, but, like her, they cannot understand the terrific workings of Macbeth's 'mind' as embodied in his speeches. Like Desdemona in the brothel scene in *Othello* (IV,ii), we understand the passion but not the words.[3] This is not to deny sense to the dialogue, for Shakespeare provides a framework of easily understood lines and phrases. These establish the ironies of his relation with Lady Macbeth, as he simultaneously honeys her with terms of affection ('love', 'dear wife', 'dearest chuck'), and refuses to confide in her ('Be innocent of the knowledge'); they also emphasise the 'dreadful' nature of the deed that is to be done – the murder of Banquo – and culminate in the Senecan *sententia* clinching the rhyming couplet at the end,

> Things bad begun make strong themselves by ill.

No one in the audience has to worry at the sense of this line. If it be granted that the scene has a sense readily grasped in the theatre, what then is the status of those grand lines which puzzle commentators, and cannot possibly be analysed in the seconds their delivery takes on stage?

Probably the commentators and the audience would agree that the power of the scene is created largely by these passages, which are probably unintelligible to many who watch the play in the theatre. If so, then their power lies not in their sense, but in what Empson was anxious to undo, their 'magic' – in this particular scene there is a literal application of the word in that Macbeth is doing something analogous to the practices of the Weird Sisters, and anticipates the moment at the beginning of Act IV when he conjures and invokes devils. Here he stops short of that, but the effect is one of incantation, or, to put it another way, in the theatre the rhetoric dominates over the sense, which permits only tortured glimpses into the dark recesses of Macbeth's state of mind, and establishes a mood in which, with Lady Macbeth, we marvel at his words; and the point of it all arguably is to bring home the extent to which

Macbeth himself understands the force of what he says, but not the implications. If there is some truth in this, then the commentators and writers on imagery may explain what cannot be grasped by an audience in the theatre, often ignore the lines that convey the dramatic 'sense' of the scene, and say little or nothing about the effect of the scene's rhetoric; and the explanations they give may have the effect of cancelling out the 'magic' of the scene, which is its most important quality in the theatre.

This scene in *Macbeth* is unusual in the complexity of Macbeth's speeches, and might be regarded as an extreme case, but the issue it raises is, I think, common enough, especially in Shakespeare's later plays. It would seem that the dramatic significance of scenes may often be conveyed in the theatre very largely by means other than those meanings of words and images which are the main concern of most commentators and critics. In order to talk about the dramatic significance it would seem in turn necessary to pay attention to such features as the rhetorical pattern of the dialogue, the mood and tone of what is spoken, all that may be summed up in a notion of style. This is more easily said than done, for little of the massive accumulation of critical work on Shakespeare's plays affords much help. What has been written relates mainly to four aspects of Shakespeare's style;[4] one is what characterises his work in distinction from that of his contemporaries; another is the way his style changes and develops, as in his exploration of the uses of prose in the period from about 1598 to 1603, or his stretching of the boundaries of blank verse in the late plays; a third is the use of a particularly marked style in a given play, such as the latinate vocabulary that is a feature of *Troilus and Cressida*; and a fourth is what John Russell Brown calls his 'dramatic style', in seeking to illustrate the 'theatrical life' of a text. In these studies, and others, there is also occasional consideration of the relation of style to character, and this bears on the questions raised by the scene quoted from *Macbeth*. In using the term 'dramatic significance' I suppose I am reaching towards some deeper idea of style than all these, as creating significances that supplement, override, deepen, or perhaps even work against the obvious verbal meaning of a scene, and which may, hence, have a controlling effect on what the audience makes of it.

Style is an elusive concept, and the difficulties of talking about it will be evident enough in what follows. Meanings of words can be checked against usage, and although commentators may disagree about the primary sense of 'crow' or 'seeling', they are generally content to emphasise one meaning and allow for a play of secondary ambiguities. With style there are no obvious checks or parameters. Some especially prominent features, like Othello's grand and strange vocabulary and rhythms, have established general agreement that there is an 'Othello music', but responses to it vary, and it has been seen as expressing both a simple nobility in the character and a 'brutal egotism', or 'habit of self-approving self-dramatisation'.[5] In this way interpretation of the dramatic significance of a style can turn on a general attitude to the proper use of language. So, for example, in an essay on *Hamlet*, L. C. Knights comments on the opening speech of Claudius as follows:

At this stage there is no need to describe in detail the forms of corruption of that Denmark in which any decent man would feel himself in prison. There is murder, of course, but even before we know that Claudius is a murderer, it is clear that on his first appearance we are intended to register something repulsive. His very first speech is a masterly example of 'the distillation of personality into style'.

> Though yet of Hamlet our dear brother's death
> The memory be green, and that it us befitted
> To bear our hearts in grief and our whole kingdom
> To be contracted in one brow of woe,
> Yet so far hath discretion fought with nature
> That we with wisest sorrow think on him,
> Together with remembrance of ourselves.

That, surely, is the tone and accent of Milton's Belial; we need know nothing of Claudius's previous activities to react to those unctuous verse rhythms with some such comment as 'Slimy beast!'. Neither the King's practical efficiency in dealing with the public affairs of his kingdom, nor his ostensible kindness towards his nephew, can wipe out that first impression.[6]

This comment seems to spring more from a dislike of any kind of stately and rhetorical utterance than from a response to the totality of the scene, for it ignores the context of a ceremonial assembly in which Claudius is not speaking privately to a friend, but addressing in public the whole court. The royal 'we' is fitting to the occasion, as is the dignified tone, which might be regarded not as 'unctuous', but rather as establishing a mood of calm authority after the sense of alarm, possible war, and 'post-haste and romage in the land', generated in the opening scene. Claudius is making a formal announcement of his marriage with Gertrude, and goes on to conduct business of state, sending ambassadors to Norway. Formal language and a formal style are appropriate, and the way Claudius speaks seems rather to represent one form of a more general court style, which is echoed in the way Gertrude, Laertes and Polonius speak in this scene. The balanced phrases, 'With mirth in funeral, and with dirge in marriage', the expansions, and the elaborate weightiness of terms like 'auspicious' and 'imperial jointness', may suggest a prepared speech, even a certain pomposity, but the speech could be regarded as a brilliant tactic by Claudius (or Shakespeare) to *conceal* rather than distil his personality. Hamlet detests Claudius, and this makes it easier for us, if we identify with Hamlet, to react in the way Knights does, even to play Claudius in that way, but the text could be held to justify a quite different reading; in this Claudius's 'personality', either absorbed into the role of monarch, or hidden from sight under the court rhetoric, except to the extent that to command the allegiance of all the court but Hamlet, and the affection of Gertrude, gains him some sympathy, is revealed only when the role no longer sustains, or the mask is dropped, notably when he attempts to pray in Act III, scene iii. There his style of utterance – simpler, more rapid, with shorter phrases, greater urgency, and sixteen uses of the first person 'I', 'Me', 'my' or 'mine' in the first twenty lines – shows us a vulnerable, troubled and self-conscious private figure.

Perhaps both ways of playing Claudius's first scene are plausible, in which case it has a kind of ambiguity not in Empson's seven types – an ambiguity of dramatic significance, which is not dependent upon verbal nuances, or the play of imagery, but on style. My immediate concern, however, is to relate this discussion of the presentation of Claudius to the scene from *Macbeth* cited earlier. Claudius's rhetoric in Act I, scene ii of *Hamlet* may be seen as predominantly a function of his personality, or as more generally related to the style of language of the court as a whole. The second of these functions points to yet another way of attending to style in Shakespeare's plays, as a shifting aspect of dramatic technique within a play, not specifically related to individual characters, or to be identified with the general style of a particular play. The passage in *Macbeth* illustrates this better than the scene in *Hamlet*, although the various functions of style overlap to a greater or lesser degree. The language of these scenes is appropriate to each play, and to the different characters, but something more is involved too. As Claudius speaks in court diction and vocabulary in his first scene, so in Act III, scene ii of *Macbeth* the strange clotted imagery, and incantatory force of Macbeth's speeches of invocation, chime in with other passages where Macbeth links his activities directly with witchcraft, in the soliloquy preceding his murder of Duncan ('Witchcraft celebrates Pale Hecate's offerings' (II,i,51)), and in Act IV, scene i, when he insists the Witches answer his questions ('I conjure you by that which you profess' (IV,i,49)). In other words, Macbeth speaks in this way when imaginatively gripped by thoughts and actions that relate him most closely to the business of witchcraft. In these speeches he is, so to speak, casting spells, and their dramatic force on stage is engendered more by their incantatory quality, forcing us, like Lady Macbeth, to 'marvel' at his words, than by their sense. To this extent their style is not a reflection of Macbeth's personality so much as a subtle means of rendering his state of mind, and of linking Macbeth at these points with the Witches. Hence although an audience may miss the sense of much of the language, they can readily grasp the dramatic significance of the speeches in Act III, scene ii as mediated in the style.

These two functions of style, as expressing personality and establishing other kinds of dramatic significance, are especially interesting because of their uneasy relation with the 'meaning' of passages as paraphrasable by commentators. A particularly difficult example is Prince Hal's soliloquy at the end of Act I, scene ii in *1 Henry IV*. If this is taken, like Claudius's opening speech, as a distillation of personality into style, then Hal is bound to appear pretty chilling in his ability to switch from an affectionate ease with Falstaff to a cold-blooded statement of his intention to reject his companions. The defiance of decorum in the early part of this scene, in which Hal is presented in the intimacy of mutual abuse with Falstaff, is breathtaking after the formality of the opening court-scene:

Falstaff. Now, Hal, what time of day is it, lad?
Prince.   Thou art so fat-witted with drinking of old sack, and unbuttoning thee after supper, and sleeping upon benches after noon, that thou hast forgotten to demand that truly which thou wouldest truly know. What a devil hast thou to do with the time of the day? Unless hours were cups of sack, and minutes capons, and clocks the tongues of bawds, and dials the signs of leaping-houses, and the blessed sun himself a fair hot wench in flame-coloured taffeta, I see no reason why thou shouldst be so superfluous to demand the time of the day.

(I,ii,I–II)

Falstaff's opening question establishes at once through its familiar 'Hal' and 'lad' that he is entirely at home in the Prince's company, but more importantly, that the Prince allows and enjoys this relationship, an effect sharpened by the contrast between the blank verse of the previous scene and the easy prose of this one. Prince Hal's response is even more startling; for one thing, his joking abuse of Falstaff suggests the exactly calculated permissiveness only possible between intimates, for whom trading insults in a way that just stops short of offence is a means both of exercising wit and fashioning their private world. Again, the insistence on the familiar 'thou' in Hal's speech, and especially perhaps the expletive, 'What a devil hast thou to do with the time of the day?', confirms the mutual ease of a long-established relationship, which alone would permit such playfulness. The sense of this is strengthened further by the accumulation of details in Hal's speech, which constitutes a kind of humorous biography of Falstaff, which reflects back upon the Prince; for if he can speak so casually of drinking, bawds, brothels, and wenches, a natural inference might be that he also is well acquainted with them, and speaks from knowledge, however much exaggeration there may be in what he says.

As an account of how Falstaff spends his days, and by implication the Prince too, the speech depicts a life of idleness and pleasure, something reinforced by the very structure of Hal's sentences, 'a succession of items joined by "and" in which the mind is not required to find an order of importance',[7] but which conveys rather the rhythm of an existence devoted to drinking, eating, wenching and sleeping. This in turn points up further the contrast with the opening scene, as that marks a brief pause in a sequence of civil broils, where men are urgently engaged in the business of state, and the King has at last found 'a time for frighted peace to pant'. Falstaff's question, 'what time of day is it?' seems idle to Hal, whose response is to discourse on the meaninglessness of 'time' in Falstaff's rhythm of life, but their exchange is far from idle in its contrast to the sense of the meaning of time generated in the opening scene, which turns on the foiling yet again of the King's 'holy purpose' (l. 102) to make a pilgrimage to Jerusalem, to 'the sepulchre of Christ' (l. 19). Having established the intimacy of Hal and Falstaff, the second scene goes on to show also the degree to which Hal remains critically aware of Falstaff's limitations, as he joins forces with Poins in plotting against him the elaborate practical joke of the Gadshill robbery. Hal's final soliloquy here requires, then, to be judged in relation to all this, and not simply as a revelation of the psychology of the Prince.

> *Prince.* I know you all, and will awhile uphold
> The unyoked humour of your idleness;
> Yet herein will I imitate the sun,
> Who doth permit the base contagious clouds
> To smother up his beauty from the world,
> That, when he please again to be himself,
> Being wanted, he may be more wondered at
> By breaking through the foul and ugly mists
> Of vapours that did seem to strangle him.

If all the year were playing holidays,
To sport would be as tedious as to work;
But when they seldom come, they wished-for come,
And nothing pleaseth but rare accidents.
So, when this loose behaviour I throw off
And pay the debt I never promisèd,
By how much better than my word I am,
By so much shall I falsify men's hopes;
And, like bright metal on a sullen ground,
My reformation, glittering o'er my fault,
Shall show more goodly and attract more eyes
Than that which hath no foil to set it off.
I'll so offend to make offence a skill,
Redeeming time when men think least I will.   (I,ii,188–210)

The return to blank verse at once relates Hal to the court, as he speaks in the mode of the court-scenes in Act I, scene i and Act I, scene iii, and so emerges with authority as Prince. These lines constitute another meditation on time, a repudiation of the life-style of Falstaff as described in Hal's opening speech. Instead of a paratactic sequence of clauses joined by 'and', all equally important (or unimportant), the clauses of Hal's soliloquy vary in weight, and the connectives emphasise not a series of equivalents but a process of thinking out, in links like 'Yet', 'That when', 'If', 'But when', and 'So when'. The structure and style of the speech, that is to say, lead to and culminate in the notion of 'Redeeming time'. In terms of dramatic significance, then, this speech seems both necessary and finely judged in relation to the King who is prevented, by the civil wars he has provoked by usurping the throne, from expiating his sins, and so redeeming time, and to Falstaff, for whom time has no importance anyway.

Yet it leaves many *readers* feeling uneasy. Perhaps this is because the study allows analysis of the imagery, which then jars with what the scene has shown. Prince Hal may reasonably see himself as the 'sun', a conventional image of royalty, but Falstaff and Poins are hardly to be equated with 'base contagious clouds', or 'foul and ugly mists'. Far from being strangled by them, he seems to have chosen their company, and to prefer them and 'playing holidays' to work. In performance, the rhetoric probably is more persuasive, and the imagery less noticeable, especially as Hal is alone when he speaks the lines, and addressing the audience, who are embraced in his opening words 'I know you all' – it is *our* humour of idleness he will uphold, to enable us to enjoy Falstaff, and for this we may be grateful. Also his statement comes over as a general argument of policy, a statement of the position he has to take, a necessary reminder of his rank and obligations, and an anticipation of glories to come, so functioning in a quasi-choric way, and not as an attack on his companions. Even in the theatre, however, the uneasiness may be felt, possibly because the life-style of the court, so far as we have seen it in Act I, scene i, has little to recommend it, and sufficient reason has not been established why Hal should prefer it to the more entertaining world of Falstaff. A modern audience no doubt responds less readily than an Elizabethan one to the obligations of royalty and the notion of 'honour' won in battle, and there perhaps remains some discomfiture – the dramatic significance of the speech seems somewhat at odds with its sense, and its relation to the psychology of Hal is therefore uncertain.

If the start of Hal's career produces this immediate problem, the end of it, as Henry V, provides an especially interesting example of Shakespeare's concern with what I have called dramatic significance. The chief interest of Act V of *Henry V* lies in Henry's wooing of Katherine, in which his main speech is the following:

King. Marry, if you would put me to verses or to dance for your sake, Kate, why you undid me; for the one I have neither words nor measure, and for the other I have no strength in measure, yet a reasonable measure in strength. If I could win a lady at leap-frog, or by vaulting into my saddle with my armour on my back, under the correction of bragging be it spoken, I should quickly leap into a wife. Or if I might buffet for my love, or bound my horse for her favours, I could lay on like a butcher, and sit like a jack-an-apes, never off. But, before God, Kate, I cannot look greenly, nor gasp out my eloquence nor I have no cunning in protestation; only downright oaths, which I never use till urged, nor never break for urging. If thou canst love a fellow of this temper, Kate, whose face is not worth sun-burning, that never looks in his glass for love of anything he sees there, let thine eye be thy cook. I speak to thee plain soldier. If thou canst love me for this, take me; if not, to say to thee that I shall die is true – but for thy love, by the Lord, no; yet I love thee too. And while thou liv'st, dear Kate, take a fellow of plain and uncoined constancy; for he perforce must do thee right, because he hath not the gift to woo in other places; for these fellows of infinite tongue, that can rhyme themselves into ladies' favours, they do always reason themselves out again. What! a speaker is but a prater: a rhyme is but a ballad. A good leg will fall; a straight back will stoop; a black beard will turn white; a curled pate will grow bald; a fair face will wither; a full eye will wax hollow. But a good heart, Kate, is the sun and the moon; or, rather, the sun, and not the moon – for it shines bright and never changes, but keeps his course truly. If thou would have such a one, take me; and take me, take a soldier; take a soldier, take a king. And what say'st thou, then, to my love? Speak, my fair, and fairly, I pray thee.   (v,ii,131–67)

This is the plain soldier indeed, protesting with some skill that he has 'no cunning in protestation', in a speech that insists on his dullness, his lack

of eloquence, his inability to express himself in poetry or even to speak
well. Up to this point in the play the King has spoken mostly in verse,
except when in disguise he wanders among the soldiers, and the excuse
Williams makes for abusing him is that he appeared then 'but as a
common man' (IV,viii,50), so that his prose in the camp scenes marks his
disguise, his distance from his normal blank-verse self. That self, in turn,
was established by Shakespeare in contrast to Prince Hal, whose 'wild-
ness' (I,i,26), together with his low-life companions and his prose, he
abandoned before the opening of the play, according to the Archbishop of
Canterbury, who praises above all his skill in reasoning, as Henry shows
himself a master of all the arts of discourse:

> Hear him debate of commonwealth affairs,
> You would say it hath been all in all his study;
> List his discourse of war, and you shall hear
> A fearful battle rendered you in music.
> Turn him to any cause of policy,
> The Gordian knot of it he will unloose,
> Familiar as his garter; that, when he speaks,
> The air, a chartered libertine, is still,
> And the mute wonder lurketh in men's ears
> To steal his sweet and honeyed sentences.   (I,i,41–50)

The Archbishop's praise may be a little overpitched, but Henry has some
notable speeches which bear out this description of him, like his fine
denunciation of the conspirators (II,ii), his 'Once more unto the breach,
dear friends' (III,i), and his meditation on ceremony (IV,i). Indeed,
having prepared his audience for the entry of the King with this account
of him, Shakespeare must have had in mind a Henry consistent with it;
and however much weight is given to the Archbishop's concern for the
wealth of the church, and his anxiety to gain the King's support for his
own political ends, there is no trace of irony in his image of Henry as 'full
of grace and fair regard'.

The Henry who woos Katherine in Act V bears, on the face of it, little
resemblance to the King the Archbishop and we have known. It would
seem perhaps possible to treat Henry's speech, which follows on Katherine's remark that the tongues of men are full of deceit, as an elaborate
trope in which Henry pretends to be almost the opposite of what he is,
but since he maintains this 'character' throughout the rest of the act, and
is engaged in what must be conveyed to the audience as a sincere and
honest wooing leading to the triumphant unity of France and England,
such an interpretation cannot be sustained. Henry has to 'believe' in what

he says, and the sense of his speech continually reinforces the tone – the plain soldier has a plain vocabulary, in which his images and references all relate to commonplace things and people: leapfrog, riding, a butcher, sun-burn, a cook, the sun and the moon. This Henry seems quite unlike either the witty Hal of *Henry IV* or the gracious blank-verse monarch of the previous acts in *Henry V*. The demands of the dramatic action at this point were more important for Shakespeare than consistency of characterisation; a rhyming lover, a Romeo, would be quite wasted on a princess with hardly any English, so Henry has to appear a plain prose Benedick instead. Beyond this, Shakespeare may also have aimed at rounding off the play by giving full weight to what Henry had become rather than what he had been. The gracious, eloquent King of the early acts merges into the war-hero of Agincourt, who in turn becomes the plain soldier of Act V who speaks in blows not words. To put it another way, the Henry of Act I has emerged from the 'courses of his youth' (I,i,24) into authority and maturity, so that whatever age we imagine him to be, dramatically the figure who can reflect so poignantly on kingship and ceremony in Act IV is a much older and wiser character than the Prince of *Henry IV*.

In seeking a way to bring *Henry V* to a joyful conclusion, Shakespeare restored to Henry his youth, by the expedient of suppressing in Act V what had suggested his maturity, and presenting him simply as a soldier. In this way he turns Henry into an inexperienced lover, who 'hath not the gift to woo in other places', and who, wooing apparently as a young and rather *gauche* lover for the first time, adds the conquest of Kate, as he prefers to call her, to his victory over France, and rounds off the play with a scene which has more in common with the romantic Comedies than with the preceding action. This is how in reading we might account for Act V, but perhaps in performance any sense of inconsistency is diminished by our instinctive response to the style of Henry's speech, which, in spite of his disclaimers, shows a remarkable skill in deploying figures of rhetoric, culminating in a notable example of parison, which, as Puttenham describes it, 'goes by clauses of equal quantity...and they give a good grace to a ditty, but specially to a prose',[8] something Shakespeare knew in having Henry say, 'A good leg will fall; a straight back will stoop; a curled pate will grow bald; a fair face will wither...', and so on. Even if we do not recognise any of his figures, in responding to the style of the speech we instinctively catch the wit and control of a very sophisticated speaker, and so although what Henry says seems a denial of the King we knew earlier, his way of speaking provides a dramatic

connection, and this prevents an audience being troubled in the theatre
by a sense that Henry has changed out of recognition.

In all the passages discussed above, the dramatic effect is generated by
something more than the sense of the words on the page. In *Macbeth*, the
words are too difficult for an audience to grasp properly, and the magic of
what he says is more important than the sense, for it is as if in the turmoil
of his mind he does not fully understand his own language. In *Hamlet*,
the style of Claudius's opening speech represents more than a distillation
of personality, though here the temptation for some critics has been to
attend to style and not to the sense, shrewd, well-balanced, and authorita-
tive, of what Claudius says. In *1 Henry IV*, Prince Hal's soliloquy at the
end of Act I, scene ii becomes explicable only if attention is given to its
dramatic placing and significance as well as to the meaning of what he
says. Finally, in *Henry V*, what appears a marked inconsistency in
characterisation and language makes sense if Henry's prose in Act V is
seen in a deeper stylistic relation to the rest of the play. It may perhaps
seem merely a commonplace to say that in the theatre our response to a
scene may be primarily in terms of its style, tone and mood, rather than
words or verbal imagery, but just as editors in the main, as in the old
Arden edition, have explained verbal difficulties to the neglect of other
matters, so criticism has concerned itself chiefly with poetic imagery,
wordplay, ambiguity, with meaning rather than with style or dramatic
significance. The passages tentatively analysed above in various ways
illustrate kinds of dramatic significance which can be realised only by
attending to other features besides meaning – in all these cases one might
say it is possible to have the meaning and miss the experience, as
Empson's explanation of 'the crow / Makes wing to the rooky wood'
suggests. So perhaps the time is ripe for the development of an approach
to Shakespeare which would ask how dramatic significance is established
in plays, and how this differs from the meanings investigated in the
process of glossing a text or studying imagery; it would necessarily
consider style, and the ways in which the demands of character over
scene, or scene over character, or play over both scene and character, may
affect Shakespeare's treatment of his material, and how an understanding
of such things may throw light on the deeper structure and significance of
a work. This is not to propose a way of at last discovering some final
significance in a play; as noted earlier in relation to Claudius, dramatic
significance has its ambiguities and leaves open a variety of interpretations. It is simply to claim that the study of verbal meaning is not

enough, however rich and complex Shakespeare's poetry may be; we need to appreciate the dramatic magic as well as the sense.

NOTES

1 London, 1930, p. 25.
2 *Ephesians* 4.30.
3 There is, of course, no way of knowing what 'the audience' really understands, and individual members will vary greatly in their response. The term is a convenience, and there must always be an element of guess-work in claims made about what happens in 'the theatre', where every performance is in any case different in however minute ways from all others.
4 The studies by George Rylands in *Words and Poetry* (London, 1928) and Richard David in *The Janus of Poets* (Cambridge, 1935) now seem pioneering efforts which deserved a better follow-up. Since Miriam Joseph catalogued *Shakespeare's Use of the Arts of Language* (New York, 1947), there has been some persuasive illustration of Shakespeare's knowledge of how to exploit these arts, most notably in Brian Vickers's *The Artistry of Shakespeare's Prose* (London, 1968). Maurice Charney focussed on a single play in terms more perhaps of imagery and meaning than of style in his *Style in 'Hamlet'* (Princeton, 1969) and John Russell Brown sought to open up a new teaching method in *Shakespeare's Dramatic Style* (London, 1970).
5 F. R. Leavis, *The Common Pursuit* (London, 1952), pp. 142, 146.
6 *An Approach to 'Hamlet'* (London, 1960), pp. 41–2.
7 G. W. Turner, *Stylistics* (London, 1973), p. 119, defining parataxis.
8 *The Arte of English Poesie*, ed. G. D. Willcock and A. Walker (Cambridge, 1936), p. 214; I have modernised the spelling. See also Lee A. Sonnino, *A Handbook to Sixteenth-Century Rhetoric* (London, 1968), p. 43.

Feliciter audax: Antony and Cleopatra, I,i,1–24

G. R. HIBBARD

		[*Enter* DEMETRIUS *and* PHILO.]
	Philo.	Nay, but this dotage of our general's
		O'erflows the measure. Those his goodly eyes,
		That o'er the files and musters of the war
		Have glowed like plated Mars, now bend, now turn,
5		The office and devotion of their view
		Upon a tawny front. His captain's heart,
		Which in the scuffles of great fights hath burst
		The buckles on his breast, reneges all temper,
		And is become the bellows and the fan
		To cool a gipsy's lust.

[*Flourish. Enter* ANTONY, CLEOPATRA, *her* Ladies, *the* Train, *with* Eunuchs *fanning her.*]

10		Look where they come!
		Take but good note, and you shall see in him
		The triple pillar of the world transformed
		Into a strumpet's fool. Behold and see.
	Cleopatra.	If it be love indeed, tell me how much.
15	*Antony.*	There's beggary in the love that can be reckoned.
	Cleopatra.	I'll set a bourn how far to be beloved.
	Antony.	Then must thou needs find out new heaven, new earth.
		[*Enter* a Messenger.]
	Messenger.	News, my good lord, from Rome.
	Antony.	Grates me! the sum.[1]
	Cleopatra.	Nay, hear them, Antony.
20		Fulvia perchance is angry; or who knows
		If the scarce-bearded Caesar have not sent
		His powerful mandate to you: 'Do this or this;
		Take in that kingdom and enfranchise that;
		Perform't, or else we damn thee.'
	Antony.	How, my love?

No other of Shakespeare's plays begins on such a full-throated note as this. That 'happy valiancy of style', which Coleridge singled out as the

tragedy's most striking and characteristic quality,[2] makes itself felt from
the very start. Philo's outburst sweeps forward in a flood-tide of verbal
splendour. Only once within the entire speech does the end of a sentence
coincide with the end of a line; and no fewer than seven lines out of the
thirteen are run on. Moreover, as befits an impetuous outburst, the
speech is both repetitive and expansive, returning time after time, but in
different terms, to the same central issue. The essence of what the soldier
has to say is already there in the first sentence: he finds Antony's
behaviour incomprehensible, exasperating, and intolerable. But this
initial statement, inadequate in its brevity to convey a depth and complexity of feeling which, like Antony's 'dotage', itself 'O'erflows the
measure', is then exemplified and further defined through two magnificent images, each rising on a wave of hyperbolical inflation that eventually breaks in the same kind of devastatingly reductive scorn: 'a tawny
front' and 'a gipsy's lust'. And then, after the colourful and spectacular
entry of the hero and the heroine, in which the effeminacy that Philo has
castigated is endorsed and given visual form in the eunuchs and the
fanning, comes the summing-up in yet another image, which follows
exactly the same pattern of development as the two previous images to
reach its conclusion in the contemptuous finality of 'a strumpet's fool',
the metrical as well as the sense counterpart to 'a tawny front' and 'a
gipsy's lust'.

The most distinctive feature of *Antony and Cleopatra* as a whole is
already apparent: Philo cannot understand why Antony should behave as
he is doing, nor can he suppress or control the mixed emotions, including
a profound sense of loss and regret as well as scorn, with which that
behaviour fills him, but he can, through the words that Shakespeare finds
for him, *express* both the incomprehension and the violent conflict of
opposing impulses that he feels within himself.[3] It is all completely and
pellucidly there, subtly shaped in such a way as to make his speech a brief
but powerful self-contained poem, deriving much of its unity from
recurrent rhythms that act like echoes. The similarities of the three long
sentences, each working out an image, of the three dismissive phrases,
and of the three exhortations to Demetrius, 'Look where they come',
'Take but good note', and 'Behold and see', give the lines a formal quality
not unlike that of a lyric or a sonnet, with the long sentences taking the
place of stanzas, and the parallel phrases and commands, so reminiscent
of each other, corresponding to rhymes.

The speech is intended to be memorable and to be remembered, because it puts a point of view which will be of the utmost importance for the tragedy it introduces, which will be reiterated time after time during its course, and which will not receive its final answer, and, I think, its ultimate refutation, until the close. That answer is, of course, Cleopatra's last speech and Charmian's coda to it (v,ii,278–326), a passage which, with a miraculous appropriateness, is, in its structure as distinct from its content, extraordinarily like Philo's prologue; for it, too, is a complete poem in itself that tends to fall into a series of irregular stanzas, punctuated and held together by commands, questions, and exclamations, nearly all of which are of the same two-foot length as his three expressions of scorn and his three exhortations: 'Give me my robe', 'put on my crown', 'Husband, I come', 'So, have you done?', 'Dost thou lie still?', 'This proves me base', 'O couldst thou speak', 'O Eastern star!', 'O break! O break!', 'What should I stay –', 'In this vile world?', 'So, fare thee well', 'Your crown's awry', recalling, with a difference, Cleopatra's 'put on my crown', and 'It is well done.'

Commenting on this speech of Cleopatra's, Middleton Murry says: 'A dying woman does not use such figures of speech; and at the pinnacle of her complex emotion, a Cleopatra would have no language to express it.' He then goes on to say: 'in the death scene of Cleopatra [Shakespeare] achieves the miracle: he makes the language completely adequate to the emotion and yet keeps it simple' (p. 39). About the simplicity I have doubts; but the rest of that statement puts the matter extremely well and can be applied, *mutatis mutandis,* to Philo's opening lines. Soldiers, particularly when exasperated, do not speak as he does, but the language he is given is 'completely adequate to the emotion'. In this respect, above all others – and there are others – his lines are the perfect prologue to the play, for *Antony and Cleopatra* is, of all Shakespeare's mature tragedies, the most expressive and luminous. In part this luminosity comes from the manner in which images are handled. The play is charged with them, and, as Maurice Charney has shown in great detail,[4] they are most intricately linked together and carry much of the total significance; but, while they often tread hard on one another's heels, as they do, for example, in Cleopatra's ecstatic picture of the Antony she knew (v,ii,79–92), they are always kept separate from one another, as they are in Philo's speech. They do not grow into and become entangled with each other, as they do, for instance, in Lady Macbeth's taunt to her husband:

Was the hope drunk
Wherein you dressed yourself? Hath it slept since,

> And wakes it now to look so green and pale
> At what it did so freely? From this time
> Such I account thy love.   (*Macbeth*, I,vii,35–9)

The compressed involution of that, so wholly in keeping with an action that occurs for the most part in darkness and mist and in which 'the torture of the mind' (III,ii,21) is a central concern, would be entirely out of place in *Antony and Cleopatra,* where the action takes place in the clear light of the Mediterranean day and the darker recesses of the human heart are left unprobed.

It is not merely the clarity and distinctness of its images that makes *Antony and Cleopatra* so expressive, though they obviously contribute to its expressiveness; Shakespeare's whole attitude towards language seems to have changed from what it was when he wrote *King Lear*. Anne Barton, in her essay, 'Shakespeare and the Limits of Language',[5] remarks, with considerable justification, that 'It is in the tragedies. . .that words are exposed to a scrutiny not only intense but, in the case of *King Lear,* distinctly unfriendly' (p. 24), and then goes on to point out how often in that play characters in their moments of extreme suffering can do no more than repeat some single word, such as 'Howl' or 'Never', time and again; how often they lapse into sheer incoherence; and how often also they actually say that what they are experiencing is quite beyond the capacity of language to formulate. She does not refer to *Antony and Cleopatra* in her subsequent discussion of the scepticism about the adequacy of words to convey man's profoundest feelings which Shakespeare, she argues, shows in much of his tragic writing, but a brief mention of it in another context (p. 23) makes it evident that she regards it as the great exception to the general idea she advances.

It is, indeed; for if the other tragedies do evince a certain distrust of language – and, in so far as *King Lear* is concerned, this seems to me undeniable – on the part of their creator, this one does precisely the opposite: in it there is an unbounded confidence in the potentialities of language, which seems capable of encompassing anything and everything, except the monstrous and the unspeakable, which it is not called on to do. In *Antony and Cleopatra* even incoherence itself, on the one occasion when it occurs, is expressed in such a convincing fashion that it becomes a kind of eloquence. In Act I, scene iii, Cleopatra, having learnt from Antony of his intention to return to Rome, reproaches him for his lack of love and then taunts him by suggesting that his reluctance to leave her is merely a piece of play-acting. Eventually she goes too far, and

brings down on herself the curt rejoinder, 'I'll leave you, lady.' There-
upon, she tries to hold him back, if only for a moment, by pretending that
she has something of great importance to say to him but cannot
remember what it is:

> Courteous lord, one word.
> Sir, you and I must part – but that's not it.
> Sir, you and I have loved – but there's not it.
> That you know well. Something it is I would –
> O, my oblivion is a very Antony,
> And I am all forgotten.   (I,iii,86–91)

In that speech the *je ne sais quoi* has been defined with completeness and
employed with assurance to 'snatch a grace beyond the reach of art'. In a
similar way but on a much larger scale the verse conjures up the
spaciousness of the Roman empire on the bare stage of the Globe theatre,
and leads the audience into accepting the reality of a heroine of whom it is
said, 'Age cannot wither her, nor custom stale / Her infinite variety'
(II,ii,239–40). Moreover, it also works as a potent unifying factor to hold
together an action that ranges over many countries and many years, takes
in events as diverse as the coming of the *Pax Romana* and a drunken
party, and is almost as much comic as it is tragic.

The verse has this unifying effect because the style of the play is
remarkably homogeneous; the style not the styles, for *Antony and Cleopatra*, unlike the other tragedies, is written in one style not several. The
tragedies which come closest to it in this respect are the other two
(excluding the very early *Titus Andronicus*) which admit only a minimal
amount of prose, less than ten per cent of the total number of lines: *Julius
Caesar* and *Macbeth*. In the former, however, a clear distinction is made
between the language of the crowd and that of the other figures, as well as
between the Attic style of Brutus and the Asiatic style of Antony in the
forum scene (III,ii). In the latter, the most obvious distinction is between
the blank verse of most of the play and the rhyme of the witches, and the
prose of the drunken Porter and, later, the prose of Lady Macbeth in the
sleep-walking scene, each providing a kind of ironic counterpoint to the
dominant manner. But in *Antony and Cleopatra* even the one character
who is wholly confined to prose, the Clown who brings the asp to
Cleopatra in the final scene, is still, like the other characters in the play,
very much an overstater, in his own malapropian fashion, describing the
worm's biting as 'immortal' and his own account of its prowess as 'most
falliable' (V,ii,246–56). At the same time, however, the Clown plainly has

his feet on the ground, so to speak, carefully defining the meaning he gives to 'immortal' by adding 'those that do die of it do seldom or never recover', and applying 'most falliable' to his unimposing but indisputable statement, 'the worm's an odd worm'.

In fact, the Clown's speeches, in their mixture of the would-be impressive and the bathetic, are a brilliant parody of the manner of Philo's opening lines, which is also the manner of the play those lines introduce, an astonishing union of the hyperbolical with the simple, the downright, and the direct. Fully conscious of the new style he has created for his play and utterly confident in its strength, Shakespeare repeatedly draws attention to the hyperbolical element in it by submitting it to parody. Charmian, consulting the Soothsayer, says:

Let me be married to three kings in a forenoon, and widow them all. Let me have a child at fifty, to whom Herod of Jewry may do homage. Find me to marry me with Octavius Caesar, and companion me with my mistress. (I,ii,26–9)

And he, not to be outdone, replies to her question, 'Prithee, how many boys and wenches must I have?', by retorting:

> If every of your wishes had a womb,
> And fertile every wish, a million.   (ll. 34–6)

This criticism of the tendency, so evident in the writing, towards a fine excess reaches its height in the opening lines of Act III, scene ii, where Agrippa and Enobarbus compete with each other in mockery of the sycophantic efforts, as they see them, of Lepidus to stand well with both Caesar and Antony, a competition which Enobarbus wins hands down when, in answer to Agrippa's judicious comment, 'Indeed, he plied them both with excellent praises', he remarks:

> But he loves Caesar best. Yet he loves Antony.
> Hoo! hearts, tongues, figures, scribes, bards, poets, cannot
> Think, speak, cast, write, sing, number – hoo! –
> His love to Antony. But as for Caesar,
> Kneel down, kneel down, and wonder.   (III,ii,14–19)

The odd thing about this speech and, indeed, about the mockery of which it is part, is that we have heard nothing from Lepidus to justify it. His manner of expressing himself is no more extreme and excessive than that of anyone else; for in *Antony and Cleopatra* Shakespeare, abandoning, for the time being, his talent for conferring life and individuality on a character by endowing him with a distinctive and often idiosyncratic idiom, a way of speaking which is peculiarly his own, relies for his characterisation on what the *dramatis personae* say, on what is said about them by others, and, of course, on what they do. It is, it must be added, quite enough. Octavia, for example, short though her part is, makes a very definite impression that sets her off from all the other characters; yet it is only the sense and the sentiment of the following lines addressed to Antony that mark them out as hers; in their movement, their appeal to Jove, their resort to the repeated superlative, and in the magnitude and vigour of their imagery they could equally well belong to almost anyone else in the play:

> The Jove of power make me, most weak, most weak,
> Your reconciler! Wars 'twixt you twain would be
> As if the world should cleave, and that slain men
> Should solder up the rift.   (III,iv,29–32)

A mere eighteen lines later, Enobarbus, also anticipating the likelihood of a war between Antony and Caesar, virtually makes my point for me when he says:

> Then, world, thou hast a pair of chaps – no more;
> And throw between them all the food thou hast,
> They'll grind the one the other.   (III,v,13–15)

In both speeches the images are epic in their scope, but far more compressed and forceful than the images of heroic poetry usually are. A much earlier use by Shakespeare of an image that is very close in essentials to that of Enobarbus will serve to illustrate the difference. In *King John*, when John and Philip of France, after the first indecisive engagement between their armies, seem on the point of renewing the battle, the Bastard cries:

> O, now doth Death line his dead chaps with steel;
> The swords of soldiers are his teeth, his fangs;
> And now he feasts, mousing the flesh of men,
> In undetermined differences of kings.   (II,i,352–5)

The image there is, because of its greater detail, more picturesque, more explicit, and much closer to the epic manner than Enobarbus's, but it does not have, if the pun may be allowed, the same crunch. In Octavia's lines, as in Enobarbus's, it is the reciprocal interplay of the grand and the familiar that creates the striking effect. A 'rift' is the chasm caused by an earthquake, not a common sight, but the verb 'solder', belonging to the language of tinkers and plumbers, bridges the gap, as it were, and brings the whole notion much nearer to everyday experience.

It is the 'heavenly mingle' of the elevated and grand with the simple and familiar which is the basic feature of the style of *Antony and Cleopatra* and the source of that 'angelic strength' which so impressed Coleridge.[6] Nor is this mingle simply a matter of images. A pair of words are often brought into a vital and unexpected relationship with each other in such a way that they interinanimate, to use a word of Donne's, each other. 'A lass unparallel'd' (v,ii,314) is a rare creature indeed, especially when the lass in question is 'with Phoebus' amorous pinches black, / And wrinkled deep in time' (I,v,28–9), simultaneously ordinary and quite extraordinary, common and yet unique, the offspring of a marriage between a native English word that first appears around the year 1300 and a neologism, deriving ultimately from the Greek, for which the *OED* gives no example prior to 1594. Furthermore, 'lasses' are usually found in the popular love poetry of Shakespeare's day, and they live in the country, witness his own song, 'It was a lover and his lass' (*As You Like It*, v,iii,14–31); whereas 'unparallel'd' comes from the world of science and of learning in general, smacks of the Inns of Court, and has more than a touch of metaphysical wit about it. 'A lass unparallel'd' is a poem in little, and its style a microcosm of the style that informs the play.

The consistency of that style in its sustained mixing of the sublime and the simple, the heroic and the amorous, suggests that Shakespeare, when writing this play, saw it as his own dramatic contribution to the Renaissance epic in which the main themes were love and war. Philo's initial speech lends strong support to this idea, for it looks like a highly original variation on the well-established epic *topos* so memorably employed by Virgil in Aeneas's description of the ghost of Hector as it appeared to him on the night of Troy's destruction. Torn, blood-stained, and covered in dust, just as Hector's body was after being dragged round the walls of Troy by Achilles, the ghost is a shocking contrast to the hero Aeneas knew:

> quantum mutatus ab illo
> Hectore, qui redit exuvias indutus Achilli
> vel Danaum Phrygios iaculatus puppibus ignis![7]

Shakespeare characteristically puts his own stamp, in the form of verbal energy and linguistic inventiveness, on the contrast he draws between Antony as he was and Antony as he is. Over against the mythological references to Mars and to Atlas, with, perhaps, a hint of Hercules as well in the latter, are set images from common life, 'the bellows and the fan'. His mastery of concentrated and significant word-play is evident in 'dotage', meaning primarily 'sexual infatuation' but also carrying overtones of 'the lack of judgement that comes with old age', and again in 'fool', denoting both 'amorous plaything' and 'dupe'. The word 'scuffles' appears nowhere else in the canon, and its occurrence here is the earliest recorded in the *OED*, though there is evidence that 'scuffling' was being used in East Anglia rather more than twenty years before;[8] and 'triple', signifying 'third' or 'one of three', is a usage peculiar, it would seem, to Shakespeare. The most important instance of linguistic adventurousness in the entire speech is, however, the pregnant and teasing phrase 'reneges all temper', which most editors, forgetting or overlooking the fact that temperance is not a quality that Philo, or anyone else for that matter, associates with Antony, gloss as 'abandons or renounces all moderation'. On the only other occasion when Shakespeare employs 'renege' (*King Lear*, II,ii,73) it means 'deny'; but a better guide to its full significance here is Maria's laughing account of Malvolio's ridiculous behaviour, in which she says of him:

Yond gull Malvolio is turned heathen, a very renegado; for there is no Christian that means to be saved by believing rightly can ever believe such impossible passages of grossness. (*Twelfth Night*, III,ii,64–8)

'To renege' is 'deliberately to deny and renounce one's faith'; and the 'temper' Philo has in mind is the temper of good steel, standing meta-phorically for the steely courage and springy resolution of Antony's heart in which his men have hitherto been able to put their trust, exactly as they have done in the temper of their swords. At the root of the soldier's bitter and regretful condemnation of his general lies his conviction that Antony is now a renegade, one who has betrayed and renounced that faith in the military virtues which he once embodied and which Philo holds still.

The stylistic daring of the speech is matched by the dramatic daring of its placing. No other of Shakespeare's tragic heroes is introduced after this fashion. It is true that we hear many harsh things about Othello before he actually appears, but, since they come from the lips of one who admits from the outset that he hates the Moor, we do not take them at their face value. We have no such reason for distrusting Philo; on the contrary, his obvious love and admiration for the Antony he once knew inspire confidence in the accuracy of what he says. His lines are a lament for fallen greatness as well as an attack on apostasy. Consequently, they also leave us asking what kind of tragedy this is to be. The other tragedies of Shakespeare's maturity all deal with a fall from greatness that happens during the course of the action, after the greatness of the hero has been

made plain to us and impressed on us by what we see him do and hear him
say; but after listening to Philo we can only conclude that Antony's
greatness is already a thing of the past, and that greatness of any kind is
the last thing Cleopatra can lay claim to. If the play is to be a tragedy, as
both the head-title and the running-title in the First Folio assure us it is,
it is bound to be radically different, as indeed it is, from the other
tragedies.

Equally remarkable and unexpected is the assignment of these crucial
lines to one who is, apparently, a minor figure with no role to play in the
subsequent action, and who will, once this scene is over, never be seen
again. The most obvious parallel to him is the 'bleeding Sergeant' in
Macbeth, who gives an epic account, in the second scene, of the battle in
which Macbeth and Banquo have so distinguished themselves, and then
disappears. But the Sergeant is, in effect, the Messenger of the play's
opening and therefore a privileged character, as it were, charged with the
task of relating actions the playwright chooses not to stage, and, to that
extent, he is a substitute for the dramatist himself. Philo, however, is no
messenger and he certainly does not speak for the author, whose attitude
towards the characters and actions of the play is, as we are about to
discover, far more complex than his, which it includes but also trans-
cends. So why does Shakespeare give these lines to the soldier? It is, I
think, his way of indicating that Philo is, in one sense, the most important
figure in the play, not on account of what he is in himself but of what he
represents. His faith in war as a kind of religion, providing the standards
by which he judges Antony's conduct, makes him the ideal Roman
soldier. Consequently, when he speaks, his voice is not so much that of an
individual as that of the flower of the Roman army; and it is this army
which will, in the end, decide whether Antony or Caesar is to emerge
from the conflict as 'Sole sir o' th' world' (v,ii,119). The political outcome
of the action is already implicit in the opening speech. Philo's is the voice
of destiny, and therefore very properly 'utters somewhat above a mortal
mouth', as Ben Jonson puts it.[9]

Yet despite the power and authority of Philo's speech, it is no sooner
out of his mouth than it begins to be undermined. Four lines, shared
equally by the two lovers, are sufficient to shake our confidence in the
fairness and accuracy of his verdict on them. As Cleopatra's initial
demand and then her teasing threat draw from Antony precisely the
affirmation and the assurance they were designed to, we hear the harmony
of concord and satisfaction replacing the harsh discord of disapproval.

There is a lilt, almost a caress, in the simple directness with which the Queen of Egypt puts the question that women have been asking their lovers since the beginning of time; and Antony's reply to it has all the weight of a long tradition of love poetry behind it. Cleverly picking up a subsidiary meaning of 'tell', namely, 'count', he dismisses all such counting as evidence of a poverty and meanness of spirit, for that is what 'beggary' denotes in this context. Somewhere behind the line lies the amorous arithmetic of Catullus, which enjoyed such a vogue in the love poetry of the early seventeenth century and which had, very recently, been heard on the stage of the Globe theatre in Ben Jonson's *Volpone*, played by Shakespeare's company, the King's Men, early in 1606. There the protagonist, in the course of his attempted seduction of Celia, borrows some lines from Catullus's Poem vii as he invites her to

> score vp summes of pleasures,
> *That the curious shall not know,*
> *How to tell them, as they flow;*
> *And the enuious, when they find*
> *What their number is, be pind.*   (III,vii,235–9)

But, whether the allusion comes through or not, Antony's essential generosity of soul is already apparent; and equally so, when Cleopatra offers to set a limit to his love, to define its bounds, is his defiance of limitation, stated in terms which, in their cosmic range, outdo the hyperboles of Philo and announce an imagistic theme which will return again and again as the action develops to reach its culmination in Cleopatra's vision of Antony as she imagined him:

> His face was as the heav'ns, and therein stuck
> A sun and moon, which kept their course and lighted
> This little O, the earth.   (V,ii,79–81)

It is already clear that the relationship between the lovers is something other than and bigger than the sordid affair which so disgusts and pains the soldier; and it may well be dawning on an audience or reader that the criteria on which Philo has based his judgement are too narrow and restricted to cope adequately with the nature and quality of the experience he has applied them to. A dialectical process, which will continue to the play's end, has begun, for we are faced with the question, which are the more important and likely to be the more rewarding, the claims of Rome and empire or the claims of Egypt and love, the pursuit of fame or the pursuit of pleasure and happiness? And behind this question lies an even bigger question of which, as yet, we have scarcely had time to become aware: are people such as these two, he the ruler of one-third of the world, and she the Queen of Egypt, in any position to make a practical, workable choice between these competing claims? To this question the play will, in due course, offer its bleak realistic answer: for the relationship to continue Antony must retain the power which the relationship itself threatens and undermines; there can be no retirement into private life for figures placed as these are.

That answer lies, however, in the future. What we are immediately faced with is the discrepancy between what Philo sees and what we, in the audience, see, and between the interpretation he puts on it and the interpretation we feel tempted to put on it. It is at this point that the see-saw movement of acquiescence and rejection, which has now started, inclines once more to Philo's side, as the exchanges of the lovers are brought to an abrupt conclusion by the entry of the Messenger bearing news from Rome. Antony's reception of him and of it is a masterly piece of condensation that asks to be rasped out. The editor of the New Arden edition of the play glosses 'Grates me! the sum' as 'offends me: be brief', while Dover Wilson renders it thus: 'news from Rome! I can't be bothered with messengers; tell it in brief'. Neither notices that 'Grates', as well as meaning 'vexes or irritates', also denotes 'grates on the ear by making a harsh creaking sound', the sense in which it is used by Hotspur in his dismissal of 'mincing poetry', of which he says:

> I had rather hear a brazen canstick turned
> Or a dry wheel grate on the axle-tree.   (*1 Henry IV*, III,i,131–2)

To Antony the mere mention of Rome is not only offensive and irritating but also positively painful, partly because it is an interruption of pleasure, jarring on and breaking off the music of his dialogue with Cleopatra, but mainly because it represents a call to a duty which he recognises as a duty but has no intention of carrying out until he is forced to do so.

Nevertheless, he is prepared, albeit grudgingly, to listen to the news, provided that it is kept brief. But Cleopatra, fully aware of the danger Rome poses to her hold on her lover, now deploys her wiles to prevent him from hearing its call. Pretending that his words have amounted to the absolute refusal to listen that she hoped for, she urges him to give audience to the Messenger, while, at the same time, making it abundantly clear that if he does he will be submitting abjectly to her two arch-enemies, his wife Fulvia and Octavius Caesar. 'Fulvia perchance is angry'

implies not only that Antony's wife is something of a virago but also that
Antony himself is hen-pecked by her; and the description of Caesar as
'scarce-bearded' is skilfully belittling, since it means that he is only just
old enough to grow a beard as well as that he is scantly bearded. Her lines
are a well-contrived challenge to Antony's manhood, and also a con-
summate piece of acting in their carefully calculated mimicry of the
authoritarian Caesar. 'Take in' is the technical military term for
'conquer' or 'capture'; and she makes her own special use of hyperbole in
having Caesar employ the royal 'we', as though he were a king, and
'damn', signifying, I think, 'devote to destruction', as though he were a
god. It is stinging, and it works. Caught off his guard by these unexpected
tactics, Antony cannot restrain his surprise and bewilderment. 'How, my
love?' carries with it the double sense of 'I don't understand; what do you
mean?' and 'How can you say such things to me?' Another aspect of his
relationship with Cleopatra has been revealed: she knows exactly how to
manipulate him, and has no hesitation about applying that knowledge. A
further eight lines from her are sufficient to complete the process and give
her a temporary victory. Antony rejects Rome, and the Messenger with
it, affirming once again his devotion to the Queen and all that she stands
for:

> Let Rome in Tiber melt, and the wide arch
> Of the ranged empire fall! Here is my space.
> Kingdoms are clay; our dungy earth alike
> Feeds beast as man. The nobleness of life
> Is to do thus [*embracing*], when such a mutual pair
> And such a twain can do't, in which I bind,
> On pain of punishment, the world to weet
> We stand up peerless.   (ll. 33–40)

This speech could well be Antony's answer to Philo's lines, though he
has not heard them; for it preserves his tone and his addiction to
hyperbole while reversing his values. Moreover, it is equally one-sided.
Philo underrates Cleopatra; Antony underrates Rome. Philo exalts the
soldierly virtues at the expense of everything else; Antony, the value of
love. His dismissal of Rome pays an unconscious tribute to its stability.
'The wide arch / Of the ranged empire' conjures up a picture of an arch
made of bricks laid in orderly rows, which is what I take 'ranged' to mean;
and such an arch is not likely to fall easily. Similarly, when, embracing
Cleopatra, whose arms, he says, are 'space' enough for him, he goes on to
assert 'The nobleness of life / Is to do thus', one cannot but recall

Coriolanus's definition of nobleness when he greets his little son thus:

> The god of soldiers,
> With the consent of supreme Jove, inform
> Thy thoughts with nobleness, that thou mayst prove
> To shame unvulnerable, and stick i' th' wars
> Like a great sea-mark, standing every flaw
> And saving those that eye thee!   (*Coriolanus*, v,iii,70–5)

Neither Rome nor the nobleness that Coriolanus defines can be disposed of in this summary fashion, not even by verse as splendid as Antony's. His lines carry their own criticism of the position he is taking up, and nowhere more so than when he threatens the world with punishment should it not obey his order to admit that he and Cleopatra 'stand up peerless' in their love. He seems either to have forgotten or, more probably, never to have realised that in rejecting Rome and empire he is depriving himself of the power to bind anyone to do anything.

Adopting a heroic manner to dismiss heroism, in the normal sense of that word, this speech is riddled with contradictions. Rightly so, for, while it states Antony's commitment to Cleopatra, what it expresses, and expresses in all its fullness, is the mental and emotional muddle he is in, and will remain in right down to his death. It is a remarkable achievement, and it is typical of what Shakespeare is doing throughout the five acts of this extraordinary play.

The last word on it may appropriately be left to T. S. Eliot, who regarded it, along with *Coriolanus,* as 'Shakespeare's most assured artistic success'.[10] It is tempting to think that *Antony and Cleopatra* was one of the works Eliot had in mind when he wrote, at the beginning of the final movement of *Little Gidding*:

> What we call the beginning is often the end
> And to make an end is to make a beginning.
> The end is where we start from. And every phrase
> And sentence that is right (where every word is at home,
> Taking its place to support the others,
> The word neither diffident nor ostentatious,
> An easy commerce of the old and the new,
> The common word exact without vulgarity,
> The formal word precise but not pedantic,
> The complete consort dancing together)
> Every phrase and every sentence is an end and a beginning,
> Every poem an epitaph.

NOTES

1 I follow Dover Wilson in reading 'Grates me!' for the 'Grates me' of Alexander and the 'Grates me,' of the Folio.

2 *Coleridge's Essays and Lectures on Shakespeare*, Everyman edition (London, 1907), p. 97.

3 See J. Middleton Murry, *The Problem of Style* (Oxford, 1922), p. 39.

4 Maurice Charney, *Shakespeare's Roman Plays* (Cambridge, Mass., 1961), pp. 79–141.

5 *Shakespeare Survey 24* (Cambridge, 1971), pp. 19–30.

6 *Coleridge's Essays*, p. 97.

7 *Aeneid*, ii, 274–6. How changed from that Hector who would come back to our lines after putting on the spoils of Achilles and hurling Phrygian fires into the ships of the Greeks!

8 For this information I am indebted to David Galloway.

9 *Discoveries*, ll. 2421–2 in vol. VIII (1947), p. 637, of *Ben Jonson*, ed. C. H. Herford and P. and E. Simpson, 11 vols. (Oxford, 1925–52). This edition (vol. V) is also used for the quotation from *Volpone*.

10 *Selected Essays* (London, 1951), p. 144.

'My name is Marina':
the language of recognition

INGA-STINA EWBANK

Marina. If I should tell my history, it would seem
Like lies disdained in the reporting.
Pericles. Prithee speak.
120 Falseness cannot come from thee, for thou lookest
Modest as justice, and thou seemest a palace
For the crowned truth to dwell in. I will believe thee,
And make my senses credit thy relation
To points that seem impossible, for thou lookest
125 Like one I loved indeed. What were thy friends?
Didst thou not say, when I did push thee back –
Which was when I perceived thee – that thou camest
From good descending?
Marina. So indeed I did.
Pericles. Report thy parentage. I think thou saidst
130 Thou hadst been tossed from wrong to injury,
And that thou thought'st thy griefs might equal mine,
If both were opened.
Marina. Some such thing I said,
And said no more but what my thoughts
Did warrant me was likely.
Pericles. Tell thy story.
135 If thine considered prove the thousandth part
Of my endurance, thou art a man, and I
Have suffered like a girl; yet thou dost look
Like Patience gazing on kings' graves and smiling
Extremity out of act. What were thy friends?
140 How lost thou them? Thy name, my most kind virgin?
Recount, I do beseech thee. Come, sit by me.
Marina. My name is Marina.   (*Pericles*, v,i,118–42)

Pericles. O Helicanus, strike me, honoured sir,
Give me a gash, put me to present pain,
Lest this great sea of joys rushing upon me
O'erbear the shores of my mortality
And drown me with their sweetness. O, come hither,

Thou that beget'st him that did thee beget;
Thou that wast born at sea, buried at Tarsus,
And found at sea again. O Helicanus,
Down on thy knees; thank the holy gods as loud
200   As thunder threatens us. This is Marina.
What was thy mother's name? Tell me but that,
For truth can never be confirmed enough,
Though doubts did ever sleep.
Marina.   First, sir, I pray,
What is your title?
205   *Pericles.* I am Pericles of Tyre; but tell me now
My drowned queen's name, as in the rest you said
Thou hast been god-like perfect, and thou art
The heir of kingdoms, and another life
To Pericles thy father.
210   *Marina.* Is it no more to be your daughter than
To say my mother's name was Thaisa?
Thaisa was my mother, who did end
The minute I began.
Pericles. Now blessing on thee! Rise; thou art my child.
(*Pericles*, v,i,191–214)[1]

Out of its context, the statement 'My name is Marina' is a very unremark-
able sample of Shakespeare's style, compared to such half-lines as
'Frailty, thy name is woman!' In its context, it has the power which a
stirring feather or a mirror beginning to mist over would have had in the
last scene of *King Lear*: to 'redeem all sorrows'. Shakespeare's style is, of
course, never a matter of words alone; the words of the text have their
peculiar life in a dramatic and theatrical context. The more a scene or a
passage depends on 'something which only the stage can convey',[2] the
more of a challenge it becomes to define what the words spoken on stage
do convey, and why. It may then be of more than local interest to explore
the style of the scene where Pericles and Marina recognise each other. At
the outset it must be remembered that the only text we have of this play is
so corrupt that it may be futile, or dangerous, to speculate on details of
expression. But I write from the conviction that, however ill-reported
and badly printed the 1609 quarto of *Pericles* is, there shines through the
structure of the dialogue in this scene, and through its connections (by
both similarities and contrasts) with other Shakespearian scenes, a sense
that, in the text which was played in 1608, Shakespeare was deliberately
attempting to dramatise *in words* the wonder of recognition.

The proper stage language of recognition would seem to be silence –
holding someone by the hand, silent, or gazing wordlessly at a statue
come alive. The proper expression of the wonder – the *admiratio* of

Renaissance dramatic theory – produced by the sudden leap, for good or ill, from one state of knowledge to another, would seem to be an inarticulate groan or at most a bare recording of sense experience: 'O, she's warm!' But, proper to whom? Natural to the character experiencing the wonder, yes; but what of the author, completing the figure in his carpet and anxious to guide his audience's experience of a climactic moment in the play towards an apprehension of the meaning as well as the intensity of this moment? The leap of recognition tends to be not only into 'woe or wonder' but also into new relations between people ('He childed as I fathered!' Edgar perceives, and Cymbeline rejoices to find himself 'A mother to the birth of three') and a new world-picture (where the time is 'out of joint', or 'free'). Aristotle saw the finest form of *anagnorisis* as one attended by *peripeteia*;[3] and it is probably not fortuitous that when, in the seventeenth chapter of the *Poetics*, he came to discuss the various methods by which discoveries, or recognitions,[4] may be brought about, nearly all his examples dealt with the discovery of the identity of persons. For in the discovery of a close relation, long thought dead or lost, recognition and reversal would seem to be particularly closely connected – dramatically virtually simultaneous, as some of Shakespeare's Comedies and all of his Romances show. The emotional shift of the wonder as such is often conveyed by spectacle or music, or both; and the sense of emotion outstripping language is, as many commentators have pointed out, an essential part of the impact of Shakespearian reunion and recognition scenes. Sometimes this sense *is* the meaning: when Cordelia finds no words but 'No cause, no cause' in response to Lear's prayer for forgiveness, then the reunion of father and daughter, emotionally overwhelming as it is, also finds its place in a structure of meanings which begins with Cordelia's refusal to 'heave / My heart into my mouth' and ends with Edgar's conclusion that we must 'Speak what we feel, not what we ought to say'. Sometimes the inexpressible is simply a rhetorical *topos*, as when Bassanio needs a whole epic simile to tell how speechless the discovery of his good fortune has made him:

> Madam, you have bereft me of all words;
> Only my blood speaks to you in my veins;
> And there is such confusion in my powers
> As, after some oration fairly spoke
> By a beloved prince, there doth appear
> Among the buzzing pleasèd multitude,
> Where every something, being blent together,

Turns to a wild of nothing, save of joy
Expressed and not expressed.

(Merchant of Venice, III,ii,176–84)

Clearly the style of Pericles and Marina has more affinity with the simple
language of Lear and Cordelia than with that of Bassanio, who holds
wonder at arm's length by talking about it. But the peculiar quality of
their language is that, in its simplicity, it gets as close, I believe, as
Shakespeare ever does to expressing the inexpressible.

At this point it may be worth remembering that the most lucid
commentator on speechlessness is Shakespeare himself who, in Act V,
scene ii of *The Winter's Tale* gives us, through the mouths of three
Gentlemen, a full explication of scenes where there is 'speech in [charac-
ters'] dumbness, language in their very gesture'. He also knew the
limitations of such 'speech'. Spectacle can figure forth 'a notable passion
of wonder', but it is weak as an analytical tool:

the wisest beholder that knew no more but seeing could not say if th' importance were joy
or sorrow – but in the extremity of the one it must needs be. (*The Winter's Tale*,
v,ii,17–19)

Music, too, can suggest; it can soothe Lear, 'awake' Hermione and
ultimately evoke almost any 'solemn and strange' emotion in *The Tempest*. But it cannot be precise about meanings. At the end of his reunion
with Marina, Pericles hears the music of the spheres, which 'nips [him]
unto listening', and in a dream vision he sees the goddess Diana who
spurs him on to the ultimate, and far more spectacular, reunion with
Thaisa. But I do not think there can be any doubt that that which nips us,
the audience, into listening, and which conveys to us that experience of
the impossible becoming possible which is so much at the heart of
Shakespeare's Last Plays, is the dialogue between father and daughter as
they approach and encompass each other's identities.

The style of a dramatist has to mediate between the experience of the
characters and that of the audience – to convey both what it feels like and
what it all adds up to. In the great Tragedies Shakespeare makes this
mediation seem very easy: Hamlet's or Macbeth's self-analysis at regular
points in the course of the play also describes the pattern of the action.
We are brought into the play as a series of moments of (imitated) human
experience, and yet also kept aware of it as a developing pattern of
complex meanings. In the Romances, Shakespeare's dramaturgy, as
Daniel Seltzer has finely described it, is concerned 'more with general
effect than with details of emotion revealing the depths of one person'.[5]

Soliloquies disappear, as does the interest in internalised motivation; character exploration becomes more shallow as plot becomes more complex; as an audience we are invited to remain outside the minds of the characters, to 'watch and marvel'.[6] *Pericles,* with the choric Gower supplying whatever linking of cause and effect is necessary, and with each episodic scene almost self-contained, would seem an extreme example of a dramatic art given less to rendering what it feels like for individual characters and more to making us marvel at what happens. No doubt this is true for the play as a whole (whether or not Shakespeare wrote the whole), but within the whole the first reunion scene forms a remarkable exception. Neither Pericles nor Marina is known to us with anything like the fullness of Lear and Cordelia, and we would not be able to describe either as 'deep' characters. Yet, in a way which I now wish to proceed to analyse, the dialogue in this scene *creates* character as well as a marvellous plot step. It enables us to share in the interaction of two minds, in the movement towards mutual discovery, and in the arrival at full recognition, with all that it means.

In neither of Shakespeare's main sources for *Pericles,* Gower's *Confessio Amantis* and Twine's *Patterne of Painefull Adventures,* is there any reference to, and still less report of, a sustained dialogue between father and daughter. Gower, who affected Shakespeare more, speaks as an omniscient observer of the mysterious bond of being 'so sibbe of bloode' which draws them together, and then makes Thaise (Shakespeare's Marina) give away the whole story of her name, parentage and fate, in reply to a single inquiry from Appolinus (Pericles), whereupon

> he tho toke hir in his arme,
> But suche a joye as he tho made,
> Was never sene, thus ben thei glade,
> That sory hadden be toforne.[7]

The reversal in Shakespeare's scene is no less extreme, but the arc which Pericles travels is made into a unique demonstration of the power of words. Pericles begins as an apathetic deaf-mute and ends up hearing the music of the spheres; Marina's first attempt to 'make a battery through his deafened ports' is met with silence, her appeal that he 'lend ear' with an inarticulate grunt, and when she persists he repulses her with a push forceful enough for her to refer to it later as 'violence'; but before long the tables are turned. Where he refused even to look at her, he is now gazing at her face, asking her to 'turn your eyes upon me'; where he would neither listen nor speak, he is now besieging her with questions. In the kind of symbolical structure which some critics like to turn the play into, the emblem of harmony provided by Marina's singing would surely have broken Pericles's unnatural isolation and healed his affliction of mind. But instead we have an almost naturalistic verbal structure, in which words act as keys to Pericles's consciousness, and a dialogue of interaction which proceeds with psychological plausibility towards the moment of full recognition. As in Strindberg's *The Stronger*, the one who speaks most is not necessarily the dominant character. Marina dominates with her brief, literal answers. Pericles hangs on her words, attempts to define her and the power she is beginning to exercise over him. His repeated questions[8] suggest a growing urgency, a thirst for simple facts, because her words begin to seem as if they would lead to some miraculous truth. And they do: 'My name is Marina.'

The fact that Marina's words can open up Pericles's mind is not presented as a purely symbolical phenomenon: she may, in the total scheme of the play, stand for the regenerative power of the new generation, but the power of her language in this scene has a particular dramatic source. For all the lack of character exploration and continuity in this play, Marina has already been established as having a kind of therapeutic literalness of speech, based in the brothel scene on a refusal to separate name and act:

Lysimachus. Now, pretty one, how long have you been at this trade?
Marina.   What trade, sir?
Lysimachus. Why, I cannot name't but I shall offend.
Marina.   I cannot be offended with my trade. Please you to name it.[9]   (IV,vi,62–7)

Marina's prototype in Gower and Twine operates quite differently. She preserves her virginity (and earns a good deal of money) by kneeling and sobbing appeals for compassion, through full accounts of her sad fate. Where her source character is defensive and pathetic, Marina is as aggressive as if her name was Beatrice. Hers is not a fugitive and cloistered virtue but one which shines forth as verbal wit, in a debate where she is ready to score moral points off that mixture of lechery and mealy-mouthedness which Lysimachus exhibits. When he tries to change his nomenclature, the results are even more unhappy:

Lysimachus. How long have you been of this profession?
Marina.   E'er since I can remember.
Lysimachus. Did you go to't so young? Were you a gamester at five, or at seven?
Marina.   Earlier too, sir, if now I be one.
Lysimachus. Why, the house you dwell in proclaims you to be a creature of sale.

Marina.   Do you know this house to be a place of such resort, and will come into't?

(IV,vi,68–76)

Thus deflated and reduced, Lysimachus is ready to be worked on by Marina's exhortation to show that he is 'born to honour'. Editors have assumed that 'in the original text Marina made a much longer and more eloquent plea than Q reports',[10] and this may of course be so. But what is interesting in the text we have, and relevant to her speech in the later scene, is that her eloquence lies in her very literalness, and that it is this quality which is therapeutic. Boult thinks she has spoken 'holy words' (IV,vi,131) to Lysimachus; but we who have overheard her speech (ll. 91–8) know that, though it has a kind of Romance framework – 'ungentle fortune' has put her in 'this unhallowed place', from which she wishes the gods to set her free, 'Though they did change me to the meanest bird / That flies i'th' purer air!' – there is nothing 'holy' about her vision of the place itself:

> this sty, where since I came
> Diseases have been sold dearer than physic.   (ll. 93–4)

Her words bite because even what looks like a metaphor has a terrifying literalness about it. She turns the nature of the 'act' as effectively against Lysimachus as Hamlet, with far more verbal elaboration, turns Gertrude's 'eyes into [her] very soul'; and she copes similarly with Boult's attempt to disarm her by defloration. So she enters the reunion scene not primarily as a symbol of 'sweet harmony' but as a vigorous heroine of social comedy, capable of working through words on people's minds.

Where, of course, Marina parts company with Beatrice or Rosalind is in the sounding-board which her background, as provided by the plot, gives to her literalness. She only has to give the true story of her birth – 'Born in a tempest, when my mother died' – for fact to sound like a metaphor. And, conversely, the plot turns her metaphors into fact:

> This world to me is as a lasting storm,
> Whirring me from my friends.   (IV,i,19–20)

Indeed the whole of her first appearance, in Act IV, scene i, with her almost obsessive recounting of her stormy birth-scene to an uninterested Leonine, suggests that with Marina Shakespeare discovered that there does not have to be a conflict between the demands of a Romance plot and the demands of characterisation. The link between the two, in her case, is a language which mediates between the strange and the true, often by simply stating the impossible, as the truth which it is.

This is her technique, and the source of her success, in the reunion scene. What penetrates Pericles's sound-barrier is a series of key-words in her opening speech – a speech in which, if we may trust the reporter, she observes the decorum of asserting her own worth before the distinguished stranger by being more abstract, solemn and dignified than in anything she says elsewhere:

> She speaks,
> My lord, that maybe hath endured a grief
> Might equal yours, if both were justly weighed.
> Though wayward fortune did malign my state,
> My derivation was from ancestors
> Who stood equivalent with mighty kings.
> But time hath rooted out my parentage,
> And to the world and awkward casualties
> Bound me in servitude.   (v,i,85–93)

Dramatic irony, of course, plays a part in the impact on us of this speech – the detached pleasure of knowing more than either speaker or listener and so being able to spot the unrecognised (by them) truth of 'equal yours', and 'justly weighed'. But in the total effect, irony is far less important than seeing and hearing the impact on Pericles, who reacts to Marina's words as they deserve. The man 'who for this three months hath not spoken / To anyone' (v,i,22–3) drags himself out of his silence, the rhythm and syntax of his response suggesting both the effort it entails and yet also the irresistible urge, like that of one hypnotised, to echo what has been said. At the same time, the slight inaccuracies of his echoes, as verbal echoes, show that he has absorbed the meaning and not merely the words:

> My fortunes – parentage – good parentage –
> To equal mine – was it not thus? What say you?   (v,i,96–7)

And quite naturalistically Marina repeats, in simpler language now, for the benefit of the strangely excited man, the point of her speech:

> I said, my lord, if you did know my parentage
> You would not do me violence.   (v,i,98–9)

The speech itself continues to haunt Pericles and to come back in remembered snatches (as in lines 129–32 of the passage quoted at the beginning of this essay); meanwhile the speaker has also been stirred to remembrance of things past:

> You're like something that – What countrywoman? –

and, as he looks at her, the image of his 'dead' wife comes back, associated with that of his 'dead' daughter:

> My dearest wife was like this maid,
> And such a one my daughter might have been. (v,i,106–7)

As he elaborates, feature by feature, on the similarity he senses, the remembered past merges with the perceived actuality, until the image of the wife who 'was' and that of the daughter who 'might have been' dissolve, as the use of the present tense shows, into the girl before him,

> Who starves the ears she feeds, and makes them hungry
> The more she gives them speech. Where do you live? (v,i,112–13)

If we note the echo here of several earlier Shakespeare passages, notably Enobarbus's description of Cleopatra,[11] we should also note that this is the only instance where the 'appetites' left unsated are for more and more 'speech'. Marina's being is still held in her words; the miracle which they have barely begun to suggest can only be approached by words, in the form of simple questions: 'Where do you live?'

This is where we finally reach the first passage quoted at the opening of my essay, chosen because it so remarkably embodies the beginning apprehension of facts more improbable than any fiction and yet also truer than any fiction. The dynamism of the scene – that which keeps it moving forward – is the pull between, on the one hand, Pericles's urge to hear and know more and more facts of Marina's life and, on the other, her awareness that these facts are, by normal standards, incredible. There is a completely naturalistic strain here: she bristles up when she has the slightest suspicion of being taken for a liar (ll. 118–19), and she persistently misinterprets the signs of emotion in Pericles:

> not to be a troubler of your peace,
> I will end here. (ll. 151–2)

> You scorn to believe me,
> 'Twere best I did give o'er. (ll. 166–7)

> Why do you weep? It may be
> You think me an impostor. (ll. 178–9)

So there is psychological motivation for the pressure towards disclosure. Previously, Lysimachus tells us,

> She never would tell
> Her parentage. Being demanded that,
> She would sit still and weep; (v,i,188–90)

but now she has to tell, as proof of her veracity, while also defiantly aware
of the precariousness of her proof:

> It may be
> You think me an impostor. No, good faith!
> I am the daughter to King Pericles,
> If good King Pericles be.   (v,i,178–81)

There is psychological motivation, too, for the most apparently symbolical stretches of the dialogue: those in which Pericles attempts to reassure
her of his trust. The verbal form taken by this attempt is interesting. He
begins by trying to describe her in emblematic metaphors. She *looks*
'modest as justice'; she *seems* 'a palace / For the crowned truth to dwell
in'; but the verbs signal a tentativeness which he then explicitly rejects:

> I will believe thee,
> And make my senses credit thy relation
> To points that seem impossible.   (v,i,122–4)

In a sense, Pericles is speaking here for the play as a whole, finding words
for its epistemology, much as Paulina does in the statue scene in *The
Winter's Tale*: 'It is required / You do awake your faith' (v,iii,94–5). He is
putting words into our mouths, too, defining that stretching of our minds
towards 'points that seem impossible' which all the Romances demand of
us. But in another sense he is speaking in character, in the language of his
own voyage towards discovery. After this, the fiction of his metaphors has
to give way to concrete and specific questions (ll. 125–8), for this way
truth lies. Much the same pattern is repeated in the Patience speech
(ll. 134–41). To describe what Marina *looks like*, he (and Shakespeare)
needs a haunting poetic image[12] – which, of course, tells us more about
her inner life than her outward appearance. But the real miracle lies in
what and who she *is*, and to determine this he need only ask a factual
question and receive a simple answer, which is felt now, at this point in
the structure, with as much impact as any poetic image: 'My name is
Marina.'

I hope it is not hair-splitting to point out that a line like this is not just a
matter of style subordinated to experience. Shakespeare has his theatre
audience in mind as much as Marina has her audience of one, and he has
to make us credit his relation to points that seem even more impossible
than Marina herself, not knowing her father, can yet imagine. His art lies
in making style and subject one, in making Marina seem to know what he
himself had expressed in Sonnet 84: that when your subject appears to

defy art, then art consists in 'Not making worse what nature made so clear'. Like Marina, the *Sonnets* poet is both haunted and spurred on by the sense of a reality which will not fit into words. Marina's mixture of assurance and resentment that her story is too strange to sound true – her

> If I should tell my history, it would seem
> Like lies disdained in the reporting –   (ll. 118–19)

rings like the poet's resentment, which itself amounts to an assertion of the worth of the beloved:

> Who will believe my verse in time to come,
> If it were filled with your most high deserts?
> ... ...
> The age to come would say 'This poet lies;...'
> ... ...
> So should my papers, yellowed with their age,
> Be scorned, like old men of less truth than tongue.   (Sonnet 17)

As in Sonnet 84, Marina *and* the play know that the best 'style' is that which 'can tell / That you are you'; and so the progress towards full recognition is charted by the most literal statements:

> My mother was the daughter of a king;
> Who died the minute I was born.   (ll. 157–8)
>
> I am the daughter to King Pericles,
> If good King Pericles be.   (ll. 180–1)
>
> This is Marina.   (l. 200)
>
> Thou art my child.   (l. 214)

Between these statements, of course, the verbal structure conveys a sequence of moments where Pericles is caught between the two kinds of knowledge: the circumstantial evidence that 'my daughter's buried' (Steevens) and the evidence of his senses that she stands before him. His reactions are reminiscent of those of other Shakespearian characters. Like many, from the lovers in *A Midsummer Night's Dream* onwards, he thinks he is dreaming (ll. 161–2). Like Lear he has to assure himself of the physical reality of the girl – that she is 'flesh and blood' and has 'a working pulse' (ll. 152–3) – and like Lear's, his first tentative acceptance of the impossible is all the more moving for being set in a fear of making a fool of himself (ll. 142–4). The pattern is that of a psychologically convincing process of approaching the truth, doubling back, hesitating, asking for still more proof. As in *King Lear,* we do not simply watch and marvel; we apprehend the wonder of the recognition *through* characters' experiences.

It may be worth stopping here for a moment to ask why it is natural to compare *Pericles* with *King Lear*, and not with any of the earlier romantic comedies. The obvious answer is thematic: Pericles is, like Lear, saved and given new life by his daughter. The reunion of Lear and Cordelia is also a recognition scene, for Lear, waking both from madness and sleep, has to assure himself both of his own reality and of Cordelia's. But another answer is to do with the function of dramatic speech. In *Pericles,* as in *King Lear,* the language of recognition passes through characters. We feel that it is part of their consciousness and their minds. In the Comedies, a verbal pattern tends to take over and, as it were, enact the recognition. We apprehend it as a fulfilled pattern and not as individual experiences. The language of recognition in Shakespearian comedy is very much in the service of the play as a whole. We do not, for example, ask, because we are not directed to ask, what it feels like for Claudio to have his 'dead' wife restored. In that scene of rather troubled and mixed tones where he learns the truth of the matter of Hero's alleged infidelity, there is a kind of short-hand, physiological record of shock –

> *Don Pedro.* Runs not this speech like iron through your blood?
> *Claudio.*   I have drunk poison whiles he uttered it –
> *(Much Ado About Nothing,* v,i,231–2)

which is not particularly memorable. Far more so is his attempt at articulating the recognition as a re-discovery –

> *Claudio.* Sweet Hero, now thy image doth appear
> In the rare semblance that I loved it first –   (v,i,237–8)

for here he is, unwittingly, providing the scenario for the final scene of the play. His one spoken reaction to that wondrous masquerade is the half-line 'Another Hero!' The function of the language in that scene of recognition and reunion is to accompany the visual conceit with words which make its meaning both evocative and precise:

> *Claudio.*   Give me your hand; before this holy friar
> I am your husband, if you like of me.
> *Hero.*   And when I lived I was your other wife;   [*Unmasking.*]
> And when you loved you were my other husband.
> *Claudio.*   Another Hero!
> *Hero.*   Nothing certainer.
> One Hero died defiled; but I do live,
> And, surely as I live, I am a maid.
> *Don Pedro.* The former Hero! Hero that is dead!
> *Leonato.*   She died, my lord, but whiles her slander lived. (v,iv,58–66)

The epigrammatic wit of Leonato's line clinches a pattern of communal discovery established by Hero's equally ingenious and equally choric lines; and, as the society of Messina turns to the *dénouement* of its other paradoxical plot, that of Beatrice and Benedick, it is for the Friar to refer to 'amazement' and 'wonder' (ll. 67 and 70). As nearly always in Shakespearian comedy, we are left to infer from thematic patterns the new self-knowledge we like to attribute to characters, and to guess at their feelings from silences. Isabella says not a word in *Measure for Measure* after the revelation that Claudio is alive, nor does Angelo; and but for the Duke's reference to seeing 'a quick'ning in his eye' we know nothing about his reaction to being 'safe' (*Measure for Measure*, v,i,492–3).

As You Like It is perhaps the play which shows most clearly the possibilities of a language of recognition operating outside the characters. Up to the *dénouement* we have been much engaged with the vigorous emotions of the heroine, and of at least some of the other characters; but we have also been prepared, as in the chorus of lovers in Act V, scene ii, to have those emotions presented in verbal patterns which remove attention from the individual. When Rosalind appears, in her own shape, in the masque-like performance of Hymen, individual reactions are entirely subordinated to the general pattern. She gives herself to her father and her lover in identical lines – 'To you I give myself, for I am yours' – and receives responses which are correspondingly de-personalised:

> Duke Senior. If there be truth in sight, you are my daughter.
> Orlando.   If there be truth in sight, you are my Rosalind.
> Phebe.   If sight and shape be true,
>   Why then, my love adieu!   (*As You Like It*, v,iv,112–15)

What Shakespeare wishes to convey to us, the audience, is not so much the joy of a particular father finding his daughter and the daughter a husband as the greater wonder of which such unions and reunions are images; and it is Hymen who is given the language to do so – a language as dense with suggestions as that of *The Phoenix and Turtle*:

> Then is there mirth in heaven,
> When earthly things made even
> Atone together.[13]   (v,iv,107–9)

In her apt comment on this passage, Agnes Latham points out how 'Shakespeare's comedy shows "things as they ought to be" in a more than trivial sense.'[14] Things as they ought to be are put into words, too, in the 'wedlock hymn' and its celebration of the 'blessèd bond of board and bed' (l. 136). The characters on stage are no doubt in a state of wonder and can

for once be *seen* engaging in that activity which is normally about to start
off stage at the end of Shakespearian comedy – to find out 'what's yet
behind' (*Measure for Measure*, last line) or 'hear the rest untold' (*Pericles*,
v,iii,84). But the Song is what we are given to *hear*:

> (*Hymen.*) Whiles a wedlock-hymn we sing,
>   Feed yourselves with questioning,
>   That reason wonder may diminish,
>   How thus we met, and these things finish.   (v,iv,131–4)

Hymen and the Song are responsible for our sense of wonder at the end of
As You Like It. They almost speak the unspeakable; and they certainly
express what from the characters' point of view would have been inexpressible. Furthermore, in the context they provide, a kind of wonder
emanates from the patterned lines of the characters, too. The 'ifs' in the
series of 'if'-clauses I quoted take on a magic quality, the very reverse of
those repeated 'ifs' through which Troilus strains *not* to recognise what
he has seen (*Troilus and Cressida*, v,ii,136–40). There *is* 'truth in sight',
and so the 'ifs' come to speak of the naturalness, the sheer possibility, of
the 'blessèd bond' and of 'earthly things' being 'made even'.

    It is, to return to *Pericles*, that simple ease – that disappearance of all
real conditionality from the 'ifs' ('If good King Pericles be') – which
dominates the latter half of the recognition scene I have been examining.
In the first ten lines of the second extract quoted at the head of this essay,
Pericles finds words for the actual recognition. What it feels like is
conveyed by a metaphor which both does and does not reverse all that the
sea has meant to him in the play. It is a 'great sea of joys', but its 'rushing
upon' him could be fatal. Mankind, as we learn both from heart special-
ists and from the death of Gloucester – whose heart ' 'Twixt two extremes
of passion, joy and grief, / Burst smilingly' – cannot always bear the shock
of recognition, however joyful. Secondly, the lines convey the clear
meaning of this recognition (ll. 196–8). I shall return to this point
presently. Next comes the spontaneous act of thanks. As G. Wilson
Knight points out, 'the new joy is proportional to the tragedy ("as loud /
As thunder threatens us") being reversed'.[15] Interestingly, though,
Helicanus is being asked to perform this religious duty on Pericles's
behalf. He himself is absorbed in the human situation ('This is Marina');
and the ebb and flow of human emotions leaves room, even in this
moment of joy, for further doubt and need for confirmation: 'What was
thy mother's name? Tell me but that . . .'

    But it is now Marina's turn for counter-questions, first a genuine one –

'First, sir, I pray / What is your title?' – and then, in reply to Pericles's insistence on his 'drownèd queen's name', a rhetorical one, in which her own recognition is beautifully conveyed by a kind of exalted understatement:

> Is it no more to be your daughter than
> To say my mother's name was Thaisa?   (ll. 210–11)

Suddenly everything has become so easy, so possible. The care Shakespeare has taken to give Marina's language a literalness in which the strange and the true meet bears fruit here, for all her earlier appearances now seem to have been rehearsals for this naming of her mother:

> Thaisa was my mother, who did end
> The minute I began.   (ll. 212–13)

Out of a wildly improbable plot, Shakespeare has created a scene with its own autonomous probability, and has done so largely through his use of language. Aristotle would not have thought very highly of the technique employed: he would, presumably, have classed this among his second type of inferior discoveries, 'which are manufactured by the poet, and which are inartistic for that reason'.[16] Shakespeare's dialogue of questions and answers could be said, too, to have slashed through that discussion which so much agitated Renaissance theorists of the drama, of the forms which recognition should take ('by natural bodily signs, by artificial signs, by memory', etc.),[17] to centre on the easy leap from a tragic past to a joyful present. In *Twelfth Night* he still used the conventional swopping of birth-marks, but made it part of a quality of wonder in the dialogue which anticipates *Pericles,* even as it confirms Olivia's exclamation of 'Most wonderful!' Sebastian and Viola establish past sufferings, contradicted as we hear them by our knowledge of the true state of affairs:

> *Sebastian.*   I had a sister
> Whom the blind waves and surges have devoured.
> Of charity, what kin are you to me?
> What countryman, what name, what parentage?
> *Viola.*   Of Messaline; Sebastian was my father.
> Such a Sebastian was my brother too;
> So went he suited to his watery tomb.
>
> (*Twelfth Night,* v,i,220–6)

The leap into joy is enacted by Sebastian's statement of the apparently impossible –

> Were you a woman, as the rest goes even,
> I should my tears let fall upon your cheek,
> And say 'Thrice welcome, drownèd Viola!' –   (v,i,231–3)

and the arrival is signalled by a kind of litany of joy between sister and brother:

> *Viola.*   My father had a mole upon his brow.
> *Sebastian.* And so had mine.   (v,i,234–5)

In a sense, the litany is a parody on the conventional exchange of recognition signs; but the structure of the dialogue – implying what in *Pericles* is stated as 'Is it no more. . .?' – proclaims wonder, not just the 'amused insouciance'[18] which some critics have found, and which productions of the play often stop at.

It is the essence of the experience of wonder that the simplest, most literal statements ('My father had a mole upon his brow') reach out to touch miracles, and that the seemingly most impossible paradoxes resolve themselves into statements of fact ('Thrice welcome, drownèd Viola'). This is how wonder becomes speakable. For those involved in the experience, almost any – or no – words will do. Not so for the dramatist. This is where I wish to return to the rightly famous[19] lines in which Pericles articulates his recognition:

> O, come hither,
> Thou that beget'st him that did thee beget;
> Thou that wast born at sea, buried at Tarsus,
> And found at sea again.   (ll. 195–8)

Semantically, the paradoxical line 196 can be paraphrased reasonably easily; but the dramatic wonder is carried by the paradox and its place in the verbal structure. The first 'beget' (strictly, 'beget'st') is metaphorical and the second literal; the syntax which connects them describes the plot and, in doing so, also gives its significance. The words, in their particular order, speak the miracle. It is, I believe,[20] not for nothing that, three times in this scene, speaking is identified with 'delivering' – including Pericles's promise to believe Marina 'by the syllable / Of what you shall deliver' (ll. 167–8). The miracle lies latent in what is happening, but it is born to us through what is spoken. Philip Edwards, who sees this line as 'the key to the play, and perhaps to the whole group of Shakespeare's late Romances', draws attention to the underlying 'ancient paradox of Christianity, in which God the father becomes the son of his own daughter, a virgin'.[21] No doubt the rhythm of the Creed similarly underlies the lines which follow. I am not concerned here with religious undertones and

symbolism as such, but with the way in which Shakespeare gives evocative power to simple words. As the saying of the Creed 'delivers' to us the
miracle of the 'plot' of the life, death and resurrection of Christ, so the
lines 'Thou that wast born at sea, buried at Tarsus, / And found at sea
again' deliver the wonder of Marina's life. The words simply refer to
what has been; the syntax – the arrangement which depends on no causal
connections but on a coordination of apparent discontinuities – summarises the episodic plot. The pattern thus formed becomes a marvellous
statement of purpose and fulfilment – one to be *known*, rather than
rationally *understood*. If there is a logic operating, it is that peculiar
closeness of word and fact which has characterised Marina throughout:

> *Pericles.*   Where were you born?
>   And wherefore called Marina?
> *Marina.*   Called Marina
>   For I was born at sea.   (v,i,152–4)

The science of language would suggest that Pericles's words, like Marina's just quoted, are 'models' of an underlying reality. Our experience in
the theatre is that they *are* reality.

In Shakespeare's Tragedies, recognitions tend to make the characters
want to see themselves as part of a general condition. When the tragic
heroes – or, as in the case of Horatio, their spokesmen – recognise the
pattern of their lives, of the 'plot' they have lived through, they tend to
interpret it. They see it as a moral phenomenon, as in *Hamlet*, or a
metaphysical one, as in *Macbeth*; or it becomes a psychological pattern, as
in Othello's self-analysis of 'one that loved not wisely, but too well'.
Always the direction is toward the general insight, from and through the
particular experience. In the Romances, the characters tend to recognise
– as in the 'most clear remembrance' of Pericles's later description of his
meeting with Marina (v,iii,12) – a self-contained significance in the
details of their own specific plot. One thinks of Gonzalo, who has been
kept speechless by the wonder of the revelations in Act V, scene i ('I have
inly wept, / Or should have spoke ere this'), but who makes up for it by
the fulness of the pattern he sees in them:

> Was Milan thrust from Milan, that his issue
> Should become Kings of Naples? O, rejoice
> Beyond a common joy, and set it down
> With gold on lasting pillars: in one voyage
> Did Claribel her husband find at Tunis;
> And Ferdinand, her brother, found a wife
> Where he himself was lost; Prospero his dukedom

In a poor isle; and all of us ourselves
When no man was his own.   (*The Tempest*, v,i,205–13)

Gonzalo is too optimistic about 'all of us'; but what matters to my
argument here is, first, his urge to see and say (or even to see through the
saying) and, secondly, the fact that the strength – poetic and dramatic – of
his language lies not in metaphor, nor in analytical or generalising
statement, but in the sheer simplicity of the account of what has happened. He *intends* this account to illustrate how 'you gods' have 'chalked
forth the way / Which brought us hither'; but it is the wonder of the facts
themselves – the 'way' – which comes to us. Such singleness of focus and
such simplicity of expression are not available in Shakespeare's tragic
endings; nor would they be adequate. Horatio's 'philosophy' may be
more single-minded than Hamlet's, and no doubt he is the only one who
could give a logical summary of what has happened in *Hamlet*; but even
his vision of the plot is a generalised nightmare

> Of accidental judgments, casual slaughters;
> Of deaths put on by cunning and forced cause;
> And, in this upshot, purposes mistook
> Fallen on th' inventors' heads.   (*Hamlet*, v,ii,374–7)

So is Macbeth's ultimate recognition of the ways of 'these juggling
fiends. . . That palter with us in a double sense' (v,viii,19ff.); and if
Coriolanus's retrospect is both single-minded and simple – 'Alone I did
it' – this speaks of his own limitations of view, not of the play's final
stance. In *King Lear* no summary is possible, beyond the sense that 'The
oldest hath borne most': the facts are before us, and before Lear, and the
final language of recognition can be no more than a stage-direction:

> Do you see this? Look on her. Look, her lips.
> Look there, look there!

If this is Shakespeare touching the limits of language, the Romances
sometimes show him reaching out to the inexpressible. In the appropriate
context, simply to 'name' – 'Did you not name a tempest, / A birth, and
death?' (v,iii,33–4) – may be to do just this. It may well be that we would
not have had *The Tempest* but for Shakespeare's discovery, in the
recognition scene in *Pericles*, of the possibilities of a peculiar one-ness of
plot, character and language.

The great events in life are discontinuous; they are not experienced as
consequences of previous actions, or as logically connected. When
Pericles expresses his joy and wonder by simply telling the fable – 'Thou

that wast born at sea. . .' – he is asserting the miraculous power of life to contain such discontinuities and illogicalities ('She is not dead at Tarsus, as she should have been'). Recognition surpasses cognition. *Pericles* is the only Shakespearian Romance where there is no moral failing involved in the separation and so no repentance or forgiveness in the reunion. But that does not mean that there is no criticism of life involved: all the more intensely it is a scene about the readiness to accept the impossible, a scene hinting at knowledge which passes understanding.

Perhaps that is the nearest we can get to describing the control which Shakespeare here, by his language, exercises over his characters and his audience. In his most illuminating analysis of this scene, Kenneth Muir has written of the effect of the meeting of Pericles and Marina: 'Shakespeare is aware that his story is too good to be true, but such fables are a criticism of life as it is, and (as some think) a statement of faith.'[22] It is the power of Shakespeare's style that it holds together the 'too good' and the 'true'.

NOTES

1 All quotations from *Pericles* in the following pages are from the New Penguin Shakespeare text of the play, edited by Philip Edwards (Harmondsworth, 1976).

2 Philip Edwards, Introduction to New Penguin *Pericles*, p. 26.

3 In Chapter 11 of the *Poetics*. See *Aristotle, On the Art of Poetry*, translated by Ingram Bywater (Oxford, 1962), p. 47.

4 Bywater translates *anagnorisis* as 'discovery', and so does T. S. Dorsch in the Penguin translation. Butcher has 'recognition', which – though it is not a word which Shakespeare would have used (the earliest record of its use in this sense – *OED*, 'Recognition', 7. – is in 'Tintern Abbey', 1798) – seems to me the more apt term for the scene between Pericles and Marina.

5 Daniel Seltzer, 'The Staging of the Last Plays', in *Later Shakespeare: Stratford-upon-Avon Studies 8*, ed. John Russell Brown and Bernard Harris (London, 1966), pp. 156–7.

6 Seltzer, 'The Staging of the Last Plays', p. 157.

7 Quoted from Geoffrey Bullough, ed., *Narrative and Dramatic Sources of Shakespeare*, 8 vols. (London, 1957–75), vol. VI (1966), p. 415.

8 Editors have suggested that repetitions in this scene may be products of 'the blundering reporter': see F. D. Hoeniger's note at V,i,160 of his New Arden edition of *Pericles* (London, 1963). But Pericles's repetitions of questions would seem to be functional.

9 It is worth remembering that contemporary social comedy made comic capital out of such hypocrisy as Lysimachus exhibits here. Freevill in Marston's *Dutch Courtesan* (1605), I,ii,97–103, has a whole list of euphemisms similar to Lysimachus's, which he uses to instruct Malheureux in the fact that "tis not in fashion to call things by their right names'.

10 Hoeniger, note at IV,vi,91–3 of New Arden *Pericles*.

11 Hoeniger cites *Hamlet*, I,ii,144–5 and Sonnet 75 as well as *Antony and Cleopatra*, II,ii,241–2: 'she makes hungry / Where most she satisfies'.

12 Kenneth Muir analyses 'this wonderful image' in *Shakespeare as Collaborator* (London, 1960), pp. 94–5.

13 We do not know whether the masque is 'plainly a charade got up by Rosalind, or whether it is pure magic, like the masque in *The Tempest*' (Agnes Latham, in her note at v,iv,107 of her New Arden edition of *As You Like It* (London, 1975)); and we can only speculate on the mode of delivery of these lines (Miss Latham thinks that 'they were perhaps a kind of recitative'). But the solemnity, and the religious undertone, of the language are unmistakable.

14 Latham, note at v,iv,109 of New Arden *As You Like It*.

15 G. Wilson Knight, *The Crown of Life* (London, 1952), p. 66.

16 Chapter 16 of the *Poetics*, quoted from T. S. Dorsch's translation in the Penguin volume of *Classical Literary Criticism* (Harmondsworth, 1965), p. 53. Bywater has 'discoveries made directly by the poet; which are inartistic for that very reason' (p. 59).

17 Madeleine Doran, *Endeavors of Art: A Study of Form in Elizabethan Drama* (Madison, 1954), p. 323.

18 Doran, *Endeavors of Art*, p. 327.

19 See C. L. Barber, '"Thou that beget'st him that did thee beget": Transformation in *Pericles* and *The Winter's Tale*', *Shakespeare Survey 22* (Cambridge, 1969).

20 Editors tend to see Marina's phrase 'delivered weeping' (l. 160) as the reporter's repetition of Pericles's words in line 105, though Hoeniger feels that 'one should not rule out the possibility that Shakespeare himself repeated the words'. It seems to me more than a possibility.

21 Edwards, New Penguin *Pericles*, p. 188.

22 Muir, *Shakespeare as Collaborator*, pp. 95–6.

Leontes and the spider:
language and speaker
in Shakespeare's Last Plays

ANNE BARTON

Hermione.   Come, sir, now
I am for you again. Pray you sit by us,
And tell's a tale.
Mamillius.   Merry or sad shall't be?
Hermione. As merry as you will.
Mamillius. A sad tale's best for winter. I have one
Of sprites and goblins.
Hermione.   Let's have that, good sir.
Come on, sit down; come on, and do your best
To fright me with your sprites; you're powerful at it.
Mamillius. There was a man –
Hermione.   Nay, come, sit down; then on.
Mamillius. Dwelt by a churchyard – I will tell it softly;
Yond crickets shall not hear it.
Hermione.   Come on then,
And give't me in mine ear.
          [*Enter* LEONTES, ANTIGONUS, Lords *and* Others.]
Leontes.   Was he met there? his train? Camillo with him?
1 Lord.   Behind the tuft of pines I met them; never
Saw I men scour so on their way. I eyed them
Even to their ships.
Leontes.   How blest am I
In my just censure, in my true opinion!
Alack, for lesser knowledge! How accursed
In being so blest! There may be in the cup
A spider steeped, and one may drink, depart,
And yet partake no venom, for his knowledge
Is not infected; but if one present
Th' abhorred ingredient to his eye, make known
How he hath drunk, he cracks his gorge, his sides,
With violent hefts. I have drunk, and seen the spider.
Camillo was his help in this, his pander.
There is a plot against my life, my crown;
All's true that is mistrusted. That false villain
Whom I employed was pre-employed by him;

50   He has discovered my design, and I
                   Remain a pinched thing; yea, a very trick
                   For them to play at will.
                                    (*The Winter's Tale*, II,i,21–52)

The Winter's Tale begins where many of Shakespeare's earlier comedies
had ended. Friendship, no longer love's rival, has found a spacious if
subordinate place for itself within the domain of marriage. Leontes enters
the play with his wife Hermione and his friend Polixenes: three people
apparently in possession of that harmonious, adult relationship which the
youthful protagonists of *Two Gentlemen of Verona, Love's Labour's Lost,
The Merchant of Venice, Much Ado About Nothing* and *All's Well That
Ends Well* had struggled painfully, over five acts, to achieve. Mamillius
and Florizel, the children whose birth is predicated at the end of so many
Shakespearian Comedies, actually exist. The story is, or should be, over.
So powerful is this sense of being in a place just beyond the normal
terminus of Shakespeare's Comedies that, even at the beginning of Act
II, when Leontes has perversely begun to un-build his paradise, it is
possible to hear the echoes of another and less disturbing winter's tale:

           Now it is the time of night
           That the graves, all gaping wide,
           Every one lets forth his sprite,
           In the church-way paths to glide.
                        (*A Midsummer Night's Dream*, V,i,368–71)

Mamillius's whispered story 'of sprites and goblins' will be as harmless as
Puck's fifth-act account of the terrors of the night: a ghost story carefully
qualified, in *A Midsummer Night's Dream*, by the final benediction of the
fairies. Safe in her warm, domestic interior, Hermione listens indulgently
to a child's tale of grave-yard horrors. Neither of them notices that, as in
Peele's *The Old Wives Tale*, someone has appeared on stage to tell
Mamillius's tale for him. It is Leontes's story of the night, not Mamillius's, that the theatre audience actually hears, and this adult fantasy is
neither harmless nor amusing.

    Leontes, like Othello before him, asserts passionately that ignorance is
bliss:

           I had been happy if the general camp,
           Pioneers and all, had tasted her sweet body,
           So I had nothing known.   (*Othello*, III,iii,349–51)

Othello's sophistical insistence that a man is robbed only if he knows he is
had concentrated attention upon Othello himself: a man constitutionally

incapable of existing – whether for good or ill – except in a state of certainty and total commitment. His false logic, engendered by the psychological pain of the moment, had been an unavailing attempt at self-delusion discredited by the speaker in the very moment of constructing it. Othello, in agony, deliberately plays with the idea of a blessed ignorance from which, through Iago's insinuations, he has effectively been debarred. He invents the gross 'pioneers' as a form of self-torture, while trying simultaneously to persuade himself that paradise would not be lost even if he were the only man who still believed in it. But he knows that he cannot any longer believe.

Leontes's speech in *The Winter's Tale*, for all its superficial similarity, is very different from Othello's. The little, inset story of the spider is palpably an old wives' tale: a piece of unnatural natural history which Leontes trots out as part of his self-defeating effort to make something out of nothing, to give substance to a bad dream. As such, it functions in ways of which the speaker is himself unaware, tells a truth he consciously rejects. If Leontes sees himself as being in Othello's situation, we do not. Othello, with some excuse, could not distinguish between Desdemona's truth and Iago's cunning falsehood. He was not the only person in the play to make this mistake. Leontes, on the other hand, inhabits a world of clear-cut black and white, one in which there is no Iago, and even the herd of anonymous gentlemen at the court always know that Hermione is innocent. Leontes's mind, as his words involuntarily but quite explicitly inform us, has poisoned itself, breeding madness from an illusory evil, even as the minds of people doomed by voodoo or black magic are supposed to do. Whether visible or not, the spider in the cup is itself innocuous: it is the human imagination that is destructive and deadly. This is the most important thing Leontes has to tell us. It is characteristic, however, of the Last Plays, that the speaker should be quite unconscious of what, for the theatre audience, is the primary meaning of his own words.

In his earlier plays, Shakespeare had very occasionally anticipated this technique. Usually, he did so for straightforward comic effect – one thinks of the word 'ass' as Dogberry indignantly applies it to himself, or as Bottom uses it, innocently, after his translation. Fools who luxuriate in words without understanding their proper meanings, as Dogberry does throughout *Much Ado About Nothing*, Touchstone's Audrey with the epithet 'foul', or Cleopatra's clown (more profoundly) with the term 'immortal', are given to making sense of a kind they would consciously repudiate. It is part of the character of the Hostess in the *Henry IV* plays that she should remain blithely unaware of the bawdy double entendres which other people detect in her speech, unintentional indecencies which tend to overbear her own meaning. Only in *Troilus and Cressida*, however, did Shakespeare exploit the device in ways that were, fundamentally, not comic. The play is conditioned throughout by the audience's foreknowledge of the fate of Troy, and of the destiny of each individual character. A unique and all-encompassing irony ensures that characters seldom speak out of their own, present moment of fictional time without an audience interpreting their words in the light of the myth as a whole. So, when Helen suggests languidly that 'this love will undo us all' (III,i,103–4), what for her is mere badinage converts instantly into a sinister and alien truth. Pandarus regards it as a jocular impossibility that Cressida should ever be false to Troilus. Should his niece falter, 'let all pitiful goers-between be called to the world's end after my name – call them all Pandars; let all constant men be Troiluses, all false women Cressids, and all brokers between Pandars. Say "Amen" ' (III,ii,195–200). It is only for the audience, painfully aware that this is precisely the significance which these names now have, that 'Amen' sticks in the throat.

Troilus and Cressida is a special case. (Indeed, it is interesting that Shakespeare should have wished to stress the ineluctable end of the Troy story in this fashion, as he did not with what might have been regarded as the equally predetermined patterns of English history.) In general, the compulsion to drive a wedge between dramatic speech and the nature and intentions of the speaker becomes important only in his late plays. One must be careful, I think, not to confuse this late stylistic development with ordinary ambiguity – the shadowy penumbra of meanings, not necessarily in the control of the speaker, which may surround a given word. Nor is it the same as that kind of implicit, underlying irony which becomes visible only when a passage is analysed in the study, or remembered from the special vantage point of the fifth act. When Henry V, before Harfleur, exhorts his soldiers to imitate tigers, greyhounds, cannons, or pitiless granite escarpments, his words are a successful incitement to action. Only in the context of the whole play, and *after the dramatic moment is past*, leaving us to confront an immobile Bardolph and Pistol, is it possible to reflect that he is asking men to be both more and considerably less than human. Obviously, Henry himself does not see the terms he employs as equivocal, an impoverishment as well as an epic magnification. The point is that, in the theatre, neither do we. Or, at least, the speech as heard projects this sense in a way that is almost subliminal.

Similarly, when Othello, in Cyprus, exclaims of Desdemona,

> Perdition catch my soul
> But I do love thee; and when I love thee not
> Chaos is come again,   (III,iii,91–3)

or Macbeth asserts, 'Had I but died an hour before this chance, / I had lived a blessed time' (II,iii,89–90), the literal but at this instant merely potential truth lurking behind the hyperbole is secondary to the meaning of the lines as the speaker intends them, but also as we hear them in the moment of utterance. Othello and Macbeth, like Pandarus and Leontes, speak more truly than they know, but the bitter prophecy inherent in their words – like the unwitting predictions of Buckingham, Lady Anne, or Richard himself ('Myself myself confound') in *Richard III* – will always be submerged in the theatre by other and more immediately arresting considerations. Even if one's mind does flicker forward to 'the tragic loading of this bed', here, in the particular stage-present of Act III, Othello's lines make themselves felt essentially as Othello himself feels them: as a spontaneous declaration of love and faith. Macbeth's cry, while it certainly prefigures his fifth-act recognition of a life fallen irremediably into the 'sear, the yellow leaf', concentrates attention as it is uttered upon the audacity of his dissembled horror. That is the primary register.

This is not, however, the way we react to Leontes's spider, or to his assertion that 'I / Play too; but so disgraced a part, whose issue / Will hiss me to my grave' (I,ii,187–9). Here, as in his angry words to Hermione,

> Your actions are my dreams.
> You had a bastard by Polixenes,
> And I but dreamed it,   (III,ii,80–2)

it is what we take to be the *primary* meaning of the speech which is concealed from the speaker. In the last example, Leontes's heavy irony functions, for us, as a simple statement of truth. This is also true of the convoluted reasoning through which he persuaded himself, in Act I, that because 'affection' may communicate with dreams, be coactive with the unreal, and because it 'fellow'st nothing' (I,ii,138–46), it may conjoin with 'something' – and has. It is interesting to compare the false logic here with Brutus's soliloquy in the orchard in *Julius Caesar*: 'Then, lest he may, prevent' (II,i,28). All of the passages from *The Winter's Tale* are entirely and almost impersonally apt as descriptions of the dramatic situation as we, but not Leontes, apprehend it. Mirrors of action almost more than of character, they do not focus attention upon Leontes's central self in the way that Othello's and Brutus's assertions had illuminated the needs and complexities of their natures.

A number of critics have felt that Shakespeare, in his Last Plays, destroyed that close relationship between language and dramatic character which had seemed the permanent achievement of his maturity. Charles Olson observed in 1950 that the later Shakespeare 'very much doesn't any longer bother to keep his music and thought inside the skin of the person and situation, able as he had been to make each person of his play make his or her individual self register its experience of reality'.[1] James Sutherland, confronting the opening lines of *Cymbeline*, suspected that 'the person who is thinking rapidly, breaking off, making fresh starts and so on, is not the character, but Shakespeare himself'.[2] For Sutherland, this dislocation between verse and character reflected a Shakespeare who, if not exactly 'bored' (Strachey's epithet), was at least a little jaded: a man to whom poetry no longer came as naturally as leaves to a tree, who had to force himself now to create at all, and had taken to writing in a strained and entirely cerebral way. S. L. Bethell also claimed that the twisted rhythms and tortured syntax of the Last Plays represented 'Shakespeare's mind, not the character's; indeed, it draws our attention *away from* the speaker to what is spoken about'.[3] Unlike Sutherland, Bethell approved of what seemed to him a new technique designed to give prominence to those metaphysical truths which alone could justify Shakespeare's use of plot material so naïve and silly. More recently, Hallett Smith has shifted the emphasis away from Shakespeare himself to the nature of the stage action. 'It is noteworthy', he says of certain passages in *Cymbeline* and *The Winter's Tale*, 'that the speeches do not so much characterize the speaker as dramatize the occasion.'[4]

Smith appears to me to have come closest to the truth. It is not easy to see why a dramatist who had so triumphantly solved what Daniel Seltzer describes as 'the problem of causing verbal expression to spring naturally from the inner life of the stage personality', who had developed 'a technique uniquely Shakespearian: that of expression, moment by moment, of an inner state and an immediate present time',[5] should suddenly decide to sacrifice the accomplishment. But then it is not easy, either, to understand the logic which impelled Michelangelo to forget everything he had painfully learned about the realistic articulation of the

human body and return, in the Rondanini *Pietà*, to the stiff, non-natural-
istic forms of Romanesque art. For whatever reason, Shakespeare at the
end of his writing life chose to subordinate character to action in ways
that seem to give Aristotle's conviction of the necessary primacy of the
μῦθος a new twist.[6]

Editors of *The Tempest* have often wished to transfer Miranda's verbal
assault upon Caliban in Act I ('Abhorrèd slave, / Which any print of
goodness wilt not take') to Prospero. It seems almost inconceivable that
her innocence and gentleness should be capable of such rugged and
uncompromising vituperation. Examination of the Last Plays as a group,
however, tends to suggest that the Folio is correct. Over and over again,
Shakespeare jettisons consistency of characterisation because he is more
interested in the impersonal quality of a moment of dramatic time. This is
what happens near the beginning of Act III of *The Tempest*, when
Miranda somewhat startlingly produces the image of a concealed preg-
nancy as the means of declaring her love to Ferdinand: 'And all the more
it seeks to hide itself, / The bigger bulk it shows' (III,i,80–1). That
Ophelia, in her madness, should reveal that she has secretly committed to
memory all the verses of a rude song about St Valentine's Day, certainly
says something about Ophelia, and about the pathos of her attempts to
look in directions sternly prohibited by Polonius and Laertes. It would
obviously be inappropriate and futile to apply the same reasoning to
Miranda's lines. They are there, not to tell us anything about sexual
repression on the island, but because – as the betrothal masque will later
make even more plain – Shakespeare is concerned, above all, to delineate
this marriage in terms of natural fertility and increase. Even so, Miranda
says to Caliban earlier what the situation, as opposed to maidenly
decorum and the pliability of her own nature, would seem to demand.

Miranda is not the only heroine to be treated in this fashion in the late
plays. As early as *Pericles*, Marina had anticipated Miranda's confrontation with Caliban in the uncharacteristic venom and masculinity of her
reproof of Boult:

> Thou art the damned doorkeeper to every
> Coistrel that comes inquiring for his Tib;
> To the choleric fisting of every rogue
> Thy ear is liable; thy food is such
> As hath been belched on by infected lungs.   (IV,vi,163–7)

The lines, however well suited to the Duke in *Measure For Measure*, are
not easy for an actress to encompass, considering that she will have spent

most of her previous scenes epitomising a kind of gentle and melancholy lyricism, coupled with an innocence incapable of even understanding the Bawd's professional instructions (IV,ii,116–23). One previous abrupt departure from Marina's normal manner, during her account to Leonine of the sea-storm of her birth (IV,i,61–6), has at least warned the performer what to expect. In both passages, Shakespeare appears to be using Marina less as a character than as a kind of medium, through which the voice of the situation can be made to speak.

Further instances of this attitude towards dramatic speech may be found most readily by turning to those passages in the late plays which, for one reason or another, have aroused critical censure or disagreement. Dr Johnson found the third-act soliloquy of Belarius in *Cymbeline* ('These boys know little they are sons to th' King') positively exasperating in its irrationality and unabashed expository purpose. Belarius is not, elsewhere, so crudely confiding, like a character in an old play. The improbability, however, of the story he has to tell has already been admitted by Shakespeare, indeed brought to our attention, in the opening dialogue between the first and second gentlemen (I,i,57–67). Belarius's speech in Act III reflects, not his own personality or feelings at the moment (elsewhere clearly enough defined), but simply the character of the events he describes: remote, fantastic, and overtly artificial. The same will be true of the highly wrought and convoluted prose in which the courtiers recount the finding of Perdita in *The Winter's Tale*, as it is of Iachimo's insistence, at the end of *Cymbeline*, upon transforming what ought to be an agonised confession of guilt into an intricate and palpable work of fiction. Iachimo's flowery and long-winded account of how Posthumus was led to wager on Imogen's chastity bears little resemblance to the episode we actually saw, back in the fourth scene of Act I. The gentlemen were not, as Iachimo claims they were, sitting at a feast praising their loves of Italy, until their hyperbole stung the melancholy Posthumus into a celebration of his wife, and then into accepting Iachimo's trial. The reality was different, and more complex than this. Iachimo has tidied it all up, brought it closer – both stylistically and in terms of fact – to a romance world. He does this for reasons which (again) have less to do with his character than with the way *Cymbeline*, in its final scene, deliberately treats its plot material as unreal.

A similar concern to express situation before character allows the wicked Queen in *Cymbeline* to speak of Britain in words that would not misbecome John of Gaunt, when she proudly refuses to pay the Roman tribute. Even Cloten, when he announces that 'Britain is / A world by itself', can expect applause (III,i,12–13). Arviragus appears to wander off the point in ways of which true grief, even in a verse play, ought to be incapable when he assures the 'dead' Fidele of the kindly attentions of the ruddock's 'charitable bill – O bill, sore shaming / Those rich-left heirs that let their fathers lie / Without a monument' (IV,ii,226–8). His brother Guiderius reproves him for playing 'in wench-like words with that / Which is so serious'. It is Arviragus, however, who is unconsciously faithful to the quality of the situation: Fidele is not dead, but merely asleep, as the result of the Queen's potion. It is interesting to compare Arviragus's lament here with the comic frenzy of the Nurse when she discovers Juliet 'dead' on her wedding day. Like Fidele, Juliet is only drugged into a semblance of death and, in this sense, the Nurse's ludicrous attempts at tragic style ('O day! O day! O day! O hateful day'; IV,5,52) are entirely appropriate to a situation which is not what it seems to be. With the Nurse, however, one is aware first and foremost of how perfectly *in character* her lamentations are. Presumably, she sounded much the same when poor Susan went to God. This is not true of Arviragus's elegy in *Cymbeline*, a speech which, if anything, seems oddly hard to square with what we know about this princely rustic.

At least two notorious problems in the Last Plays may result from Shakespeare's use of this dramatic technique. It is always hard to know what to make of Lysimachus's asseveration to Marina, at the end of their interview in the brothel, that he came 'with no ill intent; for to me / The very doors and windows savour vilely' (IV,vi,108–9). He has certainly created the impression, in the scene as a whole, that he is a man perfectly at home in a house of prostitution, and intimately acquainted with its ways. 'How now! How a dozen of virginities?' As the Bawd remarks, 'Your Honour knows what 'tis to say well enough' (IV,vi,19, 31). There is not the slightest hint that the Governor of Mytilene may be dissembling. Is his explanation to Marina a desperate attempt to save face before he too, with the other converts, goes off to 'hear the vestals sing'? Or is the answer simply that Shakespeare is not interested in Lysimachus's motivation: during the dialogue with the professionals, and with Marina, he is a young man of rank in search of a sound whore, because that is what the situation demands. Afterwards, he is not – because he is going to marry Marina. Something similar seems to be happening with Paulina's outburst to Leontes after the 'death' of Hermione.

I say she's dead; I'll swear't. If word nor oath
Prevail not, go and see. If you can bring
Tincture or lustre in her lip, her eye,
Heat outwardly or breath within, I'll serve you
As I would do the gods. But, O thou tyrant!
Do not repent these things, for they are heavier
Than all thy woes can stir; therefore betake thee
To nothing but despair. A thousand knees
Ten thousand years together, naked, fasting,
Upon a barren mountain, and still winter
In storm perpetual, could not move the gods
To look that way thou wert.   (*The Winter's Tale*, III,ii,200–11)

Paulina, of course, is lying – or, at least, she seems to be from the vantage
point of the fifth act. In the scene itself, one must assume that she is a
woman half crazed with shock and grief, expressing the truth of the
situation. For the theatre audience at this point in the play, Hermione,
unlike Fidele, is indeed dead. Paulina's voice is faithful to the action. And
it is characteristic of the Last Plays that Shakespeare should not bother,
amid the partial revelations of the final scene, to provide any explanation
of her previous behaviour.

Never a man who paid much attention to the requirements of neo-
classical decorum when constructing character, the Shakespeare of the
late plays seems to have abandoned even the basic convention by which,
earlier, his servants and lower-class characters generally expressed themselves in homely, colloquial, if vivid, prose. The gardeners of *Richard II*,
in their one, brief appearance, had been striking exceptions to this rule:
emblematic, verse-speaking custodians of a garden more symbolic than
literal and, as such, very different from Launce or Speed, Costard, the
citizenry of the Roman plays, Cade's rabble, the Dromios, Grumio,
Peter, Pompey, or the carriers at Rochester. Posthumus, on the other
hand, is a humble, private gentleman but he has mysteriously acquired,
in Pisanio, a servant of quite extraordinary verbal sophistication, who can
tell Imogen to

Forget that rarest treasure of your cheek,
Exposing it – but, O, the harder heart!
Alack, no remedy! – to the greedy touch
Of common-kissing Titan, and forget
Your laboursome and dainty trims wherein
You made great Juno angry.   (III,iv,159–64)

Even the gaoler in *Cymbeline*, although he speaks prose, seems (like
Perdita herself, though without the justification of her lineage) to smack
of something greater than himself, 'too noble for this place'. To place his

meditation on death ('O, the charity of a penny cord'; v,iv,156–207) beside that of the grave-digger in *Hamlet* is to see how little Shakespeare is concerned, now, with any attempt at social realism. Even the Old Shepherd of *The Winter's Tale*, and the fishermen Patchbreech and Pilch in *Pericles*, seem to dodge in and out of their status-defined, comic roles in ways for which there are no real parallels in earlier plays. Stephano and Trinculo, in *The Tempest*, do not do this: they are consistently (and relatively realistically) conceived throughout. Shakespeare's orthodox handling of them, however, only serves to throw into relief the inexplicably civilised verse (if not the sentiments) of Caliban.

It is a commonplace of criticism to separate Imogen from the other young heroines of the Last Plays, to see her as a sister of Rosalind, Viola, Portia, or the Julia of *Two Gentlemen of Verona*, a character existing somewhat uncomfortably in a romance world not really designed to accommodate her. There is obviously some truth in this judgement, at least when Imogen is measured against Marina, Perdita, and Miranda. She does indeed seem to be more vigorous, complex, and three-dimensional than they, to summon up memories of the earlier heroines. And yet, when Cymbeline, at the very end, recognises 'the tune of Imogen' (v,v,239), it is not easy to define just what he means. Unlike Rosalind or Viola, Imogen has seemed to manifest herself in several, divergent modes: passionate and chilly, timorous and aggressive, sometimes intensely feminine, sometimes not. This is partly the result of the way she submerges her own personality within that of the fictional Fidele, losing herself in her role, as Rosalind had not when she impersonated Ganymede, or Viola when she acted Cesario. Rosalind's mercurial, feminine self always shines through Ganymede, making Orlando's acceptance of the wooing game credible. Viola constantly reminds us, as she talks to Orsino, Feste, and Olivia, or struggles to overcome her physical cowardice when confronting Aguecheek, of the lonely, isolated girl she really is. The image is curiously double. In the theatre, an audience remains aware that Fidele is really Imogen. Yet her identity is overlaid by another: that of the 'boy' whom Guiderius, Arviragus, Belarius and (later) Lucius see. We share their viewpoint, as we never share Olivia's, Orlando's, or Orsino's. This is not because Imogen is particularly skilled at dissembling – indeed, the bluntness and impatient candour of her behaviour at court during the early scenes suggest precisely the opposite – but because Shakespeare has transformed her so completely, in her dialogue with

other characters, into the person she is pretending to be, that we intermit-
tently lose sight of the reality. It is possible that the page Fidele's lament
for his dead master,

> Alas!
> There is no more such masters. I may wander
> From east to occident; cry out for service;
> Try many, all good; serve truly; never
> Find such another master   (IV,ii,371-5)

made an imaginary situation seem so convincing that Shakespeare was
impelled to introduce the subsequent aside (ll. 378-80) in order to
remind us of the truth.

Shakespeare's handling of Imogen's disguise would seem to be a
further example of the subordination, in the Last Plays, of character to
the demands of stage action. It is also part of a new, and sometimes
perplexing, attitude towards disguise and deceit generally. Pastoral
Bohemia is a land in which ballad stories so improbable that they are
virtual synonyms for fiction can eagerly be swallowed as true. There, no
one sees through the various disguises of Autolycus, Florizel, Polixenes
and Camillo. Elsewhere, however, dissembling and deceit tend to be
transparent as they were not in earlier plays. 'Here comes the Lord
Lysimachus disguised', the Bawd remarks calmly in the fourth act of
Pericles (IV,vi,16). One almost wonders why he troubled. When one
considers how complex and vital an issue it had been in earlier
plays – both the Comedies and Tragedies – to distinguish truth from
falsehood, seeming from reality, how difficult to arrive in particular cases
at Hamlet's understanding that 'one may smile, and smile, and be a
villain', the sudden diminution or disappearance of this problem from the
Last Plays is startling. It would seem, however, to be to a considerable
extent responsible for their special character and flavour.

Where Bassanio had agonised long over the riddle of the caskets at
Belmont, Pericles solves Antiochus's conundrum without effort and at
once. Later, at Pentapolis, his rusty armour and dejected manner fail to
conceal his innate nobility and worth from King Simonides and his
daughter. Both are eager, before they know his identity, to press this
seemingly unequal marriage. Lysimachus stands more upon his dignity,
but even he requires only the assurance of a birth certificate to offer his
hand to the girl he met first in the stews. At Cymbeline's court, everyone
but the king himself can see clearly that the queen is evil and not to be
trusted, and also that Cloten is a boor, and the lowly Posthumus the only

man worthy of such a jewel as Imogen. Courts are not usually so perceptive. Cornelius will not give the queen the poisons for which she asks. Pisanio will neither betray Posthumus by entering the service of Cloten, nor believe Posthumus when he brands Imogen as unchaste. Imogen herself sees through Iachimo's slander of Posthumus. Guiderius and Arviragus know, although they cannot explain why, that Fidele is akin to them as Belarius is not.

In *The Winter's Tale*, although Antigonus misinterprets a dream (and pays heavily for it), Leontes is really the only person who believes in Hermione's guilt. Everyone else, including the nameless gentlemen of the court, sees clearly that he is deluded. Camillo tells Leontes to dissemble with Polixenes: 'with a countenance as clear / As friendship wears at feasts, keep with Bohemia' (I,ii,343–4), and the king accepts his advice. 'I will seem friendly, as thou hast advised me.' Just how successful this attempt is emerges at the end of the act, when Polixenes assures Camillo that 'I do believe thee: / I saw his heart in's face' (I,ii,446–7). Duncan had lamented that 'there's no art / To find the mind's construction in the face' (*Macbeth*, I,iv,11–12), but in the Last Plays it seems to be true more often that no art is required: faces tell all, even when, as in the case of Leontes, their owners are making strenuous attempts at hypocrisy. Prospero, through his magic art, understands the true nature of everyone on the island. The knowledge adds doubtfully to his happiness. It contributes, however, to the general sense in this, as in the other Romances, that the real problem, now, is not one of distinguishing good from evil but of deciding what to do with a knowledge which often seems to be acquired involuntarily rather than through any conscious effort at discrimination.

The involuntary plays a significantly new part in the Last Plays. Although, in general, good and evil are oddly transparent and recognisable for what they are, a few individual characters are arbitrarily deprived of this knowledge. Sealed off from everyone around them, they inhabit a strange, isolated state of consciousness in which they not only make false judgements, but cannot be reached or reasoned with by anyone else. These extreme states of mind are not arrived at, as it seems, by any logical, or psychologically comprehensible, process: they are simply 'caught', like the 'flu. This happens to Pericles towards the end of the play. He appears in Act V as a living dead man, one who has not spoken to anyone for three months. Only Marina can break through the barrier, and even she comes close to being defeated by the task. In the case of King

Cymbeline, his delusion has come upon him before the beginning of the play, an inexplicable blindness which prevents him from seeing what is apparent to everyone else. Only the death of the wicked queen releases him from the spell. *The Tempest* stands slightly apart from the other Romances, in that the trance which enwraps Alonso, Antonio, and Sebastian after the enchanted banquet is directly attributable to Prospero's art. Again, however, it has the effect of creating a distinction between a special, almost somnambulist state and a waking world of preternatural clarity and moral definition. Posthumus, in *Cymbeline*, shuts himself off from the light in Act II. Philario is a minor character, and he has never met Imogen, but even he can see that Iachimo's tale 'is not strong enough to be believed / Of one persuaded well of' (II,iv,131–2). Posthumus, however, has suddenly entered the troll kingdom of *Peer Gynt*, and no longer sees the world with the eyes of other men.

The madness of Leontes would seem to be generically like that of Pericles, Cymbeline, Posthumus and (with reservations) the three men of sin in *The Tempest*. But Shakespeare allows us to watch its inception and development at much greater length, a privilege which only serves to make the affliction itself more mysterious. Leontes comes to believe that he is the only person in Sicily capable of distinguishing truth from falsehood. In fact, he is the only person who cannot. What he describes, in the speech about the spider and the cup, as 'my true opinion' is a chimera, a self-deception of the grossest kind. And indeed, only a few lines later, he is repeating this talismanic word *true* in a sentence which means one thing to him and, as so often, something quite different to the audience: 'All's true that is mistrusted.' Editors of *The Winter's Tale* tend to feel that the phrase is sufficiently obscure to require a gloss. They explain carefully that Leontes is justifying the truth of his own suspicions about Hermione and Polixenes – and so he is. The word order, on the other hand, is oddly convoluted. (Compare Ford's superficially similar statement in a similar situation in *The Merry Wives of Windsor*: 'my intelligence is true; my jealousy is reasonable'; IV,ii,130–2.) *The Winter's Tale* inversion draws attention to a rival, and even more important, interpretation. What Leontes is telling us, without being aware that he does so, is that everything he thinks false is, in fact, true.

Throughout his writing life, Shakespeare displayed a marked predilection for analysing situations by way of contraries or antitheses. Dualities and polar opposites are a striking feature of his style, superimposed upon the individual verbal habits of particular characters: darkness and light, frost and fire, summer and winter, love and hate. Elizabethans, trained as they were in the discipline of formal rhetoric, often thought in such patterns. With Shakespeare, however, certain words seem to summon up their opposites almost automatically, as the result of an ingrained habit of mind almost more than from the requirements of a particular situation or rhetorical pattern. This is the case especially with the true–false antithesis, as even a quick glance at the two words in the Shakespeare concordance will reveal. They are surprisingly constant companions. In the Last Plays, however, something odd seems to happen to antithesis generally, and to the true–false figure in particular.

'Metaphysical' is a term frequently invoked to describe the stylistic peculiarities of the Romances. And indeed, there is much to be said for using it, in Dr Johnson's sense of heterogeneous ideas yoked together by violence, analogies so ingenious it seems a wonder they were ever found at all. Characteristic of all four plays, but of *The Winter's Tale* in particular, is a form of similitude, usually employing the conjunction *as*, in which antithesis is employed to define resemblance in a fashion both unexpected and only superficially logical. When Antonio wants to assure Sebastian that Ferdinand is surely dead, he complicates a fundamentally simple assertion by explaining that ' 'Tis as impossible that he's undrowned / As he that sleeps here swims' (II,i,228–9). Time, in *The Winter's Tale*, warns the theatre audience that he will 'make stale / The glistering of this present, as my tale / Now seems to it' (IV,i,13–15). Hermione is sure that her past life 'hath been as continent, as chaste, as true, / As I am now unhappy' (III,ii,31–3), and Paulina informs Leontes that she is 'no less honest / Than you are mad' (II,ii,70–1). Iachimo, purloining the sleeping Imogen's bracelet, finds it 'as slippery as the Gordian knot was hard' (II,ii,34). There are many other instances. In all of them, a negative and a positive statement are oddly conjoined. Moreover, although the syntax often appears to be setting up a clear-cut polarity (honest–dishonest, chaste–falsely accused), in fact the figure slides off into the oblique. The terms compared are not really antithetical: they are merely *different* in a way that makes one wonder why these particular instances have been made to confront each other at all.

The words *false* and *true* continue, in the Last Plays, to evoke one another, but Shakespeare tends to treat them, now, in an almost vertiginous way. Earlier true–false antitheses (e.g. 'As false, by heaven, as heaven itself is true'; *Richard II*, IV,i,64) had been clear cut. Although the complications attendant upon broken vows produced, in *Love's Labour's*

Lost and *King John*, three isolated examples prophetic of the future,[7] it is only in the Romances that truth and falsehood come to engage habitually in a balancing act in which, at one and the same time, they remain polarities and seem to exchange identities. In the light of similar passages in *Cymbeline* and *The Winter's Tale*, Pericles's meditation on Antiochus at the beginning of the play sounds like an authentic and uncorrupted piece of Shakespearian text:

> If it be true that I interpret false,
> Then were it certain you were not so bad
> As with foul incest to abuse your soul.   (I,i,124–6)

Even so, Cornelius, when deceiving Cymbeline's queen about the nature of the drug he gives her, describes himself as 'the truer / So to be false with her' (I,v,43–4). Pisanio performs the same gyration in Act III, when he informs the absent Cloten that 'true to thee / Were to prove false, which I will never be, / To him that is most true' (III,v,157–9), and reiterates the paradox in Act IV: 'Wherein I am false I am honest; not true to be true' (IV,iii,42). Leontes argues that even if women were as false as 'o'er-dyed blacks', as water, wind or dice, 'yet were it true / To say this boy were like me' (I,ii,134–5).

Imogen's anguished investigation of what it means 'to be false' extends the exercise:

> True honest men being heard, like false Aeneas,
> Were, in his time, thought false; and Sinon's weeping
> Did scandal many a holy tear, took pity
> From most true wretchedness. So thou, Posthumus,
> Wilt lay the leaven on all proper men:
> Goodly and gallant shall be false and perjured
> From thy great fail.   (III,iv,56–62)

Hermione on trial sees the same problem from the opposite side, but she delineates it in similar terms:

> Since what I am to say must be but that
> Which contradicts my accusation, and
> The testimony on my part no other
> But what comes from myself, it shall scarce boot me
> To say 'Not guilty'. Mine integrity
> Being counted falsehood shall, as I express it,
> Be so received.   (III,ii,20–6)

The pessimism of both women is unwarranted. Except for characters like Leontes and Posthumus, who have suddenly and arbitrarily gone blind, distinguishing between falsehood and truth as *moral* entities is no longer difficult. All of these riddling passages remind us of this fact. At the same time, they suggest, in their deliberate confounding of opposites, the presence of another kind of true–false confusion: one which is central to these plays.

On the whole, efforts to distinguish the fictional from the 'real', art from life, tales from truth, come in the Romances to replace the older, moral concern with identifying hypocrisy and deceit. It is not easy for characters to make these distinctions – nor, in some cases, for the theatre audience. Leontes, when he applies the story of the spider in the cup, mistakes a fiction of his own devising for fact, with disastrous results. He forces the imaginary to become true, even as Antonio does before *The Tempest* begins, when

> having into truth, by telling of it,
> Made such a sinner of his memory,
> To credit his own lie – he did believe
> He was indeed the Duke. (i,ii,100–3)

Both of these are false and destructive fictions, credited only by their creators. And in both plays they can be countered only by another, and benevolent, kind of illusion: Prospero's restorative art, or the pastoral make-believe of Bohemia.

In Bohemia, almost all the special techniques of the Last Plays with which this essay has been concerned are on view simultaneously. People are constantly expressing the truth of the situation without grasping what, for us, is the primary meaning of their own words – as in the reiterated description of the lowly Perdita as a 'queen'. It has often been remarked that Polixenes and Perdita, in their debate on Art and Nature, perversely argue against their own position and intentions as they understand them at this point. Polixenes, after all, has come to the sheep-shearing precisely in order to prevent his gentle scion from grafting himself onto wild stock. Perdita, for her part, intends to make just such an 'unnatural' marriage. Their words, inconsistent with the purpose of the two speakers, focus attention not upon them but upon the real nature of the situation.

Perdita dislikes acting as much as she dislikes nature's bastards in her rustic garden. It worries her that her own identity should be submerged so completely in that of the festival queen she plays, that her robes should change her disposition. In fact, she does lose herself in her part, even as Imogen had in that of Fidele, although in this case the scene in which she distributes the flowers seems to operate as a healing counterbalance to the earlier 'play' in which her father, another unwilling actor, had fancied himself hissed off the stage in the role of cuckold. It is with great reluctance that Perdita agrees to continue in her royal part after Polixenes has revealed himself. Camillo's counsel to her to 'disliken / The truth of your own seeming' (IV,iv,642–3) not only brings truth and falsehood into a linguistically dizzying relationship, in the manner characteristic of these plays; it expresses a truth beyond Camillo's ken. Like Imogen, Perdita must consent to 'disguise / That which t'appear itself must not yet be / But by self-danger' (*Cymbeline*, III,iv,143–5).

Autolycus, a man of various and willing disguises, may seem at first sight to be a hypocrite and dissembler in the manner of earlier plays. His real association, however, is with fictions rather than with genuine evil. Certainly his decision not to take the obviously profitable step of acquainting Polixenes with Florizel's intended flight – because to do so would be an honest action, and Autolycus prefers to remain true to his own falsehood – is scarcely that of a man whose villainy we can take seriously. At the end of the play, the Clown, his chief victim, is cheerfully defending his oath that Autolycus is 'as honest a true fellow as any is in Bohemia' on the grounds that 'if it be ne'er so false, a true gentleman may swear it in the behalf of his friend' (V,ii,150–1, 156–8). Justice Shallow's man Davy, pleading for the notorious Visor because 'the knave is mine honest friend' (*2 Henry IV*, V,i,47–8), never confounded the moral connotations of 'knave' and 'honest', despite his concern to mitigate the pejorative side. The Clown, on the other hand, calls precisely this polarity into doubt in ways that make it impossible for us to regard Autolycus as anything but what he is: a creator of fictions who, by not betraying Florizel to Polixenes, and by inventing a tale which frightens the Old Shepherd and the Clown into Sicily with the all-important fardel, is in fact the agent of the happy ending.

In Bohemia, people constantly confuse fact with fiction. Mopsa and Dorcas are almost obsessive in their desire to be assured that the pedlar's fantastic ballads are true. Their naïveté is comic and yet, later in the play, we find ourselves humbly sharing their impulse. The second gentleman announces that 'such a deal of wonder is broken out within this hour that ballad-makers cannot be able to express it' (V,i,23–5). The preservation of Perdita and her reunion with her father are, as Shakespeare continually reminds us, 'like an old tale', more improbable even than Autolycus's ballads. It is, however, a story that we too, in reading or watching the play, want to believe. This is even more true with the awakening of Hermione from marble to flesh, a resurrection which is as much a miracle for the theatre audience as for the characters involved. 'It is required', Paulina says, 'you do awake your faith' (v,iii,94–5). What kind of faith?

Several kinds of fiction, as it seems, have operated in *The Winter's Tale*. The comedy ending which was the original point of departure dissolved almost at once into a dark tale of sprites and goblins. Then, it metamorphosed into a traditional comedy plot. Florizel and Perdita stand together in the last moments of the play as lovers who have won through, despite parental opposition and mistakes about identity, in the immemorial way of comedy. It is true that there is something they lack. Mamillius ought to be standing beside them: Florizel's friend, as Polixenes was Leontes's. But Mamillius, like Antigonus, is dead. Hermione, too, is wrinkled and older after the passing of sixteen years. Leontes does not get back exactly what he threw away. Still, he gets back far more than men can realistically expect. *The Winter's Tale* admits something that Shakespeare's Elizabethan Comedies had tried to deny: happy endings are a fiction. A fiction, but not quite a fairy-tale.

Paulina declares of Hermione in the last scene:

> That she is living,
> *Were it but told you*, should be hooted at
> Like an old tale; but it *appears* she lives.   (v,iii,115–17: my italics)

The words are true, once again, in a way not comprehended by the speaker. It is, after all, because of the dramatic form in which this implausible fiction has been embodied, because of our complex, theatrical experience of this μῦθος, that we can give *The Winter's Tale* a kind of assent we deny to Greene's *Pandosto*. In the world as we know it, the dead do not return. Lost children generally stay lost, and shepherds' daughters do not attract the sons of kings. Ageing widows are not married off quite so neatly as Paulina. Shakespeare not only does not try to conceal, he positively emphasises the fact that his material is the archetypal stuff of legend and fairy-tale. That we respond to it as something far more powerful and engaging than 'Cinderella' or 'Beauty and the Beast' testifies to the subtlety with which Shakespeare has adjusted his language and dramatic art to the demands of a new mode: one in which plot, on the whole, has become more vivid and emotionally charged than character. And also, to a desperate artistic honesty which could admit, now, to creating fictions, while making us understand why and how much we should like those fictions to be real.

NOTES

1 Charles Olson, 'Shakespeare's Last Plays', in *Selected Writings of Charles Olson*, ed. R. Creeley (New York, 1966), p. 37.

2 James Sutherland, 'The Language of the Last Plays', in *More Talking of Shakespeare*, ed. John Garrett (London, 1959), p. 146.

3 S. L. Bethell, Introduction to *The Winter's Tale*, New Clarendon Shakespeare (Oxford, 1956), pp. 22–3.

4 Hallett Smith, *Shakespeare's Romances* (San Marino, California, 1972), p. 177.

5 Daniel Seltzer, 'Prince Hal and Tragic Style', in *Shakespeare Survey 30* (Cambridge, 1977), pp. 13, 23.

6 In *Die dramatische Technik des Sophokles* (Berlin, 1917), T. Wilamowitz argues against the idea of psychologically consistent characterisation in Sophocles, and for the centrality of action, in ways that have some bearing on Shakespeare's late style. According to Wilamowitz, Sophocles was always essentially interested in the situation of the moment, and its effect on the theatre audience. This, as opposed to any internal logic, governs the behaviour of his characters and the way we see them. (See the discussion of Wilamowitz's argument by Hugh Lloyd-Jones, 'T. Wilamowitz on the Dramatic Technique of Sophocles', in *The Classical Quarterly*, 22 (n.s.), 1972, pp. 214–28.)

7 *Love's Labour's Lost*, V,ii,760–2. *King John*, III,i,27–8 and V,iv,28–9.

Shakespeare's 'bombast'[1]

E. A. J. HONIGMANN

There is an upstart crow, beautified with our feathers, that with his *Tiger's heart wrapped in a player's hide,* supposes he is as well able to bombast out a blank verse as the best of you. (Robert Greene)

In reading some bombast speeches of *Macbeth,* which are not to be understood, [Jonson] used to say that it was horror; and I am much afraid that this is so. (Dryden)

[Shakespeare's] whole style is so pestered with figurative expressions, that it is as affected as it is obscure. (Dryden)

> And, if thou prate of mountains, let them throw
> Millions of acres on us, till our ground,
> Singeing his pate against the burning zone,
> Make Ossa like a wart! Nay, an thou'lt mouth,
> I'll rant as well as thou.   (Shakespeare)

> But he, as loving his own pride and purposes,
> Evades them with a bombast circumstance
> Horribly stuffed with epithets of war.   (Shakespeare)

Literature, we are often told, should be studied in its social-historical context. I agree; but the more eagerly I search for the social-historical background of the Elizabethan age the more inaccessible it seems – so that I sometimes wonder whether we make too much of a will-o'-the-wisp. I want to illustrate my difficulties by examining the social-historical situation of a great writer when he fights for recognition, before he is accepted as a classic. Literary critics find it hard to adjust to this situation once a writer's reputation is established – that is, to remember that for the best part of his or her career a Shakespeare, or Milton, or Jane Austen, was *not* seen by contemporaries as a classic, and that this had consequences for the writer–reader relationship, and also for the literary work itself.

No man, we know, can be a hero to his valet. Yet the valet's point of view may be a sensible one, one that could guide us towards facts that we are inclined to overlook. Contemporary critics of Shakespeare could teach us to see the great man more clearly – not because they are right and everyone else is wrong, but because we should be able to come to terms with their attitudes, without wholly swallowing them. We, in the twentieth century, have been conditioned by three hundred years of Shakespeare-worship to think of the dramatist as more than life-size, a poet apart. There are signs in Francis Meres, however, and in other early critics, that at least some contemporaries did not see Shakespeare as a 'star-ypointing pyramid', a lofty hill out-topping all the rest. He was 'our best' in tragedy – together with Lord Buckhurst, Dr Leg, Master Edward Ferris and others who have shrunk with the passage of time; he was one of 'the best for comedy'– together with 'Porter, Wilson, Hathway, and Henry Chettle', etc.[2] And the great Elizabethan poet, of course, was not Shakespeare but Spenser.

Open almost any critical essay on Shakespeare of the last thirty years, and you get the impression that Shakespeare is our best, and probably the world's best, and that every word in the canon is perfection: Caesar can do no wrong. That's an unhealthy attitude, one that ignores the social-historical context in which he wrote – and it is a form of bardolatry that many of us have practised. I remember the sense of shock when Peter Alexander said to a class, many years ago, that he would like to delete a line in *Hamlet*, a bad line that Shakespeare certainly wrote but should not have allowed to stand: 'Too much of water hast thou, poor Ophelia' (IV,vii,186). My instinctive reaction was that it's a good line, because it's spoken by Laertes and suits his insensitive character – and that's a fine example of bardolatry, the urge to defend Shakespeare at all costs. Shortly thereafter, in the first volume of *Shakespeare Survey*, Hardin Craig defended Shakespeare's 'bad poetry', the doggerel used in so many plays for prophecies, oracles, etc., arguing that it was poetry with a special function, therefore not really bad poetry. It may be so – but Craig again illustrates our modern obsession that everything in the plays is exactly right and could not be improved.

We need only move on from the dark pit of Shakespeare criticism to the sweetness and light of his editors to discover that the myth of perfection is indefensible. Should we read 'O that this too too solid flesh would melt', or 'sullied flesh'? The fact that there are thousands of variants about which editors cannot agree means that there are thousands of readings in our received texts that are thought to be less than perfect by

competent judges. If we keep in mind that the very words in the plays are
often open to dispute, this will help us to recognise that other features
(plotting, characterisation) may be less than perfect, and this in turn will
help us to see Shakespeare as his contemporaries must have seen him
before he became a classic – as a very good dramatist, but human, capable
of making mistakes. And the critical watchfulness of the public at this
point in a writer's career introduces another social-historical factor that
we today are inclined to ignore – Shakespeare's awareness of the possibility of failure, of which there are clear signs in the texts.

So much by way of preface. What, then, can we learn from contemporary
references to 'Shakespeare's styles'? I observe, first of all, that many of
them fall into one of two groups: either they express admiration for
'mellifluous and honey-tongued Shakespeare', one whose 'honey-flowing
vein' proves his 'facetious grace in writing', or they ridicule one who
'supposes he is as well able to bombast out a blank verse' as the best.[3] I
want to concentrate on the second group, and on Shakespeare's reaction
to hostile criticism – two important threads in the social-historical web,
from the writer's point of view.
    It is not always remembered that Greene's ferocious attack on Shake-
speare's bombastic style was continued, not quite so unpleasantly, by
other professional rivals. Near the beginning of *The Knight of the Burning
Pestle* the Citizen's Wife calls out 'Hold up thy head, Ralph; show the
gentlemen what thou canst do; speak a huffing part', and he knows exactly
what she wants, and declaims

> By heaven, methinks it were an easy leap
> To pluck bright honour from the pale-faced moon.

    The most persistent critic of Shakespeare's style was undoubtedly Ben
Jonson. Dryden recorded that 'in reading some bombast speeches of
Macbeth, which are not to be understood', Jonson 'used to say that it was
horror'. The same thought lies behind Jonson's note in his *Discoveries*,
that Shakespeare 'flowed with that facility, that sometime it was necessary he should be stopped. . .Many times he fell into those things, could
not escape laughter.' And it is also present, I think, in Jonson's memorial
verses to Shakespeare:

> And tell, how far thou didst our Lyly out-shine,
> Or sporting Kyd, or Marlowe's mighty line.[4]

We happen to know Jonson's more informal opinion of Marlowe's style from another passage in *Discoveries*. A true poet's language, he held, must not 'fly from all humanity, with the *Tamerlanes*, and *Tamer-Chams* of the late Age, which had nothing in them but the *scenicall* strutting, and furious vociferation, to warrant them to the ignorant gapers'.[5] Writing that Shakespeare was able to outshine Marlowe's mighty line Jonson really said, more courteously, that Shakespeare excelled in a form of composition that he didn't care for – scenical strutting, furious vociferation, bombast. In this memorial poem, honest Ben naturally toned down his criticism of Shakespeare because, as another Johnson explained, 'in lapidary inscriptions a man is not upon oath'.

A dramatist could not easily have remained unaware of hostile criticism in the much smaller London of those times; not, at least, if his critic was as aggressive as Greene or as self-righteous as Jonson. What could Shakespeare do to protect himself? There are good reasons for believing that he was sensitive about his literary reputation. We hear that he was 'much offended' when a publisher ascribed another poet's work to him and 'presumed to make so bold with his name'. He himself wrote that 'when a man's verses cannot be understood. . .it strikes a man more dead than a great reckoning in a little room'.[6] Either personally, or through his friends, he demanded an apology from Greene's literary executor, Henry Chettle, with some success; and he twice hit back at Jonson, in the War of the Theatres and in one of his last plays. Gentle Shakespeare knew that one cannot afford to be a man of straw when professional honour's at the stake.

His problem was that, like other dramatists of his age, he evidently believed that tragedy requires a high style; this could easily go too high, and indeed go off. In the Induction of Day's *Isle of Gulls* two gentlemen discuss poetry, and one calls for 'stately', 'high writ' verse, the other despises it. The Prologue then puts the dramatist's dilemma in a nutshell:

> If he compose a scene
> Of high writ poesy, fitting a true stage,
> 'Tis counted fustian.

The dramatist aimed at high writ poesy (the 'high style', as I call it below), and was not pleased to be told by his detractors that he had produced only fustian, or bombast. It must have been a familiar debate in and around London's theatres; and it helps us to see that Shakespeare could not possibly have failed to anticipate that some of his best 'high writ poesy' might be misunderstood.

The time-honoured way to insure against misunderstanding in the theatre is not to leave things to chance, but to tell the audience what to think. Tell them at least three times, experienced dramatists advise, and with luck perhaps half the audience will catch on. It sounds like common sense, but it did not satisfy Shakespeare the professional: when he wanted the audience not to miss a point he repeated it six, eight, ten times. Before Ancient Pistol's first appearance, in *2 Henry IV*, one significant word is repeated fourteen times.

Hang him, swaggering rascal! Let him not come hither; it is the foul-mouth'dst rogue in England. . .If he swagger, let him not come here. No, by my faith! I must live among my neighbours; I'll no swaggerers. (II,iv,66–70)

We can't possibly confuse Pistol's fustian with the high style, though Pistol himself does: the dramatist makes sure of that. And a similar technique is employed, the other way round, when Hamlet asks the Player to recite a speech that might be thought over-written. Describing its style before we are allowed to hear a word of it Shakespeare warns us, through Hamlet, that while there may be some who will react unfavourably, all good and true and beautiful people will of course admire it. The effect is like Ben Jonson's 'By God 'tis good, and if you like't, you may.' Or rather, more potent: it's not just assertion, it's blackmail; if you don't care for the Player's speech you convict yourself of bad taste. Notice that even if the word 'bombast' is not used, Shakespeare circles unmistakably round it:

an excellent play, well digested in the scenes, set down with as much modesty as cunning. I remember one said there were no sallets in the lines to make the matter savoury, nor no matter in the phrase that might indict the author of affectation; but called it an honest method, as wholesome as sweet. (*Hamlet*, II,ii,33–40)

More than in any other tragedy Shakespeare must have worried about the dangers of over-writing in *Hamlet*. Repeatedly, and for good reasons, the action pulls towards stylistic inflation; and this 'high writing' is all the more noticeable since so many passages of easy, conversational prose come in between. To protect himself against the charge of 'bombast' he resorted to a very simple expedient; he got in with it first. 'These are but wild and whirling words, my lord.' 'He would drown the stage with tears / And cleave the general ear with horrid speech.' 'Ay me, what act / That roars so loud and thunders in the index?' ('Thunder' could be used as a polite word for 'rant'.) 'Nay, an thou'lt mouth, / I'll rant as well as thou.'[7]

Hamlet's advice to the players seems to me a similar, but more oblique,

insurance policy against the charge of over-writing. 'O, it offends me to
the soul to hear a robustious periwig-pated fellow tear a passion to tatters,
to very rags' (III,ii,10–11) – precisely what Hamlet himself appeared to be
doing a few moments earlier, in 'O, what a rogue and peasant slave am I.'
Yet if he himself condemns 'tearing a passion to tatters', we are now
nudged to believe, it couldn't have happened – or, if it did, not quite as we
thought it did. This is a defensive manoeuvre somewhat like the first
reference to an 'antic disposition':

> How strange or odd some'er I bear myself –
> As I perchance hereafter shall think meet
> To put an antic disposition on.   (I,v,170–2)

Here Hamlet speaks of the future, yet his immediately preceding behaviour was so very antic that one can't help wondering whether he now
offers a half-apology for what has just passed. It looks like a post-dated
insurance policy, one that covers the holder against claims for damage
already done.

In *Hamlet* Shakespeare does not defend heightened speech and improbable action; he merely intimates, again and again, that he *knows* that
what he writes sounds like wild and whirling words, or croaking, prating,
mouthing, ranting, roaring, thunder, passionate speech, horrid speech,
antic or distempered language, tearing a passion to tatters. Doing this he
partly disarms criticism; he takes the 'bombast' out of its sails. In other
tragedies, however, he sometimes adopts a different policy. He does next
to nothing to protect Julius Caesar against the charge of inflated diction;
on the contrary, he draws attention to Caesar's self-delighting orotundity
by making it ebb and flow around repeated ideas and phrases, fixed points
that stand out like rocks surrounded by verbal foam:

> Caesar shall forth. . .
>
>   . . .   .
> Yet Caesar shall go forth. . .
>
>   . . .   .
> And Caesar shall go forth.
>
>   . . .   .
> And tell them that I will not come to-day.
> Cannot, is false; and that I dare not, falser;
> I will not come to-day. Tell them so, Decius.
>
>   . . .   .
> Decius, go tell them Caesar will not come.
>
>   . . .   .
> The cause is in my will: I will not come.
>
> (*Julius Caesar*, II,ii,10–71)

We may take it, I think, that Shakespeare wanted Caesar's language to sound, at times, 'ridiculous' (as Ben Jonson described it). It is also possible that Jonson's response to the language of *Macbeth* was not entirely off the mark. If he really said of 'some bombast speeches of *Macbeth*, which are not to be understood' that 'it was horror', it could be that Jonson reacted as Shakespeare intended. There are certainly speeches in this tragedy 'which are not to be understood', or are not easily understood. The disjointedness of some of the soliloquies suggests a mind under tremendous pressure, a mind that darts hither and thither to escape, like a caged animal, imprisoned as it is in an overwhelming idea.

> If it were done when 'tis done, then 'twere well
> It were done quickly. If th'assassination
> Could trammel up the consequence, and catch
> With his surcease, success; that but this blow
> Might be the be-all and the end-all here –
> But here upon this bank and shoal of time –
> We'd jump the life to come. But in these cases
> We still have judgment here.   (*Macbeth*, I,vii,1–8)

Whether or not we call it bombast, Macbeth's language here bursts upon us without apologies for wild and whirling words, thus giving its strange syntax and imagery maximum impact. I assume that Shakespeare quite deliberately resorted to verbal shock-tactics ('horror', 'not to be understood') because there are other indications of the same technique. For example, Macbeth switches several times within a single speech from and to aside, which is almost bound to bewilder an audience unfamiliar with the play.

> Macbeth. [*Aside*] Glamis, and Thane of Cawdor!
>   The greatest is behind. [*To the others*] Thanks for your pains.
>   [*Aside to Banquo*] Do you not hope your children shall be kings?
>   (I,iii,116–18)

And again:

> Macbeth. [*Aside*] Two truths are told,
>   As happy prologues to the swelling act
>   Of the imperial theme. [*To the others*] I thank you, gentlemen.
>   [*Aside*] This supernatural soliciting
>   Cannot be ill; cannot be good.   (I,iii,127–31)

All the signs suggest that Shakespeare wanted Macbeth's overleaping imagination to astound the audience, and that this is why he abstained from defensive comments on Macbeth's unusual language, even at the risk of inviting ridicule from Ben Jonson.

Of all Shakespeare's tragedies, *Othello* is the one that has stimulated the most intriguing discussions of style in recent times. F. R. Leavis, in a well-known essay that manages to suggest that all the world worships false gods but that at last Moses returns from the mountain with tablets of stone, scrutinised the 'Othello music' and found in it a 'habit of self-approving self-dramatisation', a self-idealisation which serves at times as 'the disguise of an obtuse and brutal egotism'.[8] The critical idiom has changed, but I have little doubt that the 'self-approving' quality of Othello's verse is none other than our old friend 'bombast'.

Leavis's 'Diabolic Intellect' adopts the critical stance of Ben Jonson. Yet there is a reply to Jonson built into *Othello* – for Shakespeare knew what might be said against the Moor's very special language even as he invented it. For example, Iago explains why he wasn't promoted:

> I know my price, I am worth no worse a place.
> But he, as loving his own *pride* and purposes,
> Evades them with a *bombast circumstance*
> Horribly stuffed with epithets of war.   (*Othello*, I,i,11–14: my italics)

Later, Iago describes Othello's style in similar terms:

Mark me with what violence she first loved the Moor, *but for bragging and telling her fantastical lies. To love him still for prating?* – let not thy discreet heart think it. (II,i,219–22)

We have to remember, therefore, that Leavis adopts the point of view of the liar Iago – and for anyone who thinks, as I do, that Leavis's essay offers insights that deserve pondering, this is a disturbing thought. Iago, we have reason to believe, may be an uncomfortable bed-fellow.

The very fact that it is Iago who describes Othello as proud, bombastic, one who brags, prates and tells fantastical lies, must head us away from such a perverse view of the Moor; for even if Iago's genius for misrepresentation remains unknown to the audience in the play's earlier scenes, his animus against Othello is already manifest. Shakespeare, however, complicates our response by allowing Othello to imagine himself as one who *might* boast:

> Let him do his spite.
> My services which I have done the signiory
> Shall out-tongue his complaints. 'Tis yet to know –
> Which, when I know that *boasting* is an honour,
> I shall promulgate – I fetch my life and being
> From men of royal siege; and my demerits
> May speak unbonneted to as proud a fortune
> As this that I have reached.   (I,ii,17–24)

This is something very like boasting, thinly disguised as a modest man's unwillingness to boast: and it's absolutely characteristic of Shakespeare's teasing of the audience in *Othello*.

Othello's language is, in my opinion, more dangerously inflated than that of any other Shakespearian tragic hero. Leavis noted its 'confident and magnificent buoyancy', and he found it 'truly impressive'. We must not forget, though, that from the very beginning there is a quality in the verse that reflects the Moor's love of pride, pomp and circumstance.

> The tyrant custom, most grave senators,
> Hath made the flinty and steel couch of war
> My thrice-driven bed of down. I do agnize
> A natural and prompt alacrity
> I find in hardness; and would undertake
> This present wars against the Ottomites.   (I,iii,229–34)

Is it 'magnificent buoyancy' and 'truly impressive'? I detect, here and there, a straining after magnificence, which must not be confused with true gold. As Dr Johnson said of the language of Gray's odes, 'he has a kind of strutting dignity, and is tall by walking on tip-toes'. There are times when Othello seems to throw out his chest and intone, almost chant: this is not bombast, nor is it simply a 'magnificent buoyancy'. Rather, we have here a unique fusion of the grand style and something else – one that captures the moment when ripeness approaches overripeness. I would not care to call it 'an obtuse and brutal egotism', but, on the other hand, it affects me as more complicated than straight 'nobility'.

My last example is *King Lear* – the Shakespearian tragedy with more scenes of madness and approaching madness than any other, and therefore one where high writ poesy might easily have degenerated into fustian. Here, however, the tragic hero is safe from criticism precisely because he is thought to be mad (it's a simple strategy, adopted by many lecturers). What is interesting in *King Lear* is that there is so little direct comment on Lear's 'high' language, as distinct from his merely disconnected language – that is, so few signs that Shakespeare felt that he would be accused of writing bombastic 'horror' in Lear's most impassioned speeches.

The direct and indirect comments on Lear's language fall into three groups. First, admissions of madness, hints to the audience that his thinking must be unscrambled in special ways: 'Bless thy five wits!', 'O matter and impertinency mixed! / Reason in madness!' (III,vi,56;

IV,vi,176). Second, references to Lear's rage, some of them oblique, which can also serve as excuses for disconnected speech:

> Gloucester.   My dear lord,
> You know the fiery quality of the Duke;
> How unremovable and fixed he is
> In his own course.
> Lear.   Vengeance! plague! death! confusion!
> Fiery? What quality? Why Gloucester, Gloucester,
> . . .   .
> Fiery? the fiery Duke? Tell the hot Duke that – . . .
>
>   (II,iv,89ff.)

Here, of course, Shakespeare swivels round to the fiery quality of the *king*, which immediately blazes forth in the semi-incoherence of 'Vengeance! plague!', etc. Third, references to the language of the storm:

> Blow, winds, and crack your cheeks; rage, blow.
> You cataracts and hurricanoes, spout
> Till you have drenched our steeples, drowned the cocks.
> . . .   .
> Rumble thy bellyful. Spit, fire; spout, rain.   (III,ii,1ff.)

On the stage an old man pits himself against the elements, and his voice competes with winds and hurricanoes; the storm blows and spouts, and, the play comes close to suggesting, the old man blows and spouts as well. But the suggestion lurks below the verbal surface, and could scarcely be called a bombastic dramatist's defensive manoeuvre.

Apart from reflections on Lear's own language, the play also includes its share of passing remarks about style: it mentions plain speaking (e.g. I,i,128), blunt speaking (II,ii,91), glib and oily speaking (I,i,224), railing (II,ii,23). Such passages no doubt sharpened the audience's awareness of style; and the two voices of Edgar–Poor Tom, and of Kent–Caius, must have had the same effect. Nevertheless, Shakespeare did not choose to gloss Lear's own speeches, beyond describing them as dotage, and later as madness. The fact that Lear's 'high' language requires so little apology, in the scenes in which he is enraged but not yet mad, proves, I think, that Shakespeare felt confident that verbal extravagance would not be misunderstood.

Now I return for a moment to the 'social-historical context'. *Hamlet* and *King Lear*, two tragedies in which scenes of madness and near-madness abound, differ significantly in so far as one contains many authorial asides about inflated language, whereas the other has scarcely any. How are we to account for this? We might say that *Hamlet* was written in 1600 or 1601, at the time of the War of the Theatres – very much a contemporary of Jonson's *Poetaster*, a satire in which John Marston is made to vomit some of the grotesque words and phrases in his plays that offended Jonson's delicate ear. Shakespeare, like Marston, opposed Jonson in the War of the Theatres; inflated language was a sensitive issue – so the special social-historical context made bombastic Shakespeare cautious.

But is that the only possible answer? Or could it be that Shakespeare had, quite simply, educated the theatre-going public in the five or six years that lie between *Hamlet* and *King Lear*, had trained it to accept his language on his own terms – in short, had become a classic (a writer who could take whatever liberties he chose, like Beckett today)? Or should we look for the answer in the conventions of revenge tragedy? Or, perhaps, in the character of the tragic hero – arguing that there is a connection between the critical self-awareness of Hamlet and of his creator in the act of writing the play? Here, already, we have four different ways of looking at the social-historical context – and I haven't even mentioned the Elizabethan World Picture, or the rise of capitalism, or Jacobean pessimism, or any of the weasels, camels and whales so dear to the 'historical' mind. I conclude that the social-historical context, important as it undeniably is, must remain a grey area, behind the text – too multifarious to be truly knowable, an interesting chaos, where literary critics can only grope blindly; and that, if we wish to make use of it to explain literary texts, we must do so with great caution, without putting too much faith in one-eyed historians. The text has immediacy and reality, it is accessible; we can experience *Hamlet* as immediately as the odour of a rose. The social-historical context, as distinct from second-hand generalisations concerning it, is largely inaccessible; we may *know about* it, or about small fragments of it, but we cannot truly *know* it. The coincidence that some of Shakespeare's contemporaries ridiculed his 'bombast', and that he is defensive about 'high' language in *Hamlet*, only helps a little, if at all, to explain the styles of the play: the true explanation will come from the text, not from the context.

And now for my second conclusion – which is that, if the text is all-important, Shakespeare's 'high style' surely deserves more study than it has so far received. It was not one style, but many; and it could yet become as rich a seam for criticism as Shakespeare's imagery. It was not just a crude wind-instrument, 'terms steeped in *Aqua fortis* and gunpowder' that rattle through the skies and make earthquakes in peasants'

ears.[9] Shakespeare, as much as any writer of his age, knew the difference
between language that is 'blown up' and 'russet yeas and honest kersey
noes'. He knew what his detractors would want to say about his high writ
poesy, and we can observe, in the Tragedies, how he protected himself,
when he thought it necessary. I have indicated that he chose different
strategies in different plays. But I have neglected a more difficult task – an
examination of the various kinds of high style; of the blending of one style
with another; of the effects of inflation on the audience. These are the
really difficult questions; and difficult questions, I think, are best left for
others.

NOTES

1 This paper was read at the Tenth Triennial Congress of the International Association of University Professors of English, in Poznan, Poland, in August 1977. I have
   revised it very slightly for publication. For the quotations see E. K. Chambers,
   William Shakespeare, 2 vols. (Oxford, 1930), vol. II, p. 188; Dryden, *The Dramatic
   Poetry of the Last Age* (1672), and *The Grounds of Criticism in Tragedy* (1679);
   Hamlet, v,i,274ff.; *Othello*, I,i,12ff. I have modernised all quotations.
2 See Chambers, *William Shakespeare*, vol. II, pp. 194–5.
3 *Ibid.* vol. II, pp. 188ff.
4 For Jonson's views see *ibid.* vol. II, pp. 202ff.
5 *Ben Jonson*, ed. C. H. Herford and P. and E. Simpson, 11 vols. (Oxford, 1925–52),
   vol. VIII (1947), p. 587.
6 See Chambers, *William Shakespeare*, vol. II, p. 218; *As You Like It*, III,iii,9.
7 *Hamlet*, I,v,133; II,ii,555–6; III,iv,51–2; V,i,277–8.
8 F. R. Leavis, 'Diabolic Intellect and the Noble Hero', in *Scrutiny*, 6 (1937),
   reprinted in *The Common Pursuit* (London, 1952).
9 See Gabriel Harvey's *Four Letters and Certain Sonnets* (1592).

The defence of paradox

GEOFFREY BULLOUGH

I

Shakespeare used the word 'paradox' several times, usually to mean 'witty absurdity'. Thus Ulysses in *Troilus and Cressida* describes Achilles and Patroclus mocking at the Greek leaders:

> All our abilities, gifts, natures, shapes,
> . . .   .
> Success or loss, what is or is not, serves
> As stuff for these two to make paradoxes.   (I,iii,179–84)

Hamlet to Ophelia says bitterly:

the power of beauty will sooner transform honesty from what it is to a bawd than the force of honesty can translate beauty into his likeness. This was sometime a paradox, but now the time gives it proof. (III,i,111–15)

In a passage to be quoted below the word is used by the King in *Love's Labour's Lost* when dismissing as absurd Berowne's claim that only a dark beauty is 'fair'.

As a term in rhetoric 'paradox' was used of propositions which were opposed to popular belief, often because they were manifestly absurd or self-contradictory, sometimes because they contained much truth, or could be made to appear true by manipulating logic.[1] The attempt to defend a paradox could involve much wit and eloquence in plays and poems (especially metaphysical poems) of the Elizabethan period. Paradoxical themes and situations often occurred in drama and narrative prose. A popular offshoot since classical times was the paradoxical encomium in which a person or subject not usually regarded as praiseworthy was praised for comic or ironic effect; such as Isocrates's praise of Helen of Troy, Lucian's of the fly and parasites, C. Agrippa's, and Daniel

Heinsius's praise of the ass, Erasmus's *Praise of Folly*, Harington's *Metamorphosis of Ajax*.

This essay will be concerned not so much with paradox as a rhetorical figure as with the paradoxical encomium (and its reverse) and the use of paradoxical situations and characters in some of Shakespeare's plays. I omit the poems since they demand separate treatment.

II

From the first Shakespeare seems to have regarded comedy as involving characters in unusual situations. So in *The Comedy of Errors* two pairs of twins, long separated, are brought together in Ephesus in a manner producing many misunderstandings, until they begin to fear that they have been transformed by magic in a city of witches and are in danger of losing their identities.

In *The Taming of the Shrew* the drunken tinker Sly is transported by a practical joker into an aristocratic setting and for a time acts as if he were noble. In the play proper Katherine is a paradoxical character, self-contradictory in that despite her shrewish behaviour she is really waiting for a resolute mate (himself made up of contradictory qualities) to become the ideal subservient wife, whereas her sister, the modest Bianca, is transformed by marriage into the conventional wife of the fabliaux, wilful and disobedient.

Love's Labour's Lost starts from a paradoxical situation – the oaths taken by the King of Navarre and his nobles, to 'war against your own affections / And the huge army of the world's desires', swearing for three years 'Not to see ladies, study, fast, not sleep' (I,i,9–10, 48). The underlying paradox that the love of books is more noble than the love of women is at once shown to be folly by Berowne: 'Light, seeking light, doth light of light beguile', etc., until the King exclaims, 'How well he's read, to reason against reading!' (I,i,77, 94).

The commoners in the King's entourage, who have sworn similarly, affect rhetorical terminology and forms, so it is natural for Don Armado, 'a man of fire-new words, fashion's own knight', when he falls in love, to discuss the breaking of his oath in paradoxical debate with himself:

Love is a familiar: Love is a devil. There is no evil angel but Love. Yet was Samson so tempted, and he had an excellent strength; yet was Solomon so seduced, and he had a very good wit . . . Adieu, valour; rust, rapier; be still, drum; for your manager is in love; yea, he loveth. (I,ii, 164ff.)

At the end of Act III Berowne has to face the inconsistency of his own behaviour in breaking his oath:

> And I forsooth, in love; I, that have been love's whip;
>
> · · ·   · · ·   · · ·   · · ·   · · ·
>
> And I to be a corporal of his field,
> And wear his colours like a tumbler's hoop!
>
> · · ·   · · ·   · · ·   · · ·   · · ·
>
> Go to; it is a plague
> That Cupid will impose for my neglect
> Of his almighty dreadful little might.   (III,i,164-93)

Soon Berowne watches the others forswearing themselves, and hears Longaville arguing paradoxically that to break his vow for Maria's sake is not perjury:

> A woman I forswore, but I will prove,
> Thou being a goddess, I forswore not thee;
> My vow was earthly, thou a heavenly love;
> Thy grace being gained cures all disgrace in me.   (IV,iii,60-3)

When Berowne himself admits to the King his apostasy he expatiates on the charms of his Dark Lady in terms like those used by Shakespeare in some of his Sonnets.

> *King.*   By heaven, thy love is black as ebony.
> *Berowne.* Is ebony like her? O wood divine!
>   A wife of such wood were felicity.
>   O, who can give an oath? Where is a book?
>   That I may swear beauty doth beauty lack,
>   If that she learn not of her eye to look.
>   No face is fair that is not full so black.
> *King.*   O paradox! Black is the badge of hell,
>   The hue of dungeons, and the school of night;
>   And beauty's crest becomes the heavens well.
>
>   · · ·   · · ·   · · ·   · · ·   · · ·
>
> *Berowne.* O, if in black my lady's brows be deckt,
>   It mourns that painting and usurping hair
>   Should ravish doters with a false aspect;
>   And therefore is she born to make black fair.   (IV,iii,243-57)

His friends mock at his choice with witty abuse.

> *Dumaine.*   To look like her are chimney-sweepers black.
> *Longaville.* And since her time are colliers counted bright.
>
>   · · ·   · · ·   · · ·   · · ·   · · ·
>
> *Berowne.*   I'll prove her fair, or talk till doomsday here.   (ll. 262-70)

The King ends the badinage with a challenge –

> Then leave this chat, and good Berowne, now prove
> Our loving lawful, and our faith not torn –   (ll. 280–1)

and Berowne takes it up:

> Have at you then, affection's men-at-arms.   (l. 286)

And he embarks on a paradoxical rhapsody in support of the proposition
that the proper study of mankind is Woman, and particularly ladies' eyes:

> *They are the ground, the books, the academes,*
> *From whence doth spring the true Promethean fire*   (ll. 299–300)

Recalling his remarks in the first scene of the play but in a mood of intense
lyricism and lofty idealism he utters a splendid panegyric on love as the
great vitalising principle within the human spirit, which

> gives to every power a double power,
> Above their functions and their offices.   (ll. 327–8)

Inspired by this oration the King calls them to arms:

> Saint Cupid, then! and, soldiers, to the field!   (l. 362)

They will go to war against the French princess and her ladies. But it
must be confessed that the ladies have the better of the campaign.

III

The elevation of paradox to such a high level is not typical of all the
Comedies, but the introduction of 'proofs' based on analogy and false
logic occurs in several plays, sometimes in passages of somewhat elemen-
tary wit. A few samples may be cited.

In the first scene of *The Two Gentlemen of Verona*, after Valentine has
gone to embark for Milan, the Clown Speed and Proteus keep up a
barrage of puns, quips and absurd analogies about Valentine as shepherd
and Speed as sheep.

Speed.   Nay, that I can deny by a circumstance.
Proteus. It shall go hard but I'll prove it by another.
Speed.   The shepherd seeks the sheep, and not the sheep the shepherd; but I seek my
           master, and my master seeks not me; therefore I am no sheep.
Proteus. The sheep for fodder follow the shepherd; the shepherd for food follows not the

sheep; thou for wages followest thy master; thy master for wages follows not
thee; therefore thou art a sheep.

Speed. Such another proof will make me cry 'baa'.

The spate of sheep images continues with Speed's calling himself 'a lost
mutton' and Julia 'a laced mutton' (female).

> *Proteus.* Here's too small a pasture for such store of muttons. (i,i,73–98)

This trivial jesting is of no importance in the play. Rather more significant, as reproving Olivia's inordinate grief, is this short passage of
question and answer between the lady and her clown Feste in *Twelfth
Night*.

Feste. Good madonna, give me leave to prove you a fool.
Olivia. Can you do it?
Feste. Dexteriously, good madonna.
Olivia. Make your proof.
Feste. I must catechize you for it, madonna. Good my mouse of virtue, answer me.
Olivia. Well, sir, for want of other idleness, I'll bide your proof.
Feste. Good madonna, why mourn'st thou?
Olivia. Good fool, for my brother's death.
Feste. I think his soul is in hell, madonna.
Olivia. I know his soul is in heaven, fool.
Feste. The more fool, madonna, to mourn for your brother's soul being in heaven. Take
away the fool, gentlemen.   (i,v,53–67)

One may include the famous set speech of Jaques in *As You Like It*
(II,vii,) as an example of proof by analysis of a paradoxical postulate.
Jaques is a libertine turned melancholy moralist, who wants to be a
licensed fool with 'liberty / Withal',

> as large a charter as the wind
> To blow on whom I please, for so fools have;
> And they that are most galled with my folly,
> They most must laugh.   (ll. 48–50)

At a time when in England satire was under ban by the government and
bishops for its scurrility and abuse of persons, Jaques intends to 'Cleanse
the foul body of th' infected world', but will not 'tax any private party' (ll.
47–71).

When the banished Duke expresses sorrow for the unhappy plight of
Orlando and old Adam, using the image of 'this wide and universal
theatre', Jaques takes it up, and, with little sympathy for human suffering
but a gently satiric eye on the oddities of life, makes his oration, 'All the
world's a stage',[2] a sample of his method which provides excellent

thumbnail sketches of the Seven Ages, but deprives men and women of any real dignity, for they are 'merely players' (ll. 139–66). Later, Touch-stone's mock encomium on the horn (symbol of cuckoldry) gives a jester's view of marriage:

Many a man has good horns and knows no end of them. Well, that is the dowry of his wife; 'tis none of his own getting. Horns? Even so. Poor men alone? No, no; the noblest deer hath them as huge as the rascal. (III,iii,42–54)

This was a favourite topic at the time.[3] Especially in the Comedies written after 1595 there is much highly developed discussion of ideas or manners through passages devoted to the defence or disproof of paradox. An excellent example is Shylock's defence of usury in *The Merchant of Venice* (I,iii). The play was written at a time when the taking of interest was under attack by churchmen before (after being condemned since 1571) it was made legal by Parliament in 1597.[4]

When Antonio comes to borrow three thousand ducats 'for three months', he of course expects that the Jew will charge his usual rates. Shylock defends the taking of 'advantage' by historical precedent, telling the story in Genesis 30 of Jacob's use of an alleged natural phenomenon to get the maximum number of 'eanlings [lambs] which were streaked and pied' from the new season's crop:

> *Shylock.* And when the work of generation was
> Between these woolly breeders in the act,
> The skilful shepherd pilled me certain wands,
> And in the doing of the deed of kind,
> He stuck them up before the fulsome ewes,
> Who, then conceiving, did in eaning time
> Fall parti-coloured lambs, and these were Jacob's.
> This was a way to thrive, and he was blest;
> And thrift is blessing, if men steal it not.
> *Antonio.* This was a venture, sir, that Jacob served for;
> A thing not in his power to bring to pass,
> But swayed and fashioned by the hand of heaven.
> Was this inserted to make interest good?
> Or is your gold and silver ewes and rams?
> *Shylock.* I cannot tell; I make it breed as fast.   (I,iii,77–91)

Antonio does not accept Shylock's illustration or his analogy between living animals and 'barren metal'.[5] 'The devil can cite Scripture for his purpose', he comments, but he is moved by Shylock's ingratiating offer to lend the money without interest, and enters into the 'merry bond' despite Bassanio's mistrust.

Bassanio himself, faced with the need to choose one of the three
caskets, takes a hint from the charming song, sung *'whilst Bassanio
comments on the caskets to himself'* ('Tell me where is fancy bred'), and
utters a soliloquy on the paradox that 'outward shows' may be 'least
themselves' or 'plainness' is better than 'eloquence' (III,ii,73–107) before
choosing the leaden casket. He illustrates the topic from law, religion,
morality, warfare, and physical beauty, all of which instances prove

> Thus ornament is but the guilèd shore
> To a most dangerous sea . . .
> . . .   .
> The seeming truth which cunning times put on
> To entrap the wisest.   (ll. 97–101)

Moreover, Portia's short speech on mercy in the court scene is on the
theme 'that mercy should season justice', and is more important than
mere legality – a topic which recurs in *Measure for Measure,* and which
must have seemed to others in the court besides Shylock an absurd
paradox. Portia has to concede that the Jew has law on his side, but she
saves Antonio's life by the distinction between 'flesh' and 'blood', backed
up by a Venetian law against an alien who should 'seek the life of any
citizen' (IV,i,346). After which some mercy is extended to Shylock,
though he does not appreciate it.

IV

In the English Histories, apart from rhetorical expression, paradoxical
elements in plot and character are often due to the nature of the historical
material found in Hall or Holinshed. Richard III, though single-minded
in his cruel lust for power, has a wicked humour and an ability to turn
everything to his own advantage which owes much to the portrait of him
in Sir Thomas More's *Life.* In the first scene of *Richard III* he has had
Clarence sent to the Tower while pretending earnest sympathy:

> Simple, plain Clarence, I do love thee so
> That I will shortly send thy soul to heaven,
> If heaven will take the present at our hands.   (I,i,118–20)

In the second scene Shakespeare demonstrates another side of Gloucester in the (invented) interview over the coffin of Henry VI in which he
woos Lady Anne, the widow of the murdered Prince Edward, and turns

her deadly hatred to wonder and acceptance of his professed remorse – surely one of the most extraordinary scenes in Shakespeare.

When first Richard interrupts the funeral procession she curses him as a 'dreadful minister of hell', whose presence makes the dead king's wounds 'bleed afresh'. He desires Christian charity of her, denies that he killed her husband, and ascribes his murder of Henry VI to love of her. His insistent iteration of this absurd claim in all smooth reasonableness calms her, and after she has failed to kill him with his own sword he persuades her to accept a ring. He is left on stage to gloat:

> Was ever woman in this humour wooed?
> Was ever woman in this humour won?
> I'll have her; but I will not keep her long. (I,ii,227–9)

Richard's hypocrisy and ability to create and dominate improbable situations are important features of his character. They underlie the (historical) scene (III,vii) in the gallery at Baynard's Castle in which, appearing between two bishops, he plays humble reluctance to be made king.

The murder of Clarence is not without a trace of sick humour when the Second Murderer is afflicted with a sudden attack of conscience. Fear of Gloucester and thought of the reward remedy this qualm:

1st Murderer. Where's thy conscience now?
2nd Murderer. In the Duke of Gloucester's purse!
1st Murderer. So when he opens his purse to give us our reward, thy conscience flies out.
2nd Murderer. 'Tis no matter; let it go; there's few or none will entertain it.
1st Murderer. What if it come to thee again? (I,iv,126–32)

At this the Second Murderer enters into a diatribe against Conscience as a pitiful sort of devil tempting them not to proceed:

I'll not meddle with it – it makes a man a coward: a man cannot steal, but it accuseth him; a man cannot swear, but it checks him; a man cannot lie with his neighbour's wife, but it detects him. 'Tis a blushing shamefaced spirit. . . It is turned out of towns and cities for a dangerous thing; and every man that means to live well, endeavours to trust to himself and live without it. (ll. 133–42)

Now the First Murderer begins to hesitate, and is urged:

Take the devil in thy mind, and believe him not: he would insinuate with thee but to make thee sigh. (ll. 144–6)

They kill Clarence coldly and callously, mocking at his trust in his brother Gloucester's affection. Yet now again the Second Murderer feels remorse. He refuses his fee, but his partner will take his reward and go far away.

Richard II presents many contrasts between appearance and reality, people's pretensions and their true natures; in particular it deals with questions of the King's claim to divine right, and the right of subjects to rebel. When the Duchess of Lancaster blames her husband for not avenging the murder of Thomas of Woodstock, Gaunt explains that the King was responsible, but 'I may never lift / An angry arm against His minister' (I,ii,40–1). The paradox of Richard II's nature consists in the contrast between his lofty claims and the weakness of his character:

> Not all the water in the rough rude sea.
> Can wash the balm off from an anointed King;
> The breath of worldly men cannot depose
> The deputy elected by the Lord.   (III,ii,54–7)

He puts his trust in heaven:

> Then, if angels fight,
> Weak men must fall; for heaven still guards the right.   (ll. 61–2)

When he hears that his Welsh allies have dispersed, his weak vaunts collapse into a premature acceptance of defeat:

> Say, is my kindom lost? Why, 'twas my care;
> And what loss is it to be rid of care?   (III,ii,95–6)

The idea recurs in the deposition scene. Henceforth Richard is continually aware of the contrast between his title as King and what he becomes owing to Bolingbroke's triumph, alternating between reiteration of his god-given rights ('no hand of blood and bone / Can gripe the sacred handle of our sceptre, / Unless he do profane, steal, or usurp', III,iii,79–81), and acceptance of his loss of title and name. In the deposition scene (IV,i) he sees himself as like Christ betrayed by Judas (IV,i,167ff.). Surrendering his crown, sceptre, holy oil, lands, decrees, and 'all duteous oaths', he acknowledges that he is now

> no man's lord; I have no name, no title,
> No, not that name was given me at the font,
> But 'tis usurped.
>   . . .   .
> [I] know not now what name to call myself.   (ll. 255–9)

Thus he plays on the notion of lost identity; and after he has called for,

and shattered, the mirror 'where all my sins are writ', he embarks on
another rhetorical flourish on the difference between shadows and substance. His mood shifts between abject humility and acid comments on
the traitors round him as he explores the paradoxes of his situation and
moods.

Confined in Pomfret Castle Richard peoples his cell with thoughts:

> Thus play I in one person many people,
> And none contented. . .
>
> . . .   .
>   and by and by   .
> Think that I am unkinged by Bolingbroke,
> And straight am nothing. But whate'er I be,
> Nor I, nor any man that but man is,
> With nothing shall be pleased, till he be eased
> With being nothing.   (V,V,31–41)

The play includes some discussion of the woes of exile before Hereford
leaves the country in Act I, scene iii. This introduces the classical stoic
paradox when Gaunt tries to console him:

> Thy grief is but thy absence for a time.   (l. 258)

> Call it a travel that thou tak'st for pleasure.   (l. 262)

> The sullen passage of thy weary steps
> Esteem as foil wherein thou art to set
> The precious jewel of thy home return.   (ll.265–7)

In more general terms:

> All places that the eye of heaven visits
> Are to a wise man ports and happy havens.   (ll. 275–6)

Hereford however cannot accept the situation:

> O, who can hold a fire in his hand
> By thinking on the frosty Caucasus?   (ll. 294–5)

Heart-stricken, old Gaunt soon dies, but not before he has eloquently
exposed the evils of Richard's reign in the great speech, 'This royal
throne of Kings. . .' (II,i,40–68). He trounces the King who gloats over
his illness:

> Now, He that made me knows I see thee ill;
> Ill in myself to see, and in thee seeing ill.
> Thy death-bed is no lesser than thy land
> Wherein thou liest in reputation sick;
>
> . . .   .
> Landlord of England art thou now, not King!   (II,i,93–113)

The defence of paradox

The word-play helps to indicate the self-contradictions in the King's nature which bring about his ruin.

As has often been shown, in *1 Henry IV* there are paradoxes on both sides of the conflict. The King's first words, 'So shaken as we are, so wan with care', prove that he has little joy in his accession, for in taking the throne he has taken over the royal anxieties, and is alienated from his heir and many of his nobles. On the other side Henry Percy is paradoxical indeed – endowed with a passion for glory which wins the admiration of his foes, yet rash, quick to take offence, and resentful of wise counsel.[6] Envious of the new king's authority and accusing him of ingratitude he rebukes his father and uncle for using their 'nobility and power / ...To put down Richard, that sweet lovely rose, / And plant this thorn, this canker, Bolingbroke' (I,iii,172–6). Hot for rebellion he makes hyperbolical speeches which embody his craving for honour at all costs:

> Send danger from the east unto the west,
> So honour cross it from the north to south,
> And let them grapple. O, the blood more stirs
> To rouse a lion than to start a hare!
>
> *Northumberland.* Imagination of some great exploit
> Drives him beyond the bounds of patience.
>
> *Hotspur.* By heaven, methinks it were an easy leap
> To pluck bright honour from the pale-faced moon;
> Or dive into the bottom of the deep,
> Where fathom-line could never touch the ground,
> And pluck up drownèd honour by the locks;
> So he that doth redeem her thence might wear
> Without corrival all her dignities. (I,iii, 195–207)

His uncle Worcester rightly accuses Hotspur of forgetting sense in rhetoric:

> He apprehends a world of figures here,
> But not the form of what he should attend. (ll. 209–10)

and his father calls him a 'wasp-stung and impatient fool'.

Percy despises the plebeian conduct of 'that same sword-and-buckler Prince of Wales', whom he would not be sorry to see 'poisoned with a pot of ale'. His wife and he are on familiar terms but he treats her love with scant respect: 'this is no world / To play with mammets and to tilt with lips' (II,iii,88–9). 'You are altogether governed by humours', she says (III,i,234). Hotspur, however, has too much sense to be taken in by Owen Glendower's paradoxical boasts and magical pretensions:

> *Glendower.* I can call spirits from the vasty deep.
> *Hotspur.*   Why, so can I, or so can any man;
>   But will they come when you do call for them?   (III,i,53–5)

The Welshman's dreams and prophecies are to him just 'skimble-skamble stuff' (III,i,154). They bring out the worst in each other, until Hotspur behaves with 'Defect of manners, want of government', for which Worcester reproves him (ll. 177ff.).

When Northumberland and Glendower fail to bring their forces to battle Hotspur is not daunted. The defection

> lends a lustre and more great opinion,
> A larger dare to our great enterprise.
> . . .   .
> Doomsday is near; die all, die merrily.   (IV,i,77–8, 134)

The paradoxes in the Prince's character are implied in the first scene in which he appears (I,ii), when, after the King has wished that he could exchange Henry Percy, a son 'who is the theme of honour's tongue', with his own Henry, whose brow is stained by 'riot and dishonour' (I,i,80–90), we see Hal's rapscallion friends plotting to rob the travellers at Gadshill. After some demur the Prince agrees to take part but he knows that such conduct is unworthy of a prince, and in a famous soliloquy, 'I know you all, and will a while uphold / The unyok'd humour of your idleness', he announces that he will sooner or later show himself as he really is:

> So, when this loose behaviour I throw off
> And pay the debt I never promisèd,
> By how much better than my word I am,
> By so much shall I falsify men's hopes;
> . . .   .
> I'll so offend to make offence a skill,
> Redeeming time when men think least I will.
> (I,ii,188–91, 209–10)

Somewhat disingenuously he treats his present 'loose behaviour' as a 'holiday' from responsibility; but he admits that to others it must seem habitual misconduct. So much the more praiseworthy he will appear when he turns over a new leaf. Critics who accuse Hal of cold opportunism ignore that the speech is not so much a programme for the future as a biographical summary of what actually happened. The Prince knows that some time he must 'put away childish things'; meanwhile he will enjoy to the full his wild companions, including Falstaff, without taking thought for the morrow.

The paradox in his nature is thus only temporary, and the turning-point arrives in Act III, scene ii, when Hal is rebuked by his father for 'inordinate and low desires. . .barren pleasures, rude society', behaviour which makes him more like Richard II than like Bolingbroke:

> For all the world,
> As thou art to this hour was Richard then
>
> . . .   .
>
> And even as I was then is Percy now.   (III,ii,93–6)

Promising amendment, the Prince vows

> I will redeem all this on Percy's head,
> And in the closing of some glorious day
> Be bold to tell you that I am your son.   (ll. 132–4)

After this Hal can still jest with Falstaff but he does not respond to the latter's 'Rob me the Exchequer the first thing thou dost!', but gets down at once to the business of war. He is no longer the 'nimble-footed madcap Prince. . .that daffed the world aside', but the chivalric warrior whom Vernon so finely describes (IV,i,97–110), who admires Hotspur and wishes to challenge him to single combat (V,i). Paradox is resolved, and Hal becomes the epitome of knightly honour.

The paradox of immense energy, amiable humour and verbal resource combined with complete, unblushing self-interest is the clue to Falstaff's character, with its entire lack of any sense of duty to king, country or friends. He looks forward to Hal's reign as a lawless time when highwaymen will be called 'men of good government' and there will be no gallows in England. The practical joke in which the Prince joins on Gadshill proves not only Falstaff's cowardice but also the extraordinary adroitness of the old rogue in seeking to avoid the 'open and apparent shame' of exposure (II,iv). He does not take the imminent rebellion seriously, and his mimicking of the King proves that he knows that the Prince is defiled by the company he keeps, but he cares nothing so long as he can keep his hold on Hal. The latter's jesting banishment of the 'villainous abominable misleader of youth' foreshadows the end of their relationship. Meanwhile the Prince and we enjoy the fat man's abundant wit and eloquence which cannot hide the fact that 'there is no room for faith, truth, or honesty in his bosom' (III,iii,54–5). Yet when he is given a charge of foot we can smile at his confession, 'I have misused the King's press damnably', his picture of a company so wretched that he is ashamed to march through Coventry with them, and his cynical dismissal of them as 'food for powder – they'll fill a pit as well as a better; tush, man, mortal men' (IV,ii).

Falstaff's celebrated soliloquy before the Battle of Shrewsbury, set out largely as a debate with himself, is a reply to the praise of honour expressed by Hotspur and now embodied in the Prince (v,i,127–40). He plays round ideas of wounding and death with no thought for the meaning of honour as merited fame and respect. The perpetual jester makes puns and witticisms even as he shrinks from pain and danger. Honour is useless to the dead and ephemeral to the living. He dismisses it as a mere word, at most empty heraldry.[7]

Shakespeare has brought his braggart knight to frank self-revelation as a cynical materialist. It remains to reveal his cowardice in battle. He announces his intention of avoiding Percy if possible, and of saving his own skin: 'I like not such grinning honour as Sir Walter [Blunt] hath: give me life, which if I can save, so; if not, honour comes unlooked for, and there's an end' (v,iii,57–8).

2 Henry IV repeats the pattern of its predecessor, without the passionate ardour of Hotspur or an adventure like that on Gadshill. The parallel to Falstaff's dispraise of honour comes in Act IV, scene iii after Prince John has rebuked him for coming 'when everything is ended'. Falstaff calls Prince John a 'young sober-blooded boy. . .nor a man cannot make him laugh but that is no marvel; he drinks no wine'. This leads on into a eulogy of 'your excellent sherris' and its effects on various organs and faculties (IV,iii,89–122).[8] The speech is in a tradition going back to Michael Psellus; it is excellent fooling, but has no relation to the plot.

The scene between Henry IV and Hal after the latter has taken the crown repeats the reconciliation theme of *1 Henry IV*, and finally brings into unity the two sides of the Prince as madcap and future monarch. In Act V, scene v, when he banishes Falstaff and his crew, the monarch is supreme, but that he is a man like other men is shown in *Henry V* when the King before Agincourt debates with Bates and Williams whether the deaths of soldiers in his battles should weigh upon his conscience: 'Every subject's duty is the King's; but every subject's soul is his own' (IV,i,100–225).

V

Lack of space necessitates my dealing here only with three later comedies: *All's Well That Ends Well, Measure for Measure,* and *The Tempest,* all of which contain more or less formal speeches in support or denial of paradoxes. *All's Well* certainly contains paradoxes of character and situation – Helena disproves the conventional belief that a woman must suffer in silence, by following her reluctant husband to Florence and there trapping him sexually into getting her with child, thus fulfilling a folk-tale 'impossibility'. She also embodies the well-known paradox that true nobility depends not on noble birth and breeding but on virtue of character and conduct. On the other hand Bertram, though of high rank, is unworthy of his parentage and not only cannot perceive Helena's worth but is misled by the cowardly sham, Parolles, and wishes to seduce a virtuous Florentine maiden.

Helena's intelligence and resolution appear in Act I, scene i.

> Our remedies oft in ourselves do lie,
> Which we ascribe to heaven. The fated sky
> Gives us free scope...
>
> . . . .
>
> The King's disease – my project may deceive me,
> But my intents are fixed and will not leave me. (I,i,202–15)

The King asserts the central moral theme of the play when he defends the traditional paradox that true nobility consists not in birth but in goodness.[9] Rebuking Bertram for refusing to wed a poor physician's daughter, he says:

> 'Tis only title thou disdain'st in her, the which
> I can build up.
>
> . . . .
>
> From lowest place when virtuous things proceed,
> The place is dignified by th' doer's deed;
> Where great additions swell's, and virtue none,
> It is a dropsied honour. Good alone
> Is good without a name. Vileness is so.
> The property by what it is should go,
> Not by the title.[10] (II,iii,115ff.)

Bertram's adolescent weakness is shown also in his friendship with that hollow man Parolles – 'all words' as his name implies, a foppish boaster who encourages his master's desire for martial glory. Helena knows that Parolles is 'a notorious liar, great way fool, solely a coward'. His pretensions are soon seen through by Lafeu, and by the French lords whose trick upon him exposes his cowardice and treachery.

Parolles displays some wit in his comic dispraise of virginity to Helena, in which he apes the paradoxes of the fashionable courtier to some effect.

Virginity cannot be preserved against its enemy, man, he declares, using the analogy of sieges and mines to prove it. 'It is not politic in the commonwealth of nature to preserve virginity. Loss of virginity is rational increase; and there was never virgin got till virginity was first lost' (I,i,119–21). He argues that the sooner it is lost the better; and he likens 'your old virginity' to a withered pear (I,i,151). Helena takes this lightly, but she fears that at court ('a learning-place') Bertram will encounter many temptations.

On a lower social level the Clown in Act I, scene iii carries on Parolles's paradoxical strain in his praise of cuckoldry. 'He that comforts my wife is the cherisher of my flesh and blood'; so 'he that kisses my wife is my friend' (ll. 40ff.). His little song implies praise of Helena, but he ends with a fling at women in general. 'An we might have a good woman born before every blazing star, or at an earthquake, 'twould mend the lottery well: a man may draw his heart out ere 'a pluck one' (ll. 83ff.).

The Clown lets drop a remark pertinent to Parolles's condition when he wishes that 'men could be contented to be what they are' (as he is). This is the drab lesson Parolles must learn, to abandon pretence:

> Captain I'll be no more;
>
> . . .   .
> Simply the thing I am
> Shall make me live.
>
> . . .   .
> Safest in shame. Being fooled, by foolery thrive!
> There's place and means for every man alive.   (IV,iii,308–16)

He is glad to receive charity from his enemy Lafeu.

Measure for Measure is a play full of paradoxes. There is the extraordinary situation of a young woman about to take conventual vows who finds herself obliged to plead for the life of her brother, condemned to death for a sexual misdemeanour. The magistrate, inflamed with lust, offers to let her brother live if she will surrender to him, then orders the execution of the young man. By a trick reminiscent of Helena's in *All's Well* the virgin avoids violation, and justice is finally invoked on the unjust judge.

In addition there is the paradoxical nature of Angelo, a sincere, austere puritan whose extreme love of legality and morality turns to passion, deceit, tyrannic threats and attempted murder. The virginal Isabella with her zeal for justice must also learn the importance of mercy.[11]

Apart from other paradoxical dialogue between the main figures, the play contains three passages concerned with the theme of preparation for death.

In Act III, scene i the Duke, disguised as a Friar, advises the condemned Claudio to be 'absolute' (fully prepared) for death, and offers him consolation which owes more to pagan stoic and epicurean thought than to Christian hope of immortality, e.g. to Lucretius, Seneca, and Cicero's *Tusculan Disputation* 'On the Contempt of Death' (in which he tells his interlocutor not to 'class death among the evils' (XLVII) but 'to prepare ourselves for it with a cheerful mind, thinking ourselves like men delivered from a jail'). Life is frail and ephemeral, nourished by lower natures. Death is only a sleep, whereas life is a trivial struggle, subject to change and disease, its achievements only temporary. It passes like a dream, and in old age we lose whatever made life worth while. Men should not fear death, in which we are all equal.[12]

The Friar-Duke reconciles Claudio to his fate, with hope of an after-life: 'To sue to live, I find I seek to die; / And, seeking death, find life. Let it come on' (III,i,42–3). Brave words; so long as there's no remedy.

But once Claudio learns from his sister of a way out, he seeks it, though he be fettered with lifelong shame. In a hysterical outburst he expresses a morbid horror of extinction which yet implies some experience of 'cold obstruction' and bodily decay, or maybe an after-life spent in the punishment of Hades, as in Ovid, Bk IV, and Virgil, Bk VI (dismissed as fables in Lucretius, Bk III).

Reduced to extreme fear of death Claudio's only wish is to survive and he begs Isabella to give way:

> Nature dispenses with the deed so far
> That it becomes a virtue.   (III,i,136–7)

In horrified revulsion Isabella curses her brother, but the Duke soon calms him, confirming that he must die tomorrow, and his courage is restored.

Having seen two opposed ways of facing death we are shown a third, in the person of the debased criminal Barnardine, 'a creature unprepared, unmeet for death', who, awakened by the hangman from his drunken sleep, positively refuses to come out and be hanged: 'I have been drinking hard all night, and I will have more time to prepare me, or they shall beat out my brains with billets' (IV,iii,63, 49–51). There is rough humour here. The Friar-Duke is so appalled by the 'gravel heart' of this brute, 'unfit to live or die', that he seizes on the Provost's suggestion that they use the dead pirate Ragozine's head as a substitute for Claudio's, 'whiles I / Persuade this rude wretch willingly to die'. But 'Barnardine must die this afternoon' (IV,iii,76–9). So we have heard three attitudes to death: one fortified by the consolations of philosophy; one afflicted by *pavor mortis;* and one almost subhuman in its lack of apprehension. The Barnardine episode is an example of ethical theme manipulating plot, since to introduce Barnardine at all was unnecessary. Ragozine's head was ready and waiting. But the dramatist wanted to broaden his depiction of how men face death and to add some light relief to the prison scenes; so he invented the Bohemian 'insensible of mortality and desperately mortal' (IV,ii,138).

It is a far leap from these plays to *The Tempest,* but I must regretfully omit *Othello* and *King Lear* in which the defence and denial of paradoxes are made for the most part by the villains Iago and Edmund.[13] Much of the (masque-like) comedy in *The Tempest* is based on the exercise of magic on an island which seems to be in the Mediterranean but has many features of climate and society like the newly colonised West Indies and Virginia. It is a play about wise governance overcoming villainy, the castigation of wrongdoers, apparent cruelty concealing benevolence, philosophic meditation producing power over nature and men.

The characters are grouped according to their attitudes to rule. Antonio and Sebastian, nobles ambitious and malicious, bring their evil with them and seek to destroy the harmony of the island by murdering Alonso who was himself guilty of conniving at Antonio's treachery long ago. They represent misrule in high places. On a lower level are the jester Trinculo, the drunken butler Stephano, and Caliban, native of the island and a witch's son, who plot to kill Prospero and ravish his daughter. They represent the savage anarchy of the mob. Prospero is the good governor under whose firmness the island could flourish, and whose mastery of the elements has made Ariel his servant in good works.

Where magic operates, paradoxical (improbable) incidents occur under the magician's benevolent spell. With these we are not here concerned, but with the various opinions about the island expressed by the characters. At the beginning it is a place of terrible storms, 'the still-vext Bermoothes', whose sea wrecks galleons and drowns mariners, to the horror of the listening Miranda. For Caliban the island is an untamed place of 'fresh springs, brine-pits, barren place and fertile' (I,ii,338), where he was once the solitary king, and now is imprisoned in a rock, forced to work and tormented with 'urchin-shows', spirits like apes or adders (ii,ii,1–14). For Ferdinand it is a place of grief for a lost father, of music, captivity, hard labour and love at first sight. Antonio and Sebastian mock at Gonzalo and Adrian, who point out the good qualities of the island (ii,i), its sweet air, temperate climate and 'lusty' green grass. Gonzalo especially is their target, for he is old and knows their wickedness. When he points out the remarkable freshness of their garments despite the storm and wreck, they do not believe him.

Antonio.   What impossible matter will he make easy next?
Sebastian. I think he will carry this island home in his pocket, and give it his son for an
            apple.   (ii,i,83–5)

When King Alonso is upbraided by these villains for marrying his daughter to the black King of Tunis, the well-meaning Gonzalo tries to divert him by fancifully saying what he would do 'Had I plantation of this isle' (ii,i,137–62). He would manage it in a way contrary to what is usual, and describes it by versifying a passage from Montaigne's essay 'Of Cannibals' (Bk I, Ch. XXX) in John Florio's translation (1603), which runs:

It is a nation, would I answer *Plato,* that hath no kinds of traffike, no knowledge of Letters, no intelligence of numbers, no name of magistrate. . .; no use of service, of riches or of povertie; no contracts, no successions, no partitions, no occupation but idle; no respect of kindred, but common, no apparell but natural, no manuring of lands, no use of wine, corn, or mettle. The very words that import lying, falshood, treason, dissimulations,. . . . were never heard amongst them.[14]

Montaigne commented: 'They are even savage, as we call those fruits wilde, which nature of herselfe, and of her ordinarie progresse hath produced.' And he considered their society much superior to Plato's Republic.

  Gonzalo's paradoxical Utopia would need no ruler. 'Yet', Sebastian points out, 'he would be king on't' (l. 151). Indeed, Gonzalo assumes his existence. Alas, even while he dreams aloud, the political evils banished by Montaigne are menacing Prospero's island, and only his white magic can foil them. Alonso, himself no ideal ruler, tells Gonzalo: 'Prithee, no more; thou dost talk nothing to me', and the old man admits that he spoke in jest. Yet we may set the fleeting vision of men in a happy state of nature against the perilous conditions actually present on Prospero's island, and the imperfect government of Jacobean England.

NOTES

1 Some modern authorities: A. Sackton, 'The Paradoxical Encomium in Elizabethan Drama', *Texas Studies in English*, XXVII (1949), pp. 83–104; H. K. Miller, 'The Paradoxical Encomium', *Modern Philology*, LIII (1955–6), pp. 145–78; A. E. Malloch, 'The Techniques and Function of the Renaissance Paradox', *Studies in Philology*, LIII (1956), pp. 191–203.
    Some collections of paradoxes well known in the Renaissance: M. T. Cicero, *Paradoxa Stoicorum* (edn ed. by A. G. Lee, 1953); P. Mexia, *Silva da varia lecion*, 1540, trans. by T. Fortescue as *The Forest*, 1576; O. Landi, *Paradossi*, 1543, French trans. by C. Estienne, 1553; A. Munday, *The Defence of Contraries*, 1593 (Munday defined 'Paradoxes: that is to say, things contrary to most men's present opinions: to the end, that by such discourse as is helde in them, opposed truth might appeare more cleare and apparent'); J. Donne, *Paradoxes and Problems*, 1633; T. Milles, *The Treasurie of Ancient and Modern Times*, 1613; and John Hall, *Paradoxes*, 1650 (facs. edn ed. by D. C. Allen, Gainesville, Florida, 1956; see Allen's Introduction).

2 D. C. Allen, 'Jaques' "Seven Ages" and Pedro Mexia', *Modern Language Notes*, LVI (1941), pp. 601–3, traces the history of the 'Ages' paradox.

3 At the end of Chapman's *All Fools* (1599), Valerio praises the horn.

4 Attacks on usury included H. Smith, *Examination of Usury*, 1591, and M. Mosse, *The Arraignment of Usurie*, 1595.

5 Andrew Willet, *Hexapla in Genesin*, 1605, on Genesis 30, justified Jacob, who 'chooseth that for his wages, which not by man's wit, but God's working was to take effect'.

6 T. Milles, *The Treasurie*, 1613, Bk III, Ch. 11, has a passage condemning 'Rash Valiancy'.

7 Cf. Landi, Paradox 26, 'That it is better to be timid than courageous'.

8 Munday, *Defence*, Dec. 7, 'That Drunkenness is better than sobrietie', includes a similar panegyric on wine.

9 Cf. Sir Thomas Elyot, *The Governour*, 1531, Bk II.4, 'Nobility'.

10 Cf. Landi, Paradox 23, 'That it is better to be ignoble than of noble blood'; Milles Bk II, Ch. 22, 'That the meanest place of birth or descent, maketh a Man most Noble'.

11 Cf. Sir Thomas Elyot, *The Governour*, Bk II.7, 'Mercifulness'.

12 Landi, Paradox 18, 'That it is better to die than to live on'.

13 B. Vickers, '*King Lear* and Renaissance Paradoxes', *Modern Language Review*, LXIII (1968), pp. 305–14, is useful.

14 Everyman edition, I.220.

'True, gallant Raleigh': some off-stage conversations in Shakespeare's plays

A. C. SPRAGUE

One of the most familiar of dramatic devices is the entrance of characters already in the midst of conversation. Part of their talk we hear, part we can only guess at. Few conventions have been so generally taken for granted as this one, though Sheridan pokes fun at it through Mr Puff's absurd tragedy in *The Critic*.

> [*Enter* Sir Walter Raleigh *and* Sir Christopher Hatton.]
> *Sir Christopher.*   True, gallant Raleigh –
> *Dangle.*   What, they had been talking before?
> *Puff.*   O, yes; all the way as they came along.

Shakespeare uses it a great many times, the number varying to a surprising extent from play to play. *All's Well That Ends Well* has nearly a dozen examples. *The Merry Wives of Windsor* abounds in them, as does *The Winter's Tale*, whereas *The Tempest* and *Julius Caesar* have only one apiece. The purposes which such conversations serve are varied. Economy and concentration are not the only ones. Passages exist also, though these are few, which leave us uncertain as to just what was said off stage. These deserve rather more attention than they have received.

At one point in *The Merry Wives of Windsor* what might have been a scene of some length is avoided. Falstaff, dressed as the detested old woman of Brainford, has been soundly beaten by Master Ford. Mistress Ford and Mistress Page are jubilant.

> *Mrs Ford.* Shall we tell our husbands how we have served him?
> *Mrs Page.* Yes, by all means; if it be but to scrape the figures out of your husband's brains. If they can find in their hearts the poor unvirtuous fat knight shall be any further afflicted, we two will still be the ministers. (IV,ii,190ff.)

But we never hear them tell their story. After a brief scene between the Host and Bardolf, they return with their husbands and Evans:

Evans.   'Tis one of the best discretions of a oman as ever I did look upon.
Page.   And did he send you both these letters at an instant?
Mrs Page. Within a quarter of an hour.
Ford.   Pardon me, wife. . . (IV,iv,1ff.)

Off stage we are to suppose they have recounted the whole course of Falstaff's intrigue and have suggested a new plot against him, which is now fully described and elaborated upon.[1]

Very similar is the contrivance late in *Hamlet* when Claudius, having met the onset of Laertes with courage, tries to persuade the young man to listen to his explanations. The return of Ophelia works to the King's advantage. Laertes retires with him, broken with grief. As in *The Merry Wives of Windsor* there is a brief covering scene. Then Claudius and Laertes enter once more and Claudius begins:

> Now must your conscience my acquittance seal,
> And you must put me in your heart for friend,
> Sith you have heard, and with a knowing ear,
> That he which hath your noble father slain
> Pursued my life.[2]   (IV,vii,1–5)

In the comedy, at this point, we had a long discussion as to what was to be done to Falstaff. The present scene looks forward too, with the instruction of Laertes, an apt pupil, in how he is to revenge himself upon Hamlet.

The device of substituting an off-stage conversation for spoken dialogue saves time, since the matter omitted is often, though not always, repetitive. What Rosalind has promised to accomplish is told in full to Orlando. It need not be told over again to the Duke. Enough that we find them considering the claims which she has been making, claims of an astonishing sort.

> · *Duke Senior.* Dost thou believe, Orlando, that the boy
>   Can do all this that he hath promisèd?
>   *Orlando.*   I sometimes do believe and sometimes do not.   (V,iv,1–3)

Or, returning to the misfortunes of Falstaff: since we are already familiar with the conditions which he must accept if he is to enjoy his rendezvous at Herne's Oak, Mistress Quickly can set them forth in an unheard interview. He was doomed, indeed, from the moment he agreed to this parley, and it is no surprise when, after another covering scene, we find that he has yielded: 'Prithee, no more prattling; go. I'll hold. This is the third time; I hope good luck lies in odd numbers.'

Of a different kind is the elimination of a speech made by the Duke of Florence in *All's Well That Ends Well*.

> *Duke.* So that, from point to point, now have you heard
> The fundamental reasons of this war;
> Whose great decision hath much blood let forth
> And more thirsts after.   (III,i,1-4)

He has just finished this speech. What went before is withheld, not, we may suppose, because it might have been repetitious but because of its inconsequence. The causes of this very minor war, its rights and wrongs, are without meaning for us. It exists solely for purposes of the play – a war in which Bertram distinguishes himself and Parolles is amusingly exposed. Shakespeare wastes no time over it.

Sometimes a withheld passage is succeeded by one which summarises it. Of this sort is Lear's impassioned,

> Deny to speak with me! They are sick! They are weary!
> They have travelled all the night!   (II,iv,86-7)

or the tirade of Constance in *King John* beginning:

> Gone to be married! Gone to swear a peace!
> False blood to false blood joined! Gone to be friends![3]   (III,i,1-2)

Sometimes again, the spoken words following the imagined ones are of extraordinary naturalness, 'sounding from the page' and characterising the speaker.

> *Shylock.* Three thousand ducats – well.
> *Bassanio.* Ay, sir, for three months.
> *Shylock.* For three months – well.
> *Bassanio.* For the which, as I told you, Antonio shall be bound.
> *Shylock.* Antonio shall be bound – well.   (I,iii,1-5)

The beginning of the negotiation is left for us to re-create. Its sinister progress is dramatised later in the scene. But Shylock already lives for us in those first words of his and in the pauses which accompany them.

Equally effective are the passages in which a hot discussion off stage is continued within our hearing. Instances occur in *Julius Caesar*, when Antony and Octavius are marking the names of those to be executed

(IV,i,I); in *Othello*, when the Duke and certain senators are attempting to determine where the Turks will strike (I,iii,I); and, most spirited of all, in *1 Henry IV*. There an unheard debate of the rebel lords is continued without the least pause.

> *Hotspur.*   We'll fight with him to-night.
> *Worcester.*   It may not be.
> *Douglas.*   You give him, then, advantage.
> *Vernon.*   Not a whit.
> *Hotspur.*   Why say you so? looks he not for supply?
> *Vernon.*   So do we.   (IV,iii,I–4)

Economy is not so much served as our sense of urgent haste, which is scarcely relaxed through the twenty lines that follow.

We have been considering some of the uses to which Shakespeare put a technical expedience, one already familiar in his own time and not unknown in ours. The words withheld, the conversations assumed, are of interest in themselves. Only rarely, however, does their interpretation offer difficulty. An answer will imply a question, a denial an assertion. No reader, again, has ever been at a loss to supply what preceded lines like the following.

> *Antigonus.* Thou art perfect then our ship hath touched upon
>   The deserts of Bohemia?   (*Winter's Tale*, III,iii,I–2)

> *1 Senator.* So, your opinion is, Aufidius,
>   That they of Rome are entered in our counsels
>   And know how we proceed?   (*Coriolanus*, I,ii,I–3)
> *Friar Lawrence.* On Thursday, sir? The time is very short.
>   (*Romeo and Juliet*, IV,i,I)

> *Adriana.* Ah, Luciana, did he tempt thee so?
>   Mightst thou perceive austerely in his eye
>   That he did plead in earnest?   (*Comedy of Errors*, IV,ii,I–3)
> *Duke Frederick.* Not see him since! Sir, sir, that cannot be.
>   (*As You Like It*, III,i,I)

> *Buckingham.* Will not King Richard let me speak with him?
>   (*Richard III*, V,i,I)

Such frankness in exploiting a convention might once have been called naïve. It would not, I fancy, be so described today.

Lines like those just quoted are not, of course, annotated in editions of the plays. But others, which might well be, pass unrecognised, or are dismissed perfunctorily with something like: 'This is part of a conversation already in progress.' G. L. Kittredge, among Shakespearian editors, was exceptional in the amount of attention which he gave them. So, too, was the late George Skillan in his acting versions, published over a period of many years by Samuel French. Here is a characteristic note of his on *Henry V*:

Gower.   Nay, that's right; but why wear you your leek today? Saint Davy's day is past.
Fluellen.   There is occasions and causes why and wherefore in all things.   (v,i,1ff.)

Skillan: 'Probably acquiescing to *Fluellen*'s spirited description of the origin of the leek as a badge for Welsh soldiers and an equally spirited support of the deserved honour'. Kittredge also noticed the passage, pointing out that, 'as so often is the case', we have only the close of a conversation. 'These two words [*that's right*] refer to something Fluellen has said; we have no means of knowing what.'

Indulgence of fancy appears unexpectedly in a note by Alfred Hart in his Arden edition of *Measure for Measure*. The Duke in that play visits and asks help of a Friar before undertaking his strange investigations.

> *Duke.* No, holy father; throw away that thought;
> Believe not that the dribbling dart of love
> Can pierce a complete bosom. Why I desire thee
> To give me secret harbour hath a purpose
> More grave and wrinkled than the aims and ends
> Of burning youth.   (i,iii,1–6)

Hart's note having begun with the entirely acceptable, 'Evidently the Friar suspects some love entanglement', goes on: 'Did he think the Duke wished to gain one of the nuns? as indeed he subsequently shaped his ends to.' The late J. W. Lever in the corresponding note in the New Arden edition would have the Duke suspected of seeking to arrange a rendezvous, an interpretation which is at least possible in view of the reference to a 'secret harbour'. Wisely, however, he makes no mention of nuns.

The opening of *Antony and Cleopatra* with its two, chorus-like Roman soldiers, has often been commended, but without any attempt to reconstruct what they were saying immediately before. Philo begins:

> Nay, but this dotage of our general's
> O'erflows the measure. Those his goodly eyes,
> That o'er the files and musters of the war
> Have glowed like plated Mars, now bend, now turn,
> The office and devotion of their view
> Upon a tawny front.   (i,i,1–6)

Has Demetrius been referring cynically to the fact that great soldiers have often made fools of themselves over women? If so, his tone would have been that of Enobarbus later in the play. It is possible, however, to imagine a different speech; one to which Philo's lines would still be an appropriate reply. Demetrius, as we learn presently, has come from Rome, where there were strange rumours concerning Antony. Has he cited one of these, adding that he could not believe it? Philo then explains why he should, since this new Antony is no longer the Antony they once knew. The first interpretation is perhaps the more natural of the two: I find it hard to choose between them.

The general drift of another celebrated opening, that of *Othello*, is fairly clear.

> *Roderigo.* Tush, never tell me; I take it much unkindly
> That you, Iago, who has had my purse
> As if the strings were thine, shouldst know of this.   (I,i,1–3)

'This', as we soon discover, refers to Othello's elopement; and, as Alice Walker writes in the New Cambridge edition, 'Iago has presumably denied all earlier knowledge of Othello's marriage and reaffirms his denial in l.5' –

> If ever I did dream of such a matter
> Abhor me.

On the other hand, the words which we are to supply may not have been a denial of knowledge. That came, I suggest, earlier still. Now, as Roderigo remains obstinately unconvinced, Iago suddenly takes the offensive with a personal appeal. Later in the play he says to Cassio, 'And, good Lieutenant, I think you think I love you', (II,iii,300), and later still says to Othello, 'My lord, you know I love you' (III,iii,121). So here, may he not have said something like 'but sir, be sure I love you'. If we accept this, then Roderigo's 'Tush, never tell me' fits admirably, as does his 'I take it *much unkindly.*'

The beginning of the second scene in *Othello* is clearly related to the beginning of the first. It presents serious difficulties. Iago is talking to Othello, as they enter.

> *Iago.*   Though in the trade of war I have slain men,
> Yet do I hold it very stuff o'th'conscience
> To do no contrived murder. I lack iniquity
> Sometime to do me service. Nine or ten times
> I had thought to have yerked him here under the ribs.
> *Othello.* 'Tis better as it is.

Iago.   Nay, but he prated,
And spoke such scurvy and provoking terms
Against your honour
That, with the little godliness I have,
I did full hard forbear him.   (I,ii,1–10)

Kenneth Muir, in the New Penguin edition, explains that Iago 'has
apparently told Othello that Roderigo was responsible for informing
Brabantio of Desdemona's elopement'. This is sound enough but leaves
room for elaboration. Who is the 'he'? Steevens raised the question in the
eighteenth century ('Of whom is this said? Of Roderigo?'), and Knight,
answering it in the middle of the nineteenth, made the good point that
Iago was preparing Othello for the appearance of Roderigo with Brabantio. Roderigo seems meant. Yet Stoll, disregarding or forgetting the
identification, calls the man who vilified Othello, and was nearly stabbed
by Iago for doing so, Brabantio. Iago, he insists, would have slain
Brabantio 'on the slightest provocation', adding that 'a loyalty that
repines at not having gone the length of stabbing your father-in-law for
"prating" is of itself suspicious'.[4]

The time to which Iago refers is harder to determine. In the scene of
the arousing of Brabantio, which comes first to mind, it was Iago whose
abuse of the Moor was shocking.[5] Roderigo remained polite. What is
more, Brabantio recognised Roderigo's voice, which he distinguished
from that of a 'profane wretch', somewhere in the darkness, whom he did
not know. Iago, as Kittredge used to maintain, sticks to the truth
whenever it is possible to do so. And in this instance there might be
awkwardness for the villain were Othello and Brabantio to confer.
Kittredge turned, accordingly, to an earlier time. 'Iago is reporting what
Roderigo has said to him just before the play begins' – when we may
assume that he was railing against the Moor.

About the antecedents of these last passages – the one from *Antony
and Cleopatra* and two from *Othello* – it is possible to form an opinion.
This scarcely holds true in the case of two further passages, which agree,
however, in giving us a general idea of what was said. In the theatre, if not
in the study, this should be enough. Anne Bullen is talking sadly with the
Old Lady about Katherine.

Not for that neither. Here's the pang that pinches:
His highness having lived so long with her. . .
. . .   .
To give her the avaunt, it is a pity
Would move a monster.   (*Henry VIII*, II,iii,1ff.)

The Old Lady seems to share Anne's pity. What particular humiliation she mentioned we have no way of knowing.[6] In *Antony and Cleopatra*, again, Antony is talking to Octavia about the many affronts which he has received from her brother, and Octavia, clearly enough, has been trying to excuse him. At one point Antony accepts her explanation. We know nothing more.

> Nay, nay, Octavia, not only that –
> That were excusable, that and thousands more
> Of semblable import – but he hath waged
> New wars 'gainst Pompey.   (III,iv,1–4)

Conversations begun off stage and continued within our hearing are frequent in Shakespeare's plays (there are, I should estimate, not less than 130 of them; another reader might conceivably add twenty-five or thirty more). Only a few have been considered in this essay. I have tried to bring out the variety of purposes which they serve and the interest, and often the difficulty, of the words withheld. A number of further examples might have been chosen – notably two in *All's Well That Ends Well*. In the earlier (III,vi), Bertram's reluctance to accept the worthlessness of Parolles is made clear by implication; in the later (IV,v), the seeming insistence by the Countess that her son's behaviour is deserving of the deepest blame. A final claim for this convention might be advanced, that it enlarges a little the present time, essential to drama, without recourse to narration. What has just been said, the beginning of a speech heard only in part, shares without break the *now* of their context.

NOTES

1 Alwin Thaler discusses the passage briefly but well in his book *Shakespearian Silences* (Cambridge, Mass., 1929), pp. 50, 51.
2 Cf. *2 Henry IV*, I,iii,1. (The rebels' grievances are set forth abundantly in the course of the play.)
3 Cf. also *As You Like It*, V,ii,1.
4 *Shakespeare and Other Masters* (Cambridge, Mass., 1940), p. 254.
5 Stanislavsky assumes that Iago referred to this scene, shifting his own part in it to Roderigo (*Stanislavsky Produces Othello* (London, 1948), p. 39).
6 R. A. Foakes suggests to me that Anne's first words pick up and answer Henry's reference to conscience at the end of the scene before: Anne herself, visibly present, is the reason why the King is divorcing Katherine.

Shakespeare's recollections
of Marlowe

M. C. BRADBROOK

'Who chooseth me shall gain what many men desire.'
Why, that's the lady! All the world desires her;
From the four corners of the earth they come
40   To kiss this shrine, this mortal-breathing saint.
The Hyrcanian deserts and the vasty wilds
Of wide Arabia are as throughfares now
For princes to come view fair Portia.
The watery Kingdom, whose ambitious head
45   Spits in the face of heaven, is no bar
To stop the foreign spirits, but they come
As o'er a brook to see fair Portia.

                    (*The Merchant of Venice*, II,vii,37–47)

At the moment of high ritual when the first of Portia's suitors, the Prince of Morocco, is to make his choice, a heightening of the verse attests his ardour. The dancing rhythm, with its onward flow, its panoramic view, and its refrain, is modelled on Tamburlaine's speech at the death of Zenocrate. Her apotheosis is celebrated with images of the cosmic grandeur that have marked Tamburlaine throughout, tinged here it would seem with some echoes of the Book of Revelations; Morocco uses the ritual of pilgrimage to express his reverence, although presumably his holy place is Mecca.

Morocco like Tamburlaine is a solar figure, clad in 'the shadowed livery of the burnished sun' (II,i,2), and like Tamburlaine's the conclusion of his quest is a death's head. Tamburlaine's grief at the death of Zenocrate is his first acknowledgement of mortality; he enshrines his dead Queen 'not lapped in lead, but in a sheet of gold' (*2 Tamburlaine*, II,iv,131), the gold casket of Morocco's choice.

Now walk the angels on the walls of heaven,
As sentinels to warn th'immortal souls

To entertain divine Zenocrate.
Apollo, Cynthia, and the ceaseless lamps
That gently looked upon this loathsome earth,
Shine downwards now no more, but deck the heavens
To entertain divine Zenocrate.
The crystal springs, whose taste illuminates
Refinèd eyes with an eternal sight
Like trièd silver runs through Paradise
To entertain divine Zenocrate.
The cherubins and holy seraphins,
That sing and play before the King of Kings,
Use all their voices and their instruments
To entertain divine Zenocrate.
And in this sweet and curious harmony,
The god that tunes this music to our souls
Holds out his hand in highest majesty
To entertain divine Zenocrate.   (2 *Tamburlaine*, II,iv,15–33)

The music is kept back for Bassanio, and for the last scene of all, but the
dark quality behind the choice, the hint of regality tempered with grief,
has been established. This dramatic recollection is designed to evoke
audience memories, and to give a heightened audience response in the
theatre; it is more than a literary evocation.

Marlowe is found both at Belmont and Venice; the main Marlovian
connections, though more diffused, lie in Shylock's role.

In making use of *The Jew of Malta*, Shakespeare may have drawn on
his own memories as an actor – for the play, unlike *Tamburlaine*, was not
in print; but it had been put on by Lord Strange's Men in 1592, and was
subsequently given by the Admiral's Men. If Alleyn played Barabas,
Burbage as Shylock acquired a subtler version of the stage Jew. Shakespeare took over certain situations, particularly from the role of Abigail
the Jew's daughter, but Barabas's joy at the stratagem by which his
daughter recovers his gold from its hiding place –

> O my girl,
> My gold, my fortune, my felicity!
> . . .   .
> O girl! O gold! O beauty! O my bliss! –
>   (*The Jew of Malta*, II,i,46–53)

becomes Shylock's grief at the flight of Jessica as mocked by Solanio:

> I never heard a passion so confused,
> So strange, outrageous and so variable,
> As the dog Jew did utter in the streets.
> 'My daughter! O my ducats! O my daughter!'   (II,viii,12–15)

The subtle use of one Christian to entrap another was a practice of Barabas which Shylock greatly expands, when he pleads that the law of Venice, and international confidence in its stability, demand the fulfilment of his bond. That Antonio stands surety for Bassanio is not of Shylock's contrivance, as the mutual destruction of Mathias and Lodowick is of Barabas's.

Shakespeare can assume certain conventions about his stage figure, and upon them work his own transformation. Barabas's justification for his treacheries, that 'Christians do the like', is sufficiently demonstrated; zest in planning these as a 'savage farce' had whetted the ironic plots in earlier plays, particularly *Titus Andronicus* and *Richard III*, where malignant delight in evil extrudes itself in lively action. The most direct borrowing from *The Jew of Malta*, Aaron's death speech in *Titus Andronicus*, is closely modelled on Barabas's counsel to Ithamore (*The Jew of Malta*, II,iii,165–99),

> First be thou void of these affections:
> Compassion, love, vain hope, and heartless fear;   (ll. 165–6)

but becomes active:

> Even now I curse the day – and yet, I think,
> Few come within the compass of my curse –
> Wherein I did not some notorious ill.
>
> (*Titus Andronicus*, v,i,125–7)

The list of crimes that make up Barabas's life story include unprovoked murders (though of a secret kind) and more elaborate stratagems; beginning

> As for myself, I walk abroad a-nights,
> And kill sick people groaning under walls;
> Sometimes I go about and poison wells;
>
> (*The Jew of Malta*, II,iii,172–4)

and ending with the macabre image of a man hanging himself for grief, with pinned upon his breast a long great scroll 'how I with interest tormented him'. Aaron's crimes are more openly violent, but the list ends with an equally macabre image of death; he digs up dead men and sets them at

> their dear friends' door
> Even when their sorrows almost was forgot,
> And on their skins, as on the bark of trees,
> Have with my knife carvèd in Roman letters,
> 'Let not your sorrow die, though I am dead.'
>
> (*Titus Andronicus*, v,i,136–40)

The scrolls transform these two Death figures into emblems of Judgement, which lies beyond death.

As Aaron's last dying confession, an occasion when a man was expected to give an exemplary speech, and ensure his future life by dying well, his diabolic manifesto has more force than the counsel imparted to a slave, by reason of the position which it occupies. Unquenched evil holds its addict fast. Barabas's own death speech is comparatively short and entails a triumphant acknowledgement of what he has brought about, with a final curse on Christians and Turks alike. The theological implications of his end have been studied in detail by G. K. Hunter.[1] Aaron's choice of the devil's part is explicit, and more purposefully aimed:

> If there be devils, would I were a devil,
> To live and burn in everlasting fire,
> So I might have your company in hell
> But to torment you with my bitter tongue!   (v,i,147–50)

A just doom is to set him breast deep in earth, and famish him – 'There let him stand and rave and cry for food.' This is the end meted out to the negro bond-slave in the second part of *The Pleasant History of Tom a Lincoln*: it seems symbolic of the end of Base Desire. Aaron, who would 'have his soul black like his face', is one of a line of villainous Moors, Turks and Jews, who supplied the material for atrocity plays like *Selimus* and *Lust's Dominion*; but his role in the retinue of the Empress allows for a mixture of ferocious comedy in Marlowe's manner, as he kills the nurse who has delivered the black infant born to him by the Empress, or as he instructs her sons in his own diabolic arts. This diabolic, jesting vitality has a Marlovian ring, though Shakespeare's sense of natural detail is as always much nearer the soil:

> Come on, you thick-lipped slave, I'll bear you hence;
> For it is you that puts us to our shifts.
> I'll make you feed on berries and on roots,
> And feed on curds and whey, and suck the goat,
> And cabin in a cave, and bring you up
> To be a warrior and command a camp.
> (*Titus Andronicus*, IV,ii,176–81)

Aaron initiates most of the action in the play; when at the end Tamora and her sons disguise as Revenge, Rapine and Murder, they are, as it were, entering a figurative level which Aaron has already presented. In a play as deeply indebted to Kyd's Revenge dramas as *Titus Andronicus*, the Marlovian ingredient has brought something more characteristic of

Shakespeare the poet into the remarkably well-constructed tragedy; and into its sombre and heraldic symmetries something of the countryside. Even Aaron's final catalogue of crimes includes some that sound like country witchcraft; to

> Make poor men's cattle break their necks;
> Set fire on barns and hay-stacks in the night,   (v,i,132–3)

are crimes not really worthy of the imperial court.

Shakespeare's imitations of Marlowe, even at their closest, invite consideration of the differences between the two. Marlowe's was incomparably the most powerful dramatic voice which he encountered at the beginning of his career, and Tamburlaine's were the accents which first had liberated the drama. Blended with the voice of the Jew in Aaron is the voice of Tamburlaine, especially in his opening soliloquy:

> Now climbeth Tamora Olympus' top,
> Safe out of fortune's shot, and sits aloft,
> Secure of thunder's crack or lightning flash,
> Advanced above pale Envy's threatening reach.
> . . .   .
> Away with slavish weeds and servile thoughts!
> I will be bright and shine in pearl and gold.   (ii,i,1–4, 18–19)

The superb assurance of these lines, the triumph over Fortune, is Marlovian, in so grand a style that the fact that Aaron sacrifices his pride to secure the life of his bastard comes with a startling reversal. It is as if recalling Marlowe pushed Shakespeare into a further degree of inventiveness. This was the thesis maintained by Nicholas Brooke in the most cogent study of their relationship, 'Marlowe as Provocative Agent in Shakespeare's Early Plays'.[2] As the sequence of history plays by Shakespeare and Marlowe ricochet one from another, each is seen borrowing in turn from the other. Henry VI's weakness shows the disintegrative force of a culpable innocence that lacks all will to power, and is in strongest contrast to Tamburlaine's power drive. Greene's parody from that play in his warning, addressed to Marlowe, against Shakespeare,

> O tiger's heart wrapped in a woman's hide[3]

is indeed the key to the catatonic movement by which Margaret becomes a spirit of Nemesis. Finally, as the embodiment of evil, Richard Crookback betters the Marlovian villain-heroes, for while they were pupils of Machiavelli he could 'set the murderous Machiavel to school'. His opening speech also betters theirs, for he is his own prologue, whilst they are preceded by various kinds of chorus.

Edward II, Marlowe's riposte, is clearly indebted to *Richard III*, since Mortimer's role as protector derives in some details from Richard's (see Harold Brooks's 'Marlowe and the Early Shakespeare'),[4] but, as the study of an obsession, the play lacks that wider sense of the country's plight, the desolation of England's trampled garden, so prominent in Shakespeare's counter-play, *Richard II*. Here the plot of the deposed and libertine king has many parallels with Marlowe's, but whilst for instance the ritual of the deposition scene is greatly expanded, the homosexual element is so played down that Bushy, Bagot and Green seem almost irrelevant. Some of the Marlovian magniloquence heard in the opening scenes does not come from *Edward II*, but the earlier plays.

> I would allow him odds
> And meet him, were I tied to run afoot,
> Even to the frozen ridges of the Alps.   (*Richard II*, 1,i,62–4)
>
> O, who can hold a fire in his hand
> By thinking on the frosty Caucasus?   (1,iii,294–5)

The two dramatists, contending with and reacting from each other, select their material to make contrasting effects. Richard's fall is more richly developed; 'Down, down I come like glistering Phaeton' is mirrored in the actual descent from the upper to the lower stage; in the deposition scene itself, 'Fiend, thou torments me ere I come to hell' stands in apposition to the many comparisons with Christ and evokes Dr Faustus, whose last speech is echoed in the cry

> O that I were a mockery king of snow
> Standing before the sun of Bolingbroke,
> To melt myself away in water drops!   (IV,i,260–2)

But here there is the double image of the King's present tears, and of his former heraldic badge, the sunburst, which was applied to him in the earlier scene. The effects of *Dr Faustus* are felt most powerfully where they are most indirect, in the final moments of self-knowledge at Pomfret, though here the depth of tragic knowledge is more analytic than Marlowe's.

The question remains that this rivalry in the theatre may have accompanied rivalry outside the theatre. What is the relation of *Venus and Adonis* to *Hero and Leander*? And is Marlowe the rival poet of Sonnets 85 and 86?

The order in which the two Ovidian romances were composed is not easy to decide. *Hero and Leander* was entered to John Wolf in the Stationers' Register on 28 September 1593, only a few months after Marlowe's death on 30 May; but it did not appear till Edward Blount published it in 1598. *Venus and Adonis* was entered on 18 April 1593 to Richard Field, and would probably have been in print by June. A second edition appeared in 1594 and it was frequently reprinted. G. P. V. Akrigg, in his *Shakespeare and the Earl of Southampton*,[5] called attention to the Latin poem *Narcissus* by John Clapham, secretary to Lord Burghley, which was printed by Thomas Scarlet in 1591 with a dedication to the Earl of Southampton. It was the first dedication the young Earl had received, but it may not have been particularly welcome.[6]

For this 'short and moral description of Youthful Love and especially Self-Love' was intended as a warning fable to the young ward who was refusing to accept the plans of his guardian, Burghley, that he should marry Burghley's granddaughter, Lady Elizabeth Vere, a marriage which had been in the Lord Treasurer's mind since the previous year.

The scene is England. Narcissus visits the Temple of Love – which, like the temple in *Hero and Leander*, is painted with stories of famous victims – where he is received by Venus, and instructed in Ovid and Petrarch; but Love prophesies that Narcissus will perish of self-love. Having drunk of Lethe, and thereby forfeited self-knowledge, Narcissus is borne on an untameable horse named 'Lust' to the Fountain of Self-Love, where, according to legend, he is drowned – in despair that night has removed the image of himself from the waters.

Here, then, is the warning which was extended to the recalcitrant youth, and here much of the material which Shakespeare was to catch up and present in a far less offensive guise. The prime model for *Venus and Adonis* is not Marlowe, but Clapham, who supplies the moral, as well as reason for the inset of the horse and jennet, and the version of the story, reduced to a mere illustration in the persuasion of Venus, that Narcissus drowned himself (and was not, as in Ovid, pulled into the water by amorous nymphs).

> Is thine own heart to thine own face affected?
> Can thy right hand seize love upon thy left?
> Then woo thyself, be of thyself rejected;
> Steal thine own freedom and complain on theft.
> > Narcissus so himself himself forsook,
> > And died to kiss his shadow in the brook.   (ll. 157–62)

Clapham has

> Deficiunt vires, et vox et spiritus ipse
> Deficit, et pronus de ripa decidit et sic
> Ipse suae periit deceptus imaginis umbra.   (sig. B3v)

Marlowe dimisses the story of Narcissus as a mere adjunct or mark to show Leander's surpassing beauty:

> let it suffice
> That my slack muse sings of Leander's eyes,
> Those orient cheeks and lips, exceeding his
> That leapt into the water for a kiss
> Of his own shadow, and despising many,
> Died ere he could enjoy the love of any,
> > *(Hero and Leander*, i,71–6)

as the story of Venus and Adonis is merely a tale embroidered on the hem of Hero's sleeve:

> Her wide sleeves green, and bordered with a grove,
> Where Venus in her naked glory strove
> To please the careless and disdainful eyes
> Of proud Adonis that before her lies,   (i,11–14)

and the 'hot proud horse' an image of Leander's imperviousness to the counsel of his father (ii,141–5). The Temple of Venus, where Marlowe's poem opens, may recall more precisely the same Temple in Clapham's poem: although commonplace, it fits in the catena of images linking all three poems.

Venus and Adonis shows a far closer relation with the first group of the Sonnets (1–19); the two Ovidian poems seem rather to be running parallel to each other, both deriving from Clapham. If Marlowe's poem were complete as it stands (and there are precedents for such selective treatment) it would provide a persuasion to love quite devoid of warnings. Blount of course refers to it as an 'unfinished tragedy' in his dedicatory letter to Sir Thomas Walsingham, with whom Marlowe had been residing at the time of his death. But the full story would defeat the special purpose.

In Shakespeare's poem, the natural beauty of the landscape and of the animals is totally unlike the jewelled exotic world of Marlowe's poem; Shakespeare had already brought more of the natural scene into his Marlovian portrait of Aaron, and much into *Richard II*. It is one of the distinguishing marks between the imagination of the one and the other poet.

The comedy is equally contrasted; Shakespeare's is muted, incidental:

> Her song was tedious, and outwore the night,
> For lovers' hours are long, though seeming short;
>
> . . .   .
>
> Their copious stories, often times begun,
> End without audience and are never done,   (ll. 841–2, 845–6)

whilst Marlowe's, enclosed in the taut couplet form, is more pervasive, an exultant triumph at the expense of mortals and gods, who are alike befooled, self-deceiving, and subjected to deflating comment:

> Albeit Leander, rude in love and raw,
> Long dallying with Hero, nothing saw
> That might delight him more, yet he suspected
> Some amorous rites or other were neglected.   (ii,61–4)

Both are addressing an audience whose appetite for the pure honey of Ovidian eroticism is tempered by a taste for witty 'arguments of love'. This is one of the games people play when they have to lead a good deal of their private life in public, as courtiers did. Though it is so near in theme to the Sonnets, *Venus and Adonis* is a more public affair; indeed, it was licensed for printing by the Archbishop of Canterbury himself – did he actually read it? Or was it one of his chaplains?

Kenneth Muir and Sean O'Loughlin noted the almost satiric outlook of *Venus and Adonis* in parts, and its ironic use of hyperbole.[7] This becomes appropriate in a context that asks for a 'correction' of John Clapham's sententiousness. This unwilling Adonis (not a traditional role for him) must be offered a more artful persuasion to love.

As I have indicated elsewhere,[8] I think *Venus and Adonis* was also Shakespeare's response to charges of ignorance made by Robert Greene, which were couched in the form of a warning to Marlowe, the 'famous gracer of tragedians'. It was designed to obliterate the impression he had tried to make by its implicit claim to Art, set out in its motto

> Vilia miretur vulgus; mihi flavus Apollo
> Pocula Castalia plena ministret aqua –

– Ovidian lines which Marlowe had translated

> Let base-conceited wits admire vile things,
> Fair Phoebus lead me to the Muses' springs.   (Elegy XV,35–6)

If *Venus and Adonis* is an answer to Clapham's Latin, its claim as 'Art' increases.

During the winter of 1592–3, when the theatres in London were closed by the plague, poets scattered to country retreats – the kind of retreat that Boccaccio depicted in *The Decameron*, if they were fortunate, or the kind that is suggested in *Love's Labour's Lost*. It was during this period of retreat that Shakespeare wrote *Venus and Adonis* – T. W. Baldwin dates it just a few months or weeks before publication.[9] In the seventeenth century it would have been a country house poem – as, in some respects, it is.

The danger from plague, which did not spare the young or the beautiful, lies behind its note of urgency. The plea for 'breed' was intensified by such circumstances. Here the two poets re-echo each other.

> Beauty alone is lost, too warily kept

parallels

> Beauty within itself should not be wasted,

and the familiar argument of usury re-occurs, Shakespeare here being the more succinct. Venus has been describing all the maladies that 'in one minute's fight bring beauty under', comparing the body to 'a swallowing grave' if it buries its own posterity – an act worse than suicide or parricide.

> Foul cank'ring rust the hidden treasure frets,
> But gold that's put to use more gold begets.   (ll. 767–8)

Leander's sophistry lacks this pressure but his eye certainly glances from earth to heaven. Ships were made to sail the sea, strings to play upon, brass pots to shine with use, robes to be worn, palaces to live in:

> What difference betwixt the richest mine
> And basest mould but use? For both, not used,
> Are of like worth. Then treasure is abused
> When misers keep it; being put to loan,
> In time it will return us two for one.   (i,232–6)

The familiar innuendo spices this trade catalogue, but Hero's reply, which is very brief, seems not amiss:

> Who taught thee rhetoric to deceive a maid?   (i,338)

Marlowe is not involved; and this spirited series of conflicts – between gods, between the lovers, within Hero herself – taught Shakespeare more about how to write plays, and fit conflict within conflict.

Sonnets 85 and 86, as I believe, describe a poetry contest between

Shakespeare and the Rival Poet. These contests of recitation – one thinks of the *Mastersingers* of Wagner – had been held in London since Chaucer's time at the festival of the Pui (the guild of foreign merchants); at a lower level there were scolding matches or 'flytings'.[10]

> Was it the proud full sail of his great verse,
> Bound for the prize of all-too-precious you,
> That did my ripe thoughts in my brain inhearse,
> Making their tomb the womb wherein they grew?
> Was it his spirit, by spirits taught to write
> Above a mortal pitch, that struck me dead?
> No.
>
> ...   .
>
> But when your countenance filled up his line
> Then lacked I matter; that enfeebled mine.   (Sonnet 86)

Marlowe was so often credited with 'inspiration' by his fellow poets, with the 'brave translunary things' that made his spirits 'all air and fire' that the fifth line does not derogate from the recognisable fitness of the opening lines to Marlowe and to him alone. (Chapman, chief alternative, had at this time written nothing, was only newly out of the Low Countries, and found composition extremely difficult and agonising by his own accounts.)

If Marlowe were the rival poet (and he seems to me the most likely candidate), this would explain why his verse re-occurred to Shakespeare in *The Merchant of Venice* within the high ritual atmosphere of a prize contest. In Sonnet 85 the winning poem was to 'reserve [its] character with golden quill', which was what happened to the prize poem at the festival of the Pui, where the winner was given a 'crown' for the song he had made in praise of the newly elected 'Prince' of that fraternity. It was then hung up under the 'Prince's' arms. (A mock challenge at wooing is set up in Jonson's *Cynthia's Revels*.) In *The Merchant of Venice* the contest is for a much nobler reward; Morocco, the first contestant, departs with the mournful echo of what he had read on the scroll, 'Your suit is cold':

> Cold indeed and labour lost!
> Then farewell, heat, and welcome, frost,   (II,vii,74–5)

whilst, after the interlude of Arragon (whom Nicholas Brooke compares with Marlowe's figure of the Guise in his contempt for things common), Bassanio approaches with that note of love and spring-time which is heard in the plays as well as the poems:

A day in April never came so sweet
To show how costly summer was at hand
As this fore-spurrer comes before his lord.   (II,ix,93–5)

The after-effects of *Hero and Leander* can be sensed in *Romeo and Juliet*. The resemblance is general and is a matter of the high assurance of Juliet's 'Gallop apace, you fiery-footed steeds', or Mercutio's bawdy wit (perhaps also the tragic suddenness of his death in a futile brawl may be taken to reflect Marlowe's own). The sustained note of lyric joy, the physical obstacles that separate the lovers, the blindness of destiny that opposes them do not add up to a challenge to Marlowe; they are in Shakespeare's own mode.

From time to time he looked back on Marlowe. Among Pistol's playscraps the 'hollow pamper'd jades of Asia' appear along with Callipolis and Hiren the Fair Greek. Then, in 1598, *Hero and Leander* appeared in print, and Shakespeare, for the only time in his life, identified and quoted a contemporary

Dead shepherd, now I find thy saw of might:
'Who ever loved that loved not at first sight?'
(*As You Like It*, III,v,80–1)

Two scenes earlier there had been a reference to Marlowe's death:

Touchstone. I am here with thee and thy goats, as the most capricious poet, honest Ovid, was among the Goths.
Jaques.   O knowledge ill-inhabited, worse than Jove in a thatched house!
Touchstone. When a man's verses cannot be understood, nor a man's good wit seconded with the forward child understanding, it strikes a man more dead than a great reckoning in a little room. (III,iii,4–13)

It is generally conceded that the 'great reckoning in a little room' recalls Marlowe's death in a quarrel over the reckoning in a tavern. The jest about 'honest Ovid' might have brought him to mind; but the catastrophe that when a man's verses cannot be understood it strikes him dead also recalls Sonnet 86:

Was it his spirit, by spirits taught to write
Above a mortal pitch, that struck me dead?

Not literally, of course; he had 'dried' – the actor's worst fear, a fear already described in Sonnet 23. The image here is a double one, of the reciter 'struck dead' and that later death after 'a great reckoning in a little room'. Tenderest of all is Rosalind's denial that any in six thousand years had met Leander's fate (untold in Marlowe's poem).

Leander, he would have lived many a fair year, though Hero had turned nun, if it had not been for a hot midsummer-night; for, good youth, he went but forth to wash him in the Hellespont, and, being taken with the cramp, was drowned; and the foolish chroniclers of that age found it was – Hero of Sestos. But these are all lies: men have died from time to time, and worms have eaten them, but not for love. (*As You Like It*, IV,i,83ff.)

The playfulness covering so much hesitant and withheld feeling, which is Rosalind's charm, chimes with the memory of a contest for love and favour, ended so abruptly. A later memory of Marlowe is also associated with death. Hamlet's favourite piece of verse has a distinctly Marlovian ring, though he cannot remember it exactly (' "The rugged Pyrrhus, like th' Hyrcanean beast" – 'Tis not so; it begins with Pyrrhus' (*Hamlet*, II,ii,444–5)).

This enormous icon, much bigger than life, with 'sable arms / Black as his purpose', foreshadows, with his arrested action as he stands over Priam, his sword held aloft, an image we are to see, of Hamlet himself standing over the kneeling Claudius. It is something that has risen from the depth of the mind, and that is to return; in its primitive violence and rhetorical emphasis quite un-Shakespearian, though of course very well suited to stand out from the text of this play. This, in itself, it would appear, was the reworking of a tragedy that had belonged to Marlowe's day.

Shakespeare's relation to Kyd, and to Lyly, is often of a more detailed kind than his relation to Marlowe, for what they offered were theatrical models of rhetorical speech and dramatic patterning. What Shakespeare learnt from Marlowe, the only figure whose poetic powers approached his own, was shown rather in reaction. The greatest of Marlowe's creations, *Dr Faustus*, makes the least identifiable contribution; yet as Macbeth stands waiting for the sound of the bell, there is but one scene with which it may be compared.

Psychologists affirm that the slighter the indication of an adjustment, the deeper its roots may well lie. Shakespeare reacted to Marlowe in a selective way, and as a person; that is to say, there is an emotional train of association in his borrowings. Marlowe, it is clear from *Edward II*, also reacted to Shakespeare; and Greene's warning to Marlowe may have gained in point and malice if the two were already known in some sense to be in contest for the poetic 'crown'. Such a contest, in the plague years, would have been part of the courting of favour that had survived in Spenser's day, but was by the mid 1590s not without its alternatives. To

these Shakespeare returned, throwing in his lot with the common
players.

NOTES

1 'The Theology of Marlowe's *The Jew of Malta*', *Journal of the Warburg and Courtauld
   Institutes*, XXVII (1964), pp. 211–40.
2 *Shakespeare Survey 14* (Cambridge, 1961), pp. 34–44.
3 Greene's well-known passage in his *Groatsworth of Witte* (1592):

   > There is an upstart crow, beautified with our feathers, that with his *Tiger's heart
   > wrapped in a player's hide*, supposes he is as well able to bombast out a blank verse as
   > the best of you, and being an absolute *Johannes fac totum*, is in his own conceit the
   > only Shake-scene in a country.

   This is the first reference to Shakespeare in the literature of his time. The line is
   3 Henry VI, I,iv,137.
4 In *Christopher Marlowe*, ed. Brian Morris (London, 1968).
5 London, 1968.
6 The dedication ran: 'Clarissimo et Nobilissimo Domino Henrico Comiti South-
   amptoniae; Johannes Clapham virtutis, atque honoris incrementum multosque annos
   exoptat.' For John Clapham, see Joel Hurstfield, *The Queen's Wards* (London, 1958),
   especially p. 263 where Clapham is quoted as saying Burghley oft times gratified his
   friends and servants that depended and waited on him'. It was presumably for
   Burghley's gratification, not the dedicatee's, that the poem was written. It is unfortunately not given in Bullough's *Narrative and Dramatic Sources of Shakespeare*. *STC*
   lists only the London copy (*STC* 5349).
7 See *The Voyage to Illyria* (London, 1937), pp. 44–5, where it is also said Shakespeare
   owed most to Marlowe in this poem.
8 See my article 'Beasts and Gods; Greene's *Groatsworth of Witte* and the social purpose
   of *Venus and Adonis*', *Shakespeare Survey 15* (Cambridge, 1962), pp. 62–80.
9 T. W. Baldwin, *On the Literary Genetics of Shakespeare's Poems and Sonnets* (Urbana,
   Illinois, 1950), p. 45: 'It would seem... *Venus and Adonis* was written no long time
   before its entry for publication.'
10 For the festival of the Pui see my *Shakespeare the Craftsman* (London, 1969), pp.
   31–2.

Caliban as a Red Man

G. WILSON KNIGHT

As a contribution to a book on Shakespeare's style, my essay may at first seem inappropriate, though as it develops its placing should appear more assured. I am to point to certain analogies between Caliban and the Red Men of America.[1] We cannot say what Shakespeare knew about them, but he probably heard accounts. Some aspects of Caliban, especially what others say of him, I do not stress, being concerned rather with Caliban's own outlook. In pursuance of this argument, I rely primarily on a stylistic judgement.

At his first entry he addresses Prospero and Miranda:

> *Caliban.* As wicked dew as e'er my mother brushed
> With raven's feather from unwholesome fen
> Drop on you both! A south-west blow on ye
> And blister you all o'er!
> *Prospero.* For this, be sure, to-night thou shalt have cramps,
> Side-stitches that shall pen thy breath up; urchins
> Shall, for that vast of night that they may work,
> All exercise on thee; thou shalt be pinched
> As thick as honeycomb, each pinch more stinging
> Than bees that made 'em.
> *Caliban.*   I must eat my dinner.
> This island's mine, by Sycorax my mother,
> Which thou tak'st from me. When thou cam'st first,
> Thou strok'st me and made much of me, wouldst give me
> Water with berries in't, and teach me how
> To name the bigger light, and how the less,
> That burn by day and night; and then I loved thee,
> And showed thee all the qualities o' th' isle,
> The fresh springs, brine-pits, barren place and fertile.
> Cursèd be I that did so! All the charms
> Of Sycorax, toads, beetles, bats, light on you!
> For I am all the subjects that you have,

Which first was mine own king: and here you sty me
In this hard rock, whiles you do keep from me
The rest o' th' island.   (*The Tempest*, 1,ii,321–44)

That is our introduction.

Nature is Caliban's mental stock-in-trade. It may be impregnated by the evil charm of his mother Sycorax, who is conceived as a witch of great power, as one

That could control the moon, make flows and ebbs,
And deal in her command without her power.   (v,i,270–1)

That means, presumably, could use the Moon's power without herself possessing it. Prospero calls her practices 'earthy' and her sorceries 'terrible', though 'for one thing she did / They' – the people of Argier or Algiers – 'would not take her life' (1,ii,263–73); what that was, we are not told. Such is Caliban's descent. Prospero addresses him as 'thou earth', 'tortoise', 'poisonous slave', 'hag-seed' (1,ii,314, 316, 319, 365). He threatens Caliban with more torments.

At first all had gone smoothly, till Caliban tried to violate Miranda. He had been taught language and introduced to the higher heavenly powers. Caliban in his turn showed earth-nature to Prospero, 'all the qualities o' th' isle'. He is uniquely at home with earth-nature. His curses are weighted with it, and even in his slavery he is imprisoned by Prospero 'in this hard rock' (1,ii,343).

Caliban bears certain traces of savages as they were viewed by colonial adventurers. Their talk would often have been considered meaningless. In his *Shakespeare* Mark van Doren says that Caliban's language comes with difficulty, as though speech is hard for him.[2] Prospero refers to the time

when thou didst not, savage,
Know thine own meaning, but wouldst gabble like
A thing most brutish.   (1,ii,355–7)

However brutish he may have been, his closeness to nature demands respect. He is one with the heavier elements of earth and, to some extent, water, and his contacts cover nature's springs and fertility. Most important of all for our immediate comparison is his claim that the island is *his*; as the Red Men of America, to this hour, are persistent in their claim that they have been robbed of their land. Their land, to the Red Men, was as a living entity of which they were part.

We next meet Caliban with a burden of wood, collected for Prospero, whom he still curses:

> All the infections that the sun sucks up
> From bogs, fens, flats, on Prosper fall, and make him
> By inch-meal a disease!   (II,ii,1–3)

There is thunder which Caliban, as indeed did the Red Men, regarded as coming from the spirits:

> His spirits hear me,
> And yet I needs must curse. But they'll nor pinch,
> Fright me with urchin-shows, pitch me i' th' mire,
> Nor lead me, like a firebrand, in the dark
> Out of my way, unless he bid 'em; but
> For every trifle are they set upon me;
> Sometime like apes that mow and chatter at me,
> And after bite me; then like hedgehogs which
> Lie tumbling in my barefoot way, and mount
> Their pricks at my foot fall; sometime am I
> All wound with adders, who with cloven tongues
> Do hiss me into madness.   (II,ii,3–14)

We have a new variation on animal life. As in Caliban's curses, the animals are still spiritually impregnated, but this time by spirits controlled by Prospero. Here Caliban is aware of spirits within animal forms, as the Red Men felt through animal life to spirits. This spiritual apprehension somehow, as through his curses earlier, does not prevent the animals being real to us as animals. We feel the clustering and thickly inhabited jungle, with the noise of apes and its dangerous serpents. Caliban is vividly aware of spirits in animal or human form. At Trinculo's entry he thinks him, too, a spirit; as savage tribes sometimes do when confronted by strangers. The term is used by Caliban when he first sees the whole new community of strangers from the ship: 'These be brave spirits indeed' (v,i,261).

Our 'Indian' comparisons have verbal support, though whether Indians of east or west is intended is not clear. When Stephano enters he finds Caliban and Trinculo hiding together under Caliban's 'gaberdine', and, seeing limbs only, thinks it some trick of 'savages and men of Ind' (II,ii,55). Trinculo had earlier associated Caliban with a 'dead Indian': he had a 'fish-like smell' but was 'legged like a man, and his fins like arms' (II,ii,35).

We shall next inspect passages which will show Caliban as a nature force. Whether as spirit-powers or as their ordinary selves, he is one with earth's creatures; 'all the qualities o' th' isle' (I,ii,337) come to us unmediated by any particular 'style' of expression; or we might say we have the perfection of style in its apparent absence. In Caliban's words we shall find a 'close-up' of nature, and this apparent closeness seems to be unique in Shakespeare's nature poetry. He has always a vast resource at his disposal. There are nature-spirits in *A Midsummer Night's Dream* and there is Perdita's flower-dialogue in *The Winter's Tale*. His tragedies have elemental tempests, and references to fierce animals, lion, bear, wolf and boar. There is pretty nearly every sort of nature, located or atmospheric, in reference or setting; but all are, in the comparison I am now making, used, as it were, for a literary or dramatic purpose, and so in a way distanced. Even the stallion in *Venus and Adonis*, the boar and hunted hare, yes, and the wonderful snail (ll. 1033–6), might be called descriptive triumphs and are to that extent lacking in spontaneity. I am thinking on the lines of Tolstoy's final tenets, wherein he repudiated all artistic sophistication.[3] Caliban's nature has an actuality beyond the literary; he speaks as one embedded in it, as sophisticated man cannot be. This embeddedness somehow gets across to us in his words; it may be called a matter of 'style' but if so it is a style that does not submit to analysis; even the term 'transparent' is inapposite. The literary surface is absent and reality presented as though beside us, as in a close-up, again the best phrase I can think of to give the quality of Caliban's talk.

Comparison with the Red Men is obvious. With them, animal and elemental life is throughout emphatic. They bear animal and elemental names: Black Elk, Sitting Bull, Crazy Horse, Red Cloud, Shooting Star. In their ritual dances they wear animal disguises.[4] In trance they converse with talking animals.[5] Animals and spirits are felt in unison, or identification. The earth and higher elements are remembered; in their names, in prayers and invocations, in their belief in the supernal powers of lightning and thunder. To Earth's stones and rock they attribute vitality. Like Robinson Jeffers, they felt reality rising from 'earth's stony core'; when they made a treaty, they used to call on Earth, pounding it with a staff: 'What has the earth got to say?'[6] One's feet should be able to 'hear the very heart of Holy Earth'.[7] Caliban's earthiness is, by the Red Men's standards, wholly honourable.

We now have a trio: Stephano and Trinculo, a drinking servant and a jester, who both speak in prose; and Caliban, who speaks almost wholly in poetry, the difference in style reflecting their status. Caliban is trembling with fear of what he regards as spirits sent by Prospero to torment him, and given drink by Stephano to calm him. The drink works rapidly upon him:

> These be fine things, an if they be not sprites.
> That's a brave god, and bears celestial liquor.   (II,ii,108–9)

So

> I'll swear upon that bottle to be thy true subject, for the liquor
> is not earthly.   (II,ii,116–17)

He thinks Stephano has dropped from heaven (II,ii,127). Here he corresponds exactly to the Red Men, who were easily dominated, often to their ruin, by European drink, despite the knowledge of drugs, such as mescalin, held by certain tribes; and they smoked freely.[8] Caliban's phrase 'celestial liquor' corresponds to the Red Men's name for whisky, which they called 'Holy Water'.[9]

The drink at first seems to loosen Caliban's speech to a new freedom, so that his innate feeling for nature is unleashed. He will show Stephano 'every fertile inch o' th' island' (II,ii,138). Again:

> I'll show thee the best springs; I'll pluck thee berries;
> I'll fish for thee, and get thee wood enough.
> A plague upon the tyrant that I serve!
> I'll bear him no more sticks, but follow thee,
> Thou wondrous man.   (II,ii,150–4)

Trinculo's comment is: 'A most ridiculous monster, to make a wonder of a poor drunkard'. True: Caliban has no intellectual judgement; his gifts are of another order. Next, with growing pride in his expertise:

> I prithee let me bring thee where crabs grow;
> And I with my long nails will dig thee pig-nuts;
> Show thee a jay's nest, and instruct thee how
> To snare the nimble marmoset. I'll bring thee
> To clust'ring filberts, and sometimes I'll get thee
> Young scamels from the rock.   (II,ii,157–62)

What scamels are is not known: I imagine them as limpets. Here his nature poetry is at its best. W. H. Clemen observes the amount of 'sensuous and concrete detail' contained in these lines.[10] Caliban has pleasure and just pride in revelation of nature's secrecies, her ways and habits.

Caliban's kinship with animals does not preclude hunting them. The Red Men were characterised by their simultaneous love of nature in trees and in animals together with control and use of natural resource. In that classic document of Red Indian life and culture, Longfellow's *Hiawatha* (VII), trees are cut down and shaped for a canoe. Sympathy is accorded their complaint, but they finally agree. When a woman, to make a basket, cuts the roots of a tree, she prays to it not to be angry.[11] These are compact miniatures of the Red Men's nature-philosophy. In hunting, they used every part of the buffalo, each for a special purpose, observing full respect for the creature they had killed. There was normally no hunting for pleasure and no wanton destruction of arboreal life. In human affairs they could both inflict and endure suffering; they seem to have been unique among races in acceptance, without sentimentality, of the conditions of incarnate life, both its wonders and its agonies. Caliban's words breathe natural kinship, love, and understanding, but also mastery, through man's place in the created scheme.

In *The Oregon Trail*, Francis Parkman notes

a curious characteristic of the Indians, who ascribe intelligence and a power of understanding speech to the inferior animals; to whom indeed, according to many of their traditions, they are linked in close affinity; and they even claim the honour of a lineal descent from bears, wolves, deer or tortoises. (p. 210)

The drink intoxicates Caliban. Wildly he chants his new freedom. He has in Stephano a new master, and will desert Prospero. There will be no more unwilling labour but instead

> 'Ban 'Ban Ca-Caliban
> Has a new master – Get a new man!   (II,ii,173–4)

He is quite drunk. The fall of the Red Men is often regarded as due to their having given way to the 'fire-water' brought by Europeans.[12] In 1849 Francis Parkman wrote:

With the stream of emigration to Oregon and California, the buffalo will dwindle away, and the large wandering communities who depend on them for support must be broken and scattered. The Indians will soon be abased by whisky and overawed by military posts; so that within a few years the traveller may pass in tolerable security through their country. Its danger and its charm will have disappeared together.[13]

That is at least honest. Parkman also refers often to the treachery of the Indians. He might be thinking of Caliban who now plans, perhaps because he is under the influence of the drink, to get Stephano to murder Prospero:

I am subject to a tyrant, a sorcerer, that by his cunning hath cheated me of the island. (III,ii,40–1)

Prospero's 'sorcery' corresponds – in our admittedly quite arbitrary comparison – to gunpowder and European technology in general, which the primitive mind certainly regarded as a kind of magic.

Again the reiterated – and just – complaint:

> I say, by sorcery he got this isle;
> From me he got it.   (III,ii,49–50)

The general case of the Red Men as against white robbery is well stated in the many Indian complaints compiled by T. C. McLuhan in *Touch the Earth*.[14] Caliban continues:

> I'll yield him thee asleep,
> Where thou mayst knock a nail into his head.   (III,ii,57–8)

His murderous thoughts are crude and ugly:

> Why, as I told thee, 'tis a custom with him
> I' th' afternoon to sleep; there thou mayst brain him,
> Having first seized his books; or with a log
> Batter his skull, or paunch him with a stake,
> Or cut his wezand with thy knife. Remember
> First to possess his books; for without them
> He's but a sot, as I am, nor hath not
> One spirit to command: they all do hate him
> As rootedly as I.   (III,ii,83–91)

Caliban knows that Prospero relies on his 'books'; without them he is powerless. His magic is to this extent a magic of learning, not so far away from European science; which may indeed be supposed to be covered by his early use of the term 'liberal arts' (I,ii,73), in which what we should call 'science' was embryonic. He commands spirits tyrannically and that they resent it may be true: Ariel cries for freedom. We may suppose that Prospero's command of nature-spirits and nature in general is of the same order as western callousness in using nature for our immediate ends, regardless of consequences. Today the Red Men assert regularly that they have never been guilty of ravaging, despoiling, and pollution. Respect for the rights of the environment was intrinsic to the Indian way of life. In comparison our own record is appalling. Prospero is to Caliban a callous slave-master: 'They all do hate him as rootedly as I.' That is how nature may feel under the tyranny of technology. Indians assert that the white man's greed 'has blinded him to the pain he has caused Mother Earth by his quest for what he calls natural resources'.[15]

Caliban and his companions go ahead, bent on murder. Prospero,

knowing their purpose, has set out a rich array of 'glistering apparel' to
distract them. Stephano and Trinculo are ravished by it. We have an
indirect correspondence to the Europeans' greed for gold, which the Red
Men saw as a kind of worship, driving them 'crazy';[16] and they suffered
grimly because of it, being driven from land where gold could be found.
When Trinculo first sees the 'glistering' show, Caliban's scorn registers
his superiority: 'Let it alone thou fool; / it is but trash.' His accent exactly
corresponds to the Red Men's inability to understand the Europeans'
gold-lust. He warns them a second time: 'What do you mean / To dote
thus on such luggage?' (IV,i,229–30).

They are now trapped: '*A noise of hunters heard. Enter divers* Spirits, *in
shape of dogs and hounds, hunting them about*'. Prospero uses animals, or
spirits as animals, for harsh purposes; there is no evidence in him of a
kindly approach to animal life. We heard earlier of his punishing Caliban
with the sting of bees (I,ii,329–30), and Caliban describes at length other
instances, as we have seen. The hounds are sympathetically viewed, but
then they are half humanised and used for a cruel purpose; the joy of a
hunt is innately cruel. We are given their names:

> *Prospero.* Hey, Mountain, hey!
> *Ariel.*   Silver! there it goes, Silver!
> *Prospero.* Fury, Fury! There, Tyrant, there! Hark, Hark!   (IV,i,254–6)

Two of Prospero's names are harshly toned, but Ariel's corresponds with
his own quicksilver quality. The pleasure and excitement of a hunt is
before us. They are hunting human beings; we may remember that
hounds were used to track runaway slaves. Prospero has more torments in
store:

> Go charge my goblins that they grind their joints
> With dry convulsions, shorten up their sinews
> With agèd cramps, and more pinch-spotted make them
> Than pard or cat o'mountain.   (IV,i,257–60)

Another callous reference to animals, very different from the ingrained
sympathy of Caliban's 'nimble marmoset' (II,ii,160), or his later exquisite:

> Pray you, tread softly, that the blind mole may not
> Hear a foot fall.   (IV,i,194–5)

This is perhaps Caliban's best natural 'close-up'. Prospero speaks from a
superiority, Caliban from an identity, with the animal creation.

The Tempest is full of spirits, in one shape or another; but if we concentrate on Caliban, my sole present purpose, we can say that he is sometimes aware of spirits in animals and sometimes speaks of nature direct. In both modes, the animals, as animals, are vividly present, and probably more so than when others speak of them, in *The Tempest* or elsewhere in Shakespeare. The style has an authenticity beyond that of Shakespeare's style of reference elsewhere, which may be called at the lowest 'fanciful' and at the best 'literary'.

Now what I am leading up to is this: *exactly the same applies to Caliban's style in respect of extra-sensory perceptions*. In *The Tempest* spirits may activate animals, or may, as by Caliban and once by Miranda (I,ii,409–11), be confused with human beings; or each may function alone. The general conception, widely understood, may, despite what is due to artifice and plot-fabrication, be allowed to give us a sense of spiritual reality behind or within phenomena; a reality, or essence, that makes phenomena live. So it is not strange to find that what is true of Caliban's nature poetry is true also of his spiritual poetry. His words have the same immediacy of style.

Before I approach Caliban's lines on music, it is as well to make an apology. I am working now, as not before, at what is called 'literary criticism'. As a critic rather than an interpreter, I have what may seem some strange, though tentative, judgements. I myself have always a hankering for facts. I tend to respect Byron's statement, thinking of *Marino Faliero*, in his letter to John Murray of 2 April 1817, that 'pure invention is but the talent of a liar'. I have for long been critical of *Macbeth* for subjecting its protagonist to an unfair treatment of the sources, and have often suggested that the stage record of ill luck attending performances may accordingly be due to the activity of inimical spirit-powers. My own personal books have been strongly factual, as were *Atlantic Crossing, The Dynasty of Stowe*, my poems *Gold-Dust*, and still more the biography of Jackson Knight, my brother.[17] True, imagination has given them a colouring, and factual report in the biography included, necessarily, spiritualistic experience. Faithfulness to the factual, if honest, will include much that is strange. I certainly never regard the 'factual' as excluding the 'supernatural' or things beyond ordinary sense-perception.

This emphasis on the factual, or on 'reality', accounts for my high rating of Shakespeare's accomplishment in Shylock. The poetic conception and treatment is used to present to us a Jew as a well-known figure with an aura of racial attributes; yet, as misfortune closes in on him, he has the thrust and realism of great tragedy. The coalescence of actuality and imagination is perfect. Beside him it is easy to see Macbeth and Lear as extravagances. Othello covers a racial problem, like Shylock, with a personality well realised, the all-important and dramatically dominating handkerchief being so dissolved into his personal aura that its semi-superstitious nature is discounted; but the plotting is arbitrary, as Shylock's story is not. Shylock is so well done that he is, like Falstaff, in danger of ruining the drama in which he occurs.

These are personal studies, and it may be because Macbeth and Lear are more dissolved into their separate poetic universes that they are less acceptable as persons; and that may be part of a yet greater task. I do not know. All I emphasise is that, as rounded *persons*, Shylock, Falstaff and possibly Othello stand out. For a whole play, *Timon of Athens*, discussed fully in my recent (1977) *Shakespeare's Dramatic Challenge*, has, as a whole, something of the impact I am trying to describe, exerting the pressure of reality: Hazlitt well says that of all his plays Shakespeare was here most 'in earnest'. It has no extrinsic supernatural machinery though a kind of supernature is in the action: Timon as Promethean semi-super-man, his 'god'-given Gold and his Nirvana ending. Timon's nature-contacts and critique of society correspond, point by point, to the Red Men's culture. The play has, of course, faults, presumably being in an unrevised state; and Timon, as a person, is not without looseness of delineation. In both *The Merchant of Venice* and *Timon of Athens* riches, the central concern of the European world, are a primary concern.

If all, or some, of this be allowed, then Caliban with his rich earth-contacts, which correspond so closely with those of aboriginal natives, and especially the Red Men of North America, undoubtedly qualifies as an outstanding Shakespearian delineation in the realistic mode. His nature-contacts enclose a whole range of animals. They may be blended with spirits, in his curses and his thought of Prospero's use of them to torment him, or he may feel them directly. But what I would point to is the way they affect us, whatever the reference: the 'raven's feather' of his curses, the 'tumbling hedgehogs' of his torment, the 'nimble marmoset' and 'blind mole' of direct apprehension, all are equally living and vivid presences verbally conveyed. I hazard again the suggestion that they hold a reality beyond any others in Shakespeare; the rest are more 'literary', at the best more 'imaginative'. With Caliban, as Lear says of Edgar, we have 'the thing itself' (*King Lear*, III,iv,106).

Now as the Red Indians, whom John Cowper Powys calls 'this most original and formidable race among all the children of men',[18] had wonderful spiritual apprehensions, so also does Caliban. The Red Men lived in a richly peopled universe beyond normal sensory perception. They believed in spirits within animals and men; they had superlative visionary experiences; they heard atmospheric voices, songs and music, and, above all, they dreamed; honoured dreams were a large part of their life. The record is clear in *Black Elk Speaks* (see n. 1) and elsewhere.

When Caliban and his companions hear Ariel's song, the Europeans are afraid of this invisible, ghostly music. Not so Caliban. It is to him part of his normal, clairvoyant, apprehension, and he speaks lines on the intimations around us which do not relate merely to Ariel's song, but have a purely general implication:

> Be not afeard. The isle is full of noises,
> Sounds, and sweet airs, that give delight, and hurt not.
> Sometimes a thousand twangling instruments
> Will hum about mine ears; and sometime voices
> That, if I then had waked after long sleep,
> Will make me sleep again; and then, in dreaming,
> The clouds methought would open and show riches
> Ready to drop upon me, that, when I waked,
> I cried to dream again.   (III,ii,130–8)

The riches of Caliban's vision contrast with the 'trash' of the glistening robes set to entrap them as the two aspects of riches contrast in *The Merchant of Venice* and *Timon of Athens*.

These were the lines at which my brother murmured with subdued intensity, during a performance of *The Tempest* by Charles Doran's Company which we attended together at Oxford in 1922, 'What does it mean?' – thereby prompting, perhaps inaugurating, my life's work in Shakespearian interpretation. With all the critical confidence I can muster, I assert that these few marvellous lines, like Caliban's nature poetry, and for the same deep reason, transfix us with a direct, convincing and unique report of the powers surrounding us. Our perceptions are normally constricted to an arbitrary selection of phenomena. Were they not, we might, as Alexander Pope has it, 'die of a rose in aromatic pain'.[19] The absurdity of our normal supposition that the nature of the surrounding universe is limited to our normal sense-perception has been admirably discussed in Arthur Ford, *The Life Beyond Death*, recounted by Jerome Ellison.[20] Abnormal children who have difficulties of communication may none the less have experience of voices and music unknown to

normality. As with a radio, we may not know how to turn on the switch;
but the music in the atmosphere and the voices are there for when the
switch is on, none the less. For Caliban the switch is always on; he makes
no distinction between man and spirit, the natural and the supernatural,
and sees and hears what to us is wonderful; his every accent is there to
prove it. We forget the occasion. We are, for the moment, outside *The
Tempest*, but inside the universe; a spiritualistic universe. The universe of
the Red Men.

In *Black Elk Speaks* we have a true and mainly autobiographical
account of how Black Elk as a youth was caught up into a heavenly vision
which fertilised his life, laying on him commands to serve his people. He
had extra-sensory experience, travelling back to America in spirit when
he was in Europe with a circus. He practised spiritual healing. The story
is interthreaded with animals. At his central visionary experience we are
told:

All the universe was silent, listening; and then the great black stallion raised his voice and
sang. . . His voice was not loud, but it went all over the universe and filled it. There was
nothing that did not hear, and it was more beautiful than anything can be. It was so
beautiful that nothing anywhere could keep from dancing. (Ch. III, p. 39)

We are reminded of Caliban's 'thousand twangling instruments'; it is a
similar, vast, music, travelling the universe. 'Voices', like Caliban's, of all
kinds are on page after page of Black Elk's story.

> In a sacred manner they have sent voices.
> Half the universe has sent voices.
> In a sacred manner they have sent voices to you. (Ch. XVI, p. 137)

Voices are everywhere. There are dreams too, as in Caliban's speech.
Dreams are universally respected by primitive cultures, but were probably rated more highly, and were more habitually experienced and used,
by the Red Men than by any other culture on record. Indian medicines or
charms, we are told in *The Oregon Trail*, 'are usually communicated in
dreams' (Ch. XV, p. 212). Of a healer in *Black Elk Speaks* we hear that he
performed 'after he had sung a certain sacred song that he had heard in a
dream' (Ch. II, p. 21). Dreams are the opening to the higher, visionary,
consciousness. There was 'a dreamer religion', to whose devotees dreams
were 'the sole source of supernatural power'.[21]

Finally, when Black Elk tries to recapture his early transcendent
experience while his people are wilting under European oppression and

injustice, recalling his lost vision and the failure of his life's work, at the book's heart-rending end, he cries to the great spirits:

Again, and maybe the last time on this earth, I recall the great vision you sent me. It may be that some little root of the sacred tree still lives. Nourish it then, that it may leaf and bloom and fill with singing birds. Hear me, not for myself, but for my people; I am old. Hear me that they may once more go back into the sacred hoop,[22] and find the good red road, the shielding tree!

With tears running down his cheeks, the old man raised his voice to a thin high wail, and chanted:

In sorrow I am sending a feeble voice, O Six Powers of the World. Hear me in my sorrow, for I may never call again. O make my people live!

For some minutes the old man stood silent, with face uplifted, weeping in the drizzling rain.[23]

So too Caliban weeps for the riches he had glimpsed: 'I cried to dream again.'

For Caliban nature and spirits are one; and what is true of his nature poetry is true equally of his spiritual apprehensions. Here too, I see them as out-spacing all Shakespeare's other spiritual adventures, great as they may be. Of these, the most dramatically exciting are composed of the traditional, and to that extent factual, elements: the black magic of *Macbeth*, traditional folklore; the Ghost in *Hamlet*, a blend of folklore and theology; the vision of Jupiter in *Cymbeline*, Roman mythology; the angels in *Henry VIII*, Christian. Though great as drama, and often the greater for their use of tradition, they remain artefacts. For equivalents to Caliban's lines, where the extra-sensory is so cogently, yet simply, experienced, bearing every impress of actuality, we can point to Joan's defence in *1 Henry VI* (v,iv,36–53); to Glendower's spirit-music in *1 Henry IV* (III,i,226–8, 233–5); to the healing scene in *All's Well That Ends Well*;[24] and to the resurrection of Hermione in *The Winter's Tale*, which comes from the will to place esoteric possibilities within a normal plot. These do not, however, so wonderfully compact the whole truth as Caliban's lines; which indeed, in their statement of mysteries beyond ordinary perception, may be allowed to make good sense of Shakespeare's symbolic powers elsewhere. They might even be seen as an introduction to the Shakespearian universe; and perhaps this has something to do with *The Tempest*'s being placed first in the Folio. Caliban's lines are comprehensive and unique. This may be, as with his nature poetry, a question of

style, though its style is, necessarily, slightly different. It does not, as
psychic descriptions so often do, lack vigour, but is fully, and imagisti-
cally, alive, to be experienced by the reader, or listener, as an immediacy.

If, as Dr Johnson said,[25] there is always in criticism room for an appeal
beyond literature to life itself, then the quality of Caliban's poetry, in
both its natural and supernatural contacts, becomes apparent. In it
Shakespeare forecasts what may be the future of world-literature, concerned less with the fictional than the factual, but with a factuality that
encompasses the supernatural.

In the story, Caliban realises his foolishness in thinking Stephano a
god, and seeks for 'grace' (v,i,295). That is a reasonable ending, which we
might set beside the conclusion to *Hiawatha*, where the Red Men are to
be converted to Christianity; which again, given the period of composition, we may regard as a normal conclusion. What is important, however,
is not the end, but the events that form the main substance.

Something, but far from all, of Caliban's natural kinship and its higher
extensions is given by Robert Browning's *Caliban upon Setebos*, so
admirably studied in Thomas Blackburn's *Robert Browning*.[26] There is
more in Beerbohm Tree's approach, in costume, make-up, and general
sympathy, as recorded in his illustrated souvenir edition of *The Tempest*.[27] Tree's sensitivity to Shakespeare's poetry is evident from his
bird-song interlude in his production of *Much Ado About Nothing*, long
before Caroline Spurgeon's researches into Shakespeare's imagery, and
his Weird Women actually seen floating in 'fog and filthy air' in *Macbeth*
(I,i,12); as well as in his own vocal recordings from *Richard II*, *Julius
Caesar* and *Hamlet*. But never was his status in poetic understanding
more evident than in his electing to act Caliban himself, and his building
up of the part even at the cost of some overbalance. I am thinking of his
conclusion, as pictorially illustrated in the souvenir, showing Caliban
alone on the island rocks, and looking out sadly, according to the
stage-direction, on the departing ship. A copy is shown in my *Shakespearian Production*.[28]

Here our analogy collapses. The Red Men would have been glad
enough to see the last of the Europeans.

Postscript, October 1977

Since composing my essay, my attention has been drawn by Professor
Gāmini Salgādo to Leslie A. Fiedler's *The Stranger in Shakespeare*,[29]

which contains a careful study of *The Tempest* in relation to its forecast of colonisation, paying exact regard to Caliban. Some of my own points are made: see especially the reference to European 'technology' (Ch. IV, p. 238). Mr Fiedler observes throughout 'a kind of music' and 'natural rhythm' in Caliban's talk (p. 235). I should point also to the 'brilliant analyses in D. G. James's *The Dream of Prospero*.[30]

I have concluded recent performances of my dramatic recital[31] with a short delineation of Caliban in Red Indian guise.

NOTES

1 For my Red Indian material I rely on the following books: John G. Neihardt, *Black Elk Speaks* (London, 1974; first published 1961); Frank Waters, *Masked Gods* (New York, 1973; first published 1950); Ralph T. Coe, Catalogue of the 'Sacred Circles' Exhibition, Hayward Gallery, London, October 1976–January 1977 (Arts Council of Great Britain, 1977); Carlos Castaneda, *The Teachings of Don Juan* (Harmondsworth, 1976; first published 1968); Francis Parkman, *The Oregon Trail* (Harmondsworth, 1949; first published 1849); T. C. McLuhan, *Touch the Earth* (London, 1973; first published 1972).

2 Mark van Doren, *Shakespeare* (New York, 1939), pp. 325–6. In his notes on *The Tempest*, Dr Johnson quotes Warburton as follows: 'It was a tradition, it seems, that Lord Falkland, Lord C. J. Vaughan, and Mr Seldon concurred in observing, that Shakespeare had not only found out a new character in his Caliban, but had also devised and adapted a *new manner of language* for that character' (*Johnson on Shakespeare*, ed. Walter Raleigh (London, 1908, repr. 1909), p. 66).

3 Relevant thoughts on Tolstoy are developed in my *Christian Renaissance* (London, 1962), Ch. III, pp. 38–40.

4 Waters, *Masked Gods*, Part Two.

5 Neihardt, *Black Elk Speaks*, Ch. III, pp. 28–9, 42.

6 Murray Hickey Ley, Papers lodged at Notre Dame University (South Bend, Indiana, USA), *Introductions* [booklet], pp. 24, 27.

7 McLuhan, *Touch the Earth*, p. 90.

8 For drugs, see Castaneda, *The Teachings of Don Juan*.

9 Neihardt, *Black Elk Speaks*, Ch. X, p. 100.

10 *The Development of Shakespeare's Imagery* (London, 1951), Ch. XIX, p. 187.

11 McLuhan, *Touch the Earth*, p. 40.

12 McLuhan, *Touch the Earth*, pp. 83, 102, 104, 141, 161.

13 *The Oregon Trail*, Ch. XIV, p. 176.

14 See pp. 85, 87, 91–2, 96–7, 107, 131, 156, 169.

15 Letter by a group of Indians to President Nixon, quoted in McLuhan, *Touch the Earth*, p. 170.

16 Neihardt, *Black Elk Speaks*, Ch. II, p. 18.

17 *Jackson Knight: A Biography* (Osney Mead, Oxford, 1975).

18 In his *Autobiography* (London, 1934), Ch. XI, p. 548.

19 *An Essay on Man*, I, 200.

20 London, 1974 (first published 1972), Ch. I, pp. 38–41, also Ch. V, p. 114.

21 McLuhan, *Touch the Earth*, pp. 56, 178n.

22 For the importance of 'hoops' or circles in Red Indian culture, see the Catalogue for 'Sacred Circles', noted above (n. 1), pp. 18–19. Also see McLuhan, *Touch the Earth*, p. 178.

23 Postscript to Neihardt, *Black Elk Speaks*, pp. 190–1.

24 Discussed in my *The Sovereign Flower* (London, 1958), Ch. II, pp. 148–54.

25 'Preface to Shakespeare', in *Johnson on Shakespeare* (see n. 2, above), p. 16.

26 London, 1967, Ch. IV, pp. 155–61.

27 London, 1904.

28 London, 1964.

29 London, 1973.

30 Oxford, 1967, pp. 81, 106, 111–14.

31 Described in *Shakespeare's Dramatic Challenge* (London and New York, 1977).

Shakespeare's Dark Lady:
a question of identity

S. SCHOENBAUM

My mistress' eyes are nothing like the sun;
Coral is far more red than her lips' red;
If snow be white, why then her breasts are dun;
If hairs be wires, black wires grow on her head.
I have seen roses damasked, red and white,
But no such roses see I in her cheeks;
And in some perfumes is there more delight
Than in the breath that from my mistress reeks.
I love to hear her speak, yet well I know
That music hath a far more pleasing sound;
I grant I never saw a goddess go –
My mistress when she walks treads on the ground.
    And yet, by heaven, I think my love as rare
    As any she belied with false compare.   (Sonnet 130)

It was, I believe, Aldous Huxley who once spoke of the imbecile earnestness of lust. Shakespeare can certainly be earnest on the subject; witness the tremendous sonnet (just preceding the one quoted) in which, in an explosively forceful series of self-lacerating modifiers, he excoriates a passion that post-coitally he despises, and which yet tyrannises over body and spirit. But Sonnet 130 reflects another mood; the lover is at once clear-eyed and high spirited. His mistress's attractions can survive his own denigration of them. So she withstands the anti-Petrarchan assault of the three quartets – the reference to disagreeable breath seems especially devastating in an age of oral hygiene – to assert her allure, and attendant mystery, in a concluding couplet that draws its special force from *not* being dependent upon romantic illusion.

This is the Dark Lady who, more than three and a half centuries ago, sauntered into the best-loved sequence of lyric poems in the language. They describe with a playwright's art how she captivated the poet, against his reason, and seduced the golden youth he adored. One of the great sorceresses of literature, she has since added innumerable readers to the tally of her conquests. My subject is this intriguing personage, and especially how men have responded to her wiles, first in the imaginative achievements of art, and then in the more prosaic endeavours of scholarship, by embarking upon a quest for her real-life identity.

One may grant straightaway that the Dark Lady of the Sonnets is no Helen of Troy, and that her pursuers include among their number no Schliemann of literary excavation. This dusky phantom eludes us still, although every now and then somebody makes a stir by announcing to a momentarily attentive world that he has solved the riddle. Perhaps the questors would have done well to apply to the mistress the malediction carved on Shakespeare's gravestone. Yet the story of the search for the Dark Lady, which begins with an eccentric Scottish antiquary in the late eighteenth century, and ends (more likely pauses) with an idiosyncratic English historian in the twentieth, brings its own rewards. If on the whole we learn more about the seekers than the sought, such knowledge nevertheless holds an interest of its own for those who savour the vagaries of human behaviour. The story has moments of farce, and also of poignance. Success of a sort unexpectedly emerges out of failure. For the critic this question of identity raises the larger perennial issue of the relations between a poet's experience and the well-wrought urn that is the vehicle of his experience. The Shakespeare life-record is no blank, as the uninformed have supposed, but it is destitute of the intimate revelations which only letters, diaries, and the like can furnish. In their absence, the Sonnets – clearly more private than the plays – urge on us an autobiographical reading. Do we legitimately yield to their pressure?

I

Familiar as the poems are, it may be well to begin by piecing together what we can about the Dark Lady from the revelations, sometimes obscure or contradictory, that they afford. She makes her entrance obliquely, a felt presence rather than a directly introduced member of the dramatis personae. 'Base clouds' suddenly overcast a sunny day. Somehow the poet's friend has given offence. We hear of a wound, of disgrace and shame, and of penitent tears. The trespass, the next sonnet (35) reveals, was theft, and the fault 'sensual'. Five poems later the nature of the larceny becomes clearer, although not yet explicit. 'Take all my loves, my love', the poet cries, 'yea, take them all.' It seems that the friend has taken Shakespeare's mistress.

At last, in Sonnet 41, indirections cease, the circumlocutions of tact and poetical conceit give way; what has happened is starkly stated:

> Gentle thou art, and therefore to be won,
> Beauteous thou art, therefore to be assailed;
> And when a woman woos, what woman's son,
> Will sourly leave her till she have prevailed?

So she – whoever she is – has taken the role of aggressor, and the beauteous friend has succumbed. It is an interesting triumph. The lovely boy is high-born, the poet's patron, and of ambiguous masculinity. Nature has fashioned him to be a woman, and given him a woman's face; but rather spoilt things for the heterosexual poet by outfitting her exquisite creation with a male organ. The emotional and psychological weight of these poems resides in the relationship between the two men. The woman who has come between them is still only a shadow – or cloud.

Later she comes into her own. In Sonnet 127 we meet her properly and for the first time learn about the colouration that sets her apart. Black wires grow upon her head, Sonnet 130 adds, and 'If snow be white, why then her breasts are dun', which the Oxford Dictionary helpfully defines as 'of a dull or dingy brown colour; now *esp.* dull greyish brown, like the hair of the ass and mouse'. If the Dark Lady is beautiful, hers is an unfashionable beauty; but some question emerges as to whether she is beautiful by any standard:

> In faith, I do not love thee with mine eyes,
> For they in thee a thousand errors note.

This is 141; just two sonnets earlier the poet has commended her 'pretty looks'. Are all these poems, one may wonder, addressed to the same woman? Or is it merely that we are witnessing a lover's varied moods? The old adage holds that beauty lies in the eye of the beholder; perhaps the report shifts, not the object reported. It is one of many puzzles.

Elsewhere we tread on firmer ground. We learn that the lady is musical, and (in Sonnet 128) catch a charming glimpse of her seated at the virginals. Perhaps she sings as she plays. Her fingers dance over the wooden keys, the jacks leaping nimbly up to kiss the inside of her hand. Her lover, envying the jacks, kisses his mistress on the lips. It is rather like a seventeenth-century Dutch genre painting.

Other poems show the Dark Lady as a *belle dame sans merci*, tyrannising over her lover. She breaks her bed-vow – does this mean she is married, as most have assumed, or merely that she has broken a vow made to her lover when they were in bed together? About her sexual appetite and promiscuity, however, there is no question; she is 'the bay where all men ride'. Even when with the poet she humiliates him by eyeing other men. Older than his mistress – 'my days', he laments, 'are past the best' – and consequently insecure, he wearily accepts her infidelities, and deludes himself into crediting 'her false-speaking tongue'. The word *lies* furnishes an opportunity for rueful word-play:

> Therefore I lie with her, and she with me,
> And in our faults by lies we flattered be.

Will, another key word, could mean 'carnal desire or appetite'. It might also signify the male or female genitalia. And of course the poet's name was Will. He plays with all these meanings simultaneously in Sonnet 135, where (in the 1609 quarto) the word *will* is italicised – with an uppercased *W* – seven out of the thirteen times it appears:

> Whoever hath her wish, thou hast thy Will,
> And Will to boot, and Will in over-plus;
> More than enough am I that vex thee still,
> To thy sweet will making addition thus.
> Wilt thou, whose will is large and spacious,
> Not once vouchsafe to hide my will in thine?

The only thing virginal about this lady is the musical instrument she fingers so fluently.

In an extraordinary sonnet (151) the poet contemplates her powers of conjuration over another instrument, which stands erect at the mere mention of her name: 'flesh stays no farther reason, / But, rising at thy name, doth point out thee / As his triumphant prize'. What are we to make of a mistress who can be thus addressed? Was she, as some have thought, a common prostitute? Standards of propriety of course vary with the times and with individuals; one man's grossness is another's refreshing candour. If we may occasionally lament the loss of past reticences, a flesh-and-blood Shakespeare is perhaps preferable to the impassive statuary of the culture-worshippers who wend their pious way to the Stratford shrines and cough through a performance at the Royal Shakespeare Theatre. We do well every now and then to remind ourselves that Shakespeare, father of three, had a penis.

The 144th Sonnet sets in perspective the complex triangle involving Poet, Fair Youth, and Dark Lady:

> Two loves I have, of comfort and despair,
> Which like two spirits do suggest me still;
> The better angel is a man right fair,
> The worser spirit a woman coloured ill.
> . . .   .
> But being both from me, both to each friend,
> I guess one angel in another's hell.
>   Yet this shall I ne'er know, but live in doubt,
>   Till my bad angel fire my good one out.

This seems straightforward enough: Hell fits nicely into a scheme that includes good and bad angels, saint and devil, and gains here another dimension by alluding to the game of barley-break, in which the last couple playing found itself 'in hell'. But hell was also a cant word for the female organ; hence the sexual innuendo of: 'I guess one angel in another's hell.' The last line possibly harbours a grimmer allusion. 'To fire out', which meant originally 'to smoke a fox out of its den' – cf. *King Lear*, V,iii,23: 'fire us hence like foxes' – also signified 'to communicate a venereal disease'.

A similar allusiveness may help to explain the otherwise puzzling last two poems of Shakespeare's sonnet sequence. These, as a recent critic sums up,

are generally looked upon as an appendix not connected with the story, which Shakespeare or the printer added simply to enlarge the collection. Both tell a fanciful story about the origins of a medicinal spring, brought into being when a nymph extinguished Cupid's torch in a well, which 'took heat perpetual' from this fire.[1]

'I, sick withal, the help of bath desired', the poet reports, 'and thither hied, a sad distempered guest.' The Greek Anthology, the ultimate source of these poems, makes no reference to the curative powers of the waters. As early as the eighteenth century, a commentator queried, 'Whether we shall read *Bath* (i.e. the city of that name)?' Bath is still celebrated for its medicinal hot springs, the fountains of the town proudly displaying the dubious motto, 'Water is best.' Although in Shakespeare's day it had not yet become a fashionable spa, Elizabethans sought out the waters of Bath for curative purposes: the title-page of the 1572 quarto of *The Baths of Bath's Aid*, by John Jones, physician, commends them as 'wonderfull & most excellent agaynst many Sicknesses', and William Turner, doctor in physic, contributed an appendix on 'the rare treasure of the English Bathes' to Thomas Vicary's *The Englishman's Treasure* (1587 edn). True, the word *bath* is not capitalised, or placed in italics, in Sonnets 153 and 154 in the 1609 edition, as are other proper nouns (*Cupid, Dian's*); but one cannot expect nice distinctions to be scrupulously maintained by a typesetter unchecked by authorial supervision. A topographical identification is in any event not required: there were other spas, and the reference may point, not to natural springs, but to the sweating tubs, filled with hot water, used by the victims of venereal infection. Some such allusiveness seems to be indicated by the sexual innuendoes of these two sonnets.

'I, my mistress' thrall, / Came there for cure', Shakespeare concludes in the last lines of his last sonnet, but the waters appear to have vouchsafed no cure, only the awareness that: 'Love's fire heats water, water cools not love.' Thus, ingloriously does the cycle end. If this reading is correct, and underneath their fanciful surface Sonnets 153 and 154 reveal the unpleasant medical consequences of an illicit affair, they perhaps afford an autobiographical clue to the sex-nausea that so many critics have remarked on in *Hamlet, Troilus and Cressida*, and *King Lear*.

Whatever the merits of such speculation, the Dark Lady is (within the limits of lyric poetry) as vitally realised a dramatic creation as Cressida, with her wanton spirits looking out from every joint and motive of her body, and some have wondered whether both portraits were drawn to the life from the same sitter. Never mind; we have enough to occupy us with the Dark Lady on her own, although the information is not always so clear cut as either one would wish or some have surmised. To sum up: she is younger than the poet, musical, raven-haired and raven-eyed, dark-skinned (how dark is not clear), and either unattractive or unconventionally beautiful, depending upon the viewer and the viewer's mood. She is certainly seductive, gives free rein to her appetite, may be married, and is possibly infected with venereal disease. In character she is a *femme fatale*: proud, fickle, overbearing, and deceitful. No wonder scholars have sought to find for her a local habitation and a name.

II

That the quest got under way relatively late is also not surprising, in view of the early publishing history of the Sonnets. Thomas Thorpe's 1609 quarto, the copy-text followed by all modern editors, bristles with perplexities, but represents an authentic text, even if the author himself failed to proofread it. The edition published thirty years later by John Benson is another matter. This is a pirated text with which the stationer tampered by omitting the celebrated dedication to Mr W.H., altering some of the male pronouns, and mischievously rearranging the poems, to which he gave misleading titles. Thus he destroyed their character as a sonnet cycle. The Sonnets were not included in any form in the First Folio in 1623 or in the three succeeding folios, which represented for seventeenth-century readers *the* collected edition of Shakespeare. In 1709 Nicholas Rowe called his six-volume collection *The Works of Mr William Shakespear,* but he too left out the Sonnets. These a publisher's hack supplied in an unauthorised seventh volume, unfortunately basing his text on Benson. The poems could by then be described as 'these less known works of *Shakespear*'.

Why were the Sonnets so negligently handled by their early editors? The simple answer seems to be that the literati then entertained no very high regard for them. Thus Charles Gildon, the aforementioned hack, acknowledged (while answering) current opinion that 'they are not valuable enough to be reprinted, as was plain by the first Editors of his Works who wou'd otherwise have join'd them altogether'.[2] Pope enshrined Gildon as a blockhead in *The Dunciad,* but he too ignored the Sonnets in his edition, leaving them to another hack, the physician George Sewell, to furnish in an appendix volume. It remained for Edmond Malone, justly described as 'the prince of Sonnet editors and commentators',[3] to bring out the first careful edition, complete with annotation. This he did in 1780. Even so, when thirteen years later George Steevens published his fifteen-volume edition, he adamantly refused to admit the Sonnets, sneering,

We have not reprinted the Sonnets, &c. of Shakspeare, because the strongest act of Parliament that could be framed, would fail to compel readers into their service. . . Had Shakspeare produced no other works than these, his name would have reached us with as little celebrity as time has conferred on that of Thomas Watson, an older and much more elegant sonnetteer.[4]

Steevens's low opinion of the sonnet form had previously been abundantly demonstrated in the notes he contributed in 1780 to Malone's *Supplement to the Edition of Shakspeare's Plays Published in 1778.* There (vol. 1, p. 682n.) he wrote: 'That a few of these trifles deserving a better character may be found, I shall not venture to deny; for chance cooperating with art and genius, will occasionally produce wonders.' Steevens's perversity is fully appreciated, but his opinion of sonnets in general, and of Shakespeare's in particular, provoked no contemporary outrage. I know of no more striking illustration of the changes wrought in sensibility by the whirligig of time. One should perhaps not too lightly discount the possibility one day of a Watson revival.

The great Malone resisted the temptation to speculate on the identity of the poet's mistress; a forbearance that his contemporary George Chalmers would have done well to emulate. Today pretty well forgotten, Chalmers is an interesting minor character, the early biographer of Daniel Defoe and Thomas Paine, and compiler of *Caledonia*, a notable repository of antiquarian Scottish lore. On the subject of Shakespeare's *Sonnets*, however, there befell Chalmers what has afflicted others since: his sanity deserted him. In his *Apology for the Believers in the Shakspeare-Papers* (1797), a tome swollen to over six hundred pages, Chalmers proposes in dead earnest that the *Sonnets*, apparently all of them, are addressed to Queen Elizabeth. That Shakespeare urges his adored friend to marry and procreate, and that Elizabeth was (by Chalmers's own reckoning) then past sixty, does not deter him. Nor is Chalmers perturbed by the tell-tale masculine pronouns in the poems. The Elizabethans did funny things with pronouns, the Queen was 'often considered as a man' – that is, various writers, including Spenser and Bacon, refer to her as a prince – and anyway: 'When Shakspeare draws his topics of praise from metaphysics, he is, like other metaphysicians, cold, dark, and unintelligible.' Greeted with indifference or derision, Chalmers responded two years later with a six-hundred-page sequel volume, *A Supplemental Apology for the Believers in the Shakspeare-Papers*, in which he reaffirms and elaborates his position. He is one of the moral scholars, his aim being to demonstrate how Shakespeare – 'a husband, a father, a moral man' – could not have 'addressed a hundred and twenty, nay, a hundred and twenty-six *Amourous* Sonnets to a *male* object'. Chalmers even reproduces Sonnet 20 and fails to detect a ribald pun in the concluding couplet:

> But since she [Nature] pricked thee out for women's pleasure,
> Mine be thy love, and thy love's use their treasure.

'To *prick*', Chalmers sagaciously notes, 'is often used by Shakspeare for to *mark*, as indeed the word is used sometimes at present. . .'. As Chalmers elsewhere remarks, apropos of the same issue: 'It is for impure minds only, to be continually finding something obscene in objects, that convey nothing obscene, or offensive, to the chastest hearts.'[5]

A similarly chaste motive impels the few critics who identify the *Sonnets'* enchantress with Shakespeare's wife, alternatively referred to as 'poor Anne' or 'the Stratford beauty'. In view of the fact that the guilt-ridden sonnets about lust are even more unsettling – and certainly more puzzling – if inspired by a wife rather than a mistress, the whole endeavour has its self-defeating aspect. Still, the theory is not a dead loss, as it has at least yielded a limerick:

> Bill Shakespeare wrote many a sonnet:
> He gave one, instead of a bonnet,
> Each Easter to Anne –
> He gave it – then ran –
> And left her to meditate on it.[6]

More creditable than these wayward fancies are the claims of Mary Fitton, a Victorian favourite. She was one of the Queen's Maids of Honour, but notable neither for maidenhood nor honour; for she became the mistress of William Herbert, the third Earl of Pembroke, and had the mischance to bear him a short-lived son. The Earl, having taken his pleasure, declined matrimony, and the Queen, not amused, made him cool his heels for a while in the Fleet prison. Mary went on to bear Sir Richard Leveson two bastard daughters before marrying a Captain William Polwhele. A contemporary described this mettlesome minx putting off her head-dress, tucking up her clothes, taking a large white cloak, and marching off as a man to her assignation with the Earl. Mary has the right morals – or lack of conventional morals – for the Dark Lady role, but of course this particular identification depends upon acceptance of Pembroke as Fair Youth of the Sonnets. The Earl has not wanted distinguished advocates, and that his claim still thrives is shown by the publication, in 1975, of J. H. Padel's essay on the Sonnets, 'That the Thought of Hearts Can Mend', in *The Times Literary Supplement*.

Whatever may be said on behalf of Mary Fitton, this whole episode in literary scholarship has its special interest less because of her than, rather, on account of the obscure individual who championed her cause. Thomas Tyler put the case in his 1890 edition of the *Sonnets*, which bears every appearance of having been printed at his own expense. And Tyler himself lives because, as a regular reader at the British Museum in the 1880s, he chanced to strike up an acquaintance with a writer of genius. Long afterwards, on the eve of the Great War, Bernard Shaw set down his grotesquely poignant description of this middle-aged gentleman, in a slightly shabby frock coat and tall hat, who was 'of such astonishing and

crushing ugliness that no one who had once seen him could ever thereafter forget him'.

His figure was rectangular, waistless, neckless, ankleless, of middle height, looking
shortish because, though he was not particularly stout, there was nothing slender about
him. . .Attached to his face from the left ear to the point of his chin was a monstrous
goitre, which hung down to his collar bone, and was very inadequately balanced by a
smaller one on his right eyelid. . .When you first met Thomas Tyler you could think of
nothing else but whether surgery could really do nothing for him. But after a very brief
acquaintance you never thought of his disfigurements at all, and talked to him as you
might to Romeo or Lovelace; only, so many people, especially women, would not risk the
preliminary ordeal, that he remained a man apart and a bachelor all his days.

A pessimist, Tyler

delighted in a hideous conception which he called the theory of the cycles, according to
which the history of mankind and the universe keeps eternally repeating itself without the
slightest variation throughout all eternity; so that he had lived and died and had his goitre
before and would live and die and have it again and again and again.[7]

For him Mary Fitton assumed the force of an obsession; the elaborate-
ness and ingenuity of his arguments for her as the Dark Lady can only be
suggested here. Accepting (with others) that the reference to a broken
bed-vow required Shakespeare's mistress to be married, and aware that
1607, the year of Mary Fitton's wedding, is too late for the *Sonnets*, Tyler
demonstrates, with contortions of ingenuity, that Mary had previously
taken a husband, as a young girl, but that this marriage had been declared
illegal and void. Tyler detects a pun on Fitton (= the fit one) in the bawdy
151st sonnet, a discovery to which one responds with an involuntary
double-take, for the phrase 'fit one' does not occur in the poem. He
sought out Mary's tomb at Gawsworth in Cheshire, and delightedly
announced that her monument, begrimed with the dust of centuries,
showed traces of paint indicating her dark hair and complexion. The
Tyler story illustrates one of the uses of scholarship: in the arms of this
wraith he found solace; Mary Fitton became his surrogate mistress.

She deceived him, as she had misled others. 'It would be very desir-
able', Tyler wrote in his edition, 'that Shakespeare's graphic delineation
in the Sonnets should be compared with a coloured portrait of Mrs
Fitton, if such could be found, and could be adequately certified.'[8] That
was in 1890. Seven years later Lady Newdigate-Newdegate, whose
husband, Sir Edward, was Mary Fitton's great-great-great-great-great-
grandson, reproduced in her *Gossip from a Muniment-Room* two portraits
of Mary. They show an English beauty with brunette hair, grey eyes, and

fair complexion. For Shaw and others the portraits settled the question, although Tyler continued his lonely crusade – he denounced the pictures as fakes – until he died, 'sinking unnoted like a stone in the sea'.

Still Tyler's advocacy has won its belated converts, most notably that scoundrel Frank Harris, and Mr Anthony Burgess has in his *Shakespeare* respectfully cited her candidacy for the role of Dark Lady. But she has yielded to rivals. Inevitably it occurred to someone that the dusky mistress might be black in the sense in which we use that word today. The German poet and novelist, Wilhelm Jordan – author of *Demiurgos*, a work which, according to the 11th *Britannica*, 'attempted to deal with the problems of human existence' but 'found little favour' – first made the suggestion as early as 1861. He noted the lady's black wires; so her hair must be curly and twisting. 'My mistress when she walks treads on the ground', Shakespeare wrote – aha, so she was flat-footed! There is a certain literalness about Jordan, and his preoccupation with race and blood has a dishearteningly familiar aspect. In any event, from these references, as well as other clues – her musical aptitude and 'hot-blooded coquetry' – Jordan concluded that the Dark Lady hailed 'from the West Indian colonies, was of creole descent with an admixture of African blood'; maybe a mulatto or a quadroon.[9] There the matter rested until 1933, when G. B. Harrison came up with a real-life woman from Shakespeare's London: Lucy Negro, a courtesan who plied her trade in the stews of Clerkenwell. A Gray's Inn entertainment of 1594 pays ironical tribute to Lucy as the Abbess of Clerkenwell, with her choir of nuns who, with their burning lamps, chant *placebo* to Inns of Court gallants and other young men-about-town.[10] The possibility of miscegenation involving the National Poet caused predictable unease in some quarters. Hyder Rollins, compelled to report the Black Lady theory, does so with fastidiously controlled distaste. To Edgar I. Fripp, Unitarian minister and Stratford antiquary, there is a way round the embarrassment: the Abbess of Clerkenwell is someone whose loose tongue and manners the poet perhaps observed, and around whom he amusedly wove 'his strange, sometimes gross fancies'; not a woman whose dark mysteries he physically explored.[11] Mr Burgess will have none of such prurient evasions. He takes an artist's view of the putative liaison: 'Possibly Shakespeare's falling for a dark skin was no poetic eccentricity [there being no colour prejudice in those days], though the initial contact may have come from poetic curiosity.'[12]

It remained for Leslie Hotson to track down the Lucy Negro of

London's demimonde.[13] He found she was not what her name suggests,
but white: one Luce Morgan, who belonged in the late seventies and early
eighties to the company of the Queen's familiar gentlewomen, and was
more than once favoured with gifts from her Majesty. At some
time – when is not known – she quit the court in disgrace. Worse and
worse days succeeded the former, and Luce Morgan made a new career
for herself as madame of a brothel in St John Street, Clerkenwell. She
contracted syphilis and obligingly shared it. In 1600 the Court of
Aldermen, in one of their periodic crackdowns on urban immorality,
committed this 'notorious and lewd woman' to Bridewell, where with
other bawds she beat hemp for her hard labour. An epitaph printed in
1656 reports that she turned Catholic and died of the pox, when we don't
know. Is this Shakespeare's Dark Lady? Dr Hotson believes she is, and
further (if I read him correctly) that he has removed a stain from
Shakespeare's reputation. To Harrison, he declares, belongs 'the dis-
credit of believing Shakespeare's fair enslaver a blackamoor'. Why dis-
credit? Better, one gathers, that Shakespeare should take up with a
syphilitic brothel-keeper than share his bed with a West Indian coquette.
But, of course, once the Dark Lady is found to be fair, she ceases to be a
Dark Lady, and Mistress Morgan is surely too old, being (by Hotson's
calculation) some four years Shakespeare's senior; the *Sonnets* explore his
infatuation with a younger woman. Once again the Dark Lady, seemingly
ensnared, has eluded her pursuers.

   Other players have drawn scattered applause, then retired to the
wings. There is Jacqueline Field, championed by Charlotte Carmichael
Stopes, who left it to her daughter Marie to eulogise married love, finding
it distasteful herself. Jacqueline was the wife of Richard Field, a former
Stratford neighbour of the Shakespeares who had set up shop as a printer
in London, and who had published Shakespeare's two early narrative
poems. Her sole qualification is that she was French; therefore dark-eyed,
sallow complexioned, endowed with indefinable charm, and presumably
an enthusiast of *amour*, married or not. It is curious the way this quest
invokes the old stereotypes, racial or national. If an aristocrat is preferred
to a bourgeois, one may wish to consider the daughter of the first Earl of
Essex, Penelope Rich, who (in the discreet words of one memorialist)
'had from the first an attenuated regard for the marriage tie'. Does not
Shakespeare allude to her in Sonnet 146, when he writes, 'Within be fed,
without be *rich* no more'? Lady Rich is of course Sir Philip Sidney's
Stella, and it is doubtful that she made a double killing in the sonnet

sweepstakes. She has had few supporters. In fact nobody in recent years has dominated the field. The stage was set for Dr Rowse.

On 29 January 1973, *The Times* carried a feature article, headed 'Revealed at Last, Shakespeare's Dark Lady', by A. L. Rowse. Once published, *The Times* article was summarised in newpapers and magazines the world over. For weeks afterwards the correspondence columns of the paper reverberated with responses – heated, facetious, or merely informative. Even Dame Agatha Christie entered the lists. Dr Rowse had made a stir.

In his controversial biography of Shakespeare, Dr Rowse claimed to have solved all the problems of the *Sonnets* but one; everything 'except for the identity of Shakespeare's mistress, which we are never likely to know'. That was in 1963. At the Bodleian Library, Dr Rowse was then working his way through the case-books of Simon Forman. A contemporary of Shakespeare – Forman was born in 1552 and died in 1611 – this remarkable individual was a physician, astrologer, and lecher, at all three of which vocations he enjoyed considerable success. He has long been known to Shakespeare scholars by reason of his manuscript *Book of Plays*, in which he gives eye witness accounts of performances at the Globe of *Macbeth*, *The Winter's Tale*, and *Cymbeline*. But apparently nobody before Rowse had undertaken to examine the mass of other papers. Here, in one of the case-books, among the mingle-mangle of English and Latin and diagrammed astrological forecasts, Dr Rowse discovered his Dark Lady.

She was Emilia Lanier, *née* Bassano, the daughter of Baptist Bassano and Margaret Johnson, who, although unmarried, lived together as man and wife. The Bassanos were a family of court musicians who had come to England from Venice to serve Henry VIII. Their descendants stayed on at court in the same capacity; Baptist's will describes him as 'the Queen's musician'. Emilia was only six when her father died, and by the time she was seventeen, in 1587, she was an orphan with a dowry of £100 – not a negligible sum in those days when a skilled artisan earned sixpence for a day's work – but she was hardly an heiress. She mended her fortune, however, by becoming the mistress of Henry Carey, 1st Lord Hunsdon, then well advanced in years. As Lord Chamberlain he supported the players in their sporadic skirmishes with the municipal authorities, and he was himself the patron of an acting troupe; for a while, just before his death, in 1596, he sponsored Shakespeare's company, the Chamberlain's Men. Finding herself pregnant by the noble lord, Emilia (according to

Rowse) covered up by taking as a husband a court minstrel, William Lanier, several years her junior. Not suprisingly, the marriage didn't go too well. Emilia told Forman, whom she visited in 1593 to have her horoscope cast, that

> she hath been favoured much of her Majesty and of many noblemen, hath had great gifts and been made much of – a nobleman that is dead hath loved her well and kept her. But her husband hath dealt hardly with her, hath spent and consumed her goods. She is now very needy, in debt and it seems for lucre's sake will be a good fellow, for necessity doth compel.

She will be a good fellow; so she was promiscuous. She was also, Dr Rowse reported, dark: Forman describing her as 'very brown in youth', with 'a wart or mole in the pit of the throat or near it'. Would she, Emilia asked the wizard, ever be a Lady? Forman, for his part, tried to have *halek* with her. *Halek* is his code word for sexual intercourse. At first she drew away – she was a coquette – but later dispatched her maid to fetch him to her. 'I went with them', he records in his diary, 'and stayed all night.' She told him tales about the invocation of spirits. In January 1600 Emilia Lanier sent for Forman, and he wondered 'whether she intendeth any more villainy'. By then he was finished with her.

This, in sum, is the story of Emilia Lanier, as it emerges from the pages of the case-books of the astrologer Simon Forman. His case established, Dr Rowse re-wrote his 1963 biography of Shakespeare, mainly (one guesses) to give Emilia a showcase, and published it in 1973 as *Shakespeare the Man*. In the preface to the emended second printing he claims that the resurfacing of Emilia 'has triumphantly vindicated the answers I have put forward all along, and the method by which they were found. . .The discovery of the Dark Lady completely corroborates, and puts the coping-stone on, my previous findings' – i.e. the chronology of the *Sonnets* and the identity of Fair Youth, Rival Poet, and Mr W.H. And a page later, with breathtaking confidence:

> Perhaps I should add now merely that it will be found quite impossible to impugn any of them, for they are the definitive answers. It should be encouraging for research to think that Elizabethan problems, which have awaited their answer for centuries, can still be resolved at this late date.

In the same year Rowse brought out a revised version of his edition of the *Sonnets*, titled *Shakespeare's Sonnets: The Problems Solved*, complete with paraphrases for those who prefer to read their poems as prose, and with sufficient reference to Emilia in the annotations.

But is she the Dark Lady? She was promiscuous, and her dates do accord with Dr Rowse's dating of the *Sonnets*. Coming as she did from a musical family, she may well have been accomplished at the virginals. Dr Rowse observes that the husband's christian name, William, makes an admirable basis for puns, lending another dimension to the word-play of the Will sonnets:

> Whoever hath her wish, thou hast thy Will,
> And Will to boot, and Will in over-plus.

Over-plus indeed! But Rowse is wrong about the name of the lady's husband: she married Alfonso, not William, Lanier. Alfonso is not such a good name for puns. And was Emilia dark? An odd phrase, 'very brown in youth', as though brownness of coloration diminished with the passage of the years. Stanley Wells was the first to look more closely at the words in Forman's diary, which Rowse conveniently reproduced in his *Shakespeare the Man*. The word, Dr Wells noted, is not *brown* at all, but *brave*: she was very brave in youth. It is not even a very difficult reading. *Brave* here means 'splendid', 'fine', 'showy'; no help. We cannot, then, even say on the basis of the evidence that Emilia Bassano, or Lanier, was dark. So we are left with a promiscuous lady. There must have been others in Elizabethan London – else why such an outcry about venereal disease? Even had Dr Rowse got all of his facts straight, his argument would have been no more than a tissue of conjecture; very interesting conjecture, to be sure, but conjecture none the less. No wonder that *The Times*, which had announced in a front-page headline 'A. L. Rowse discovers Shakespeare's Dark Lady', quickly beat a prudent retreat, and for the correspondence which followed used the non-committal heading, 'Another Dark Lady'.

This episode has a curious aftermath. The facts about Emilia and her husband were not long in coming to light after Dr Rowse published his *Shakespeare the Man*. The next year, in 1974, he had a chance to retrace his steps in his biography of Simon Forman. Again he tells Emilia's story. She is now brave, not brown, and her husband's name is correctly given, in passing, as Alfonso. Nowhere does Dr Rowse allude to past errors, and about his thesis he remains impenitent. 'I am all the more convinced', he asserts, '. . .that here in this Italianate woman we have the Dark Lady.' As one item of evidence he cites 'her brief affair with the player-poet of the Company'.[14] Thus what one sets out to prove becomes, almost magically, the proof itself. In Dr Rowse's latest life, *Shakespeare the*

Elizabethan,[15] speculation is accorded the status of fact, and the dust-wrapper duly hails 'his unanswerable identification of Shakespeare's Dark Lady'.

III

Emilia Lanier brings to a close my selective survey of Dark Ladies; the quest, pursued with so much energy, learning, and ingenuity, fizzles out with yet another failure. Could it have been otherwise? Surely the puzzle contains too many imponderables to admit of a solution. So long as scholars continue to debate the identity of Mr W.H. and the Fair Youth, and to disagree about the dating of the *Sonnets*, so long is the Dark Lady likely to retain her mystery; these problems are interrelated. External evidence alone – a reference in some contemporary diary or correspondence – can silence the sceptics, and that is the card some of us were hoping Dr Rowse had up his sleeve. Probably it was foolish to think such a card could ever have existed. Rowse and the others assume that the *Sonnets* comprise rhymed fourteen-line entries in a personal diary, and that their revelations represent the raw materials of experience. But poets wear masks. May not much of what is intimate about these poems be private and interior, and what is exterior – derived from the world of events – transmuted and ordered by the implacable necessities of art? The opposition between Fair Youth and Dark Lady is, after all, comprehensible in terms of poetic and moral symbolism; whether or not Shakespeare in his own life kept a mistress of this hue, he required her services for his poetry. I wouldn't wish to suggest a simple choice between the *Sonnets* as autobiographical record and the *Sonnets* as literary exercises, although critics have been drawn towards these polarities. Polarities are reductive. Between them exist innumerable gradations, which should wonderfully serve to encourage caution, the biographical virtue Dr Rowse most conspicuously lacks. In conflating art with life, he and his predecessors run the risk of being no less naïve than the visitors to Verona who gaze, moved, at Juliet's balcony.

Must we then in the last resort conclude with Edward Dowden, 'We shall never discover the name of that woman'?[16] Perhaps so. (Dowden's pejorative *that* is symptomatic. Commentators tend to endorse without hesitation the poet's estimate of his mistress; her whorish nature is a commonplace of criticism. But of course we see her only through the eyes of her restlessly dissatisfied lover; she is a creation of the male ego. Could she speak, the mistress's view of herself, her lover, and the affair might instructively differ.) One can appreciate J. W. Mackail's unillusioned judgement that 'all the labour that has been spent upon it [her pursuit] is pure waste'.[17] In his recent (1977) edition of *Shakespeare's Sonnets*, Stephen Booth takes a similar line, thus demonstrating a reticence not otherwise greatly evident in his stimulating if over-elaborate commentary. 'Speculation on her identity', Booth tersely remarks, 'has ranged from wanton to ludicrous and need not be illustrated.'[18]

Perhaps I have unwisely failed to heed these counsels, although I would hope that something might be said in defence of my approach. A contemporary of Shakespeare speaks of 'God's revenging aspect upon every particular sin to the despair and confusion of mortality'. If I have sported with folly rather than sin, the theme has its Jehovan aspect: we witness the consequences of credulity and error, and are accordingly chastened. That is to emphasise the negative. The quest for the Dark Lady has brought its own scholarly rewards, although ironically these are not what the questors sought. They have recovered Mary Fitton and Luce Morgan and Emilia Lanier, and surely we should be grateful to them for retrieving from the buried past these vital and passionate women; minor personages no doubt, and ones who did not influence the sweep of public events, but such obscure lives convey some of the flavour of history which the careers of princes and prelates cannot.

There is more to it. When Dr Rowse published his findings about Emilia, a university lecturer in Belfast, Roger Prior, pursued the trail a little further, and discovered that in 1611 she had published a slender volume of poems, *Salve Deus Rex Judaeorum*. This quarto survives in eight copies, several of them defective. As the title indicates, the temper of the poems is religious, with the authoress taking a stern line with respect to 'wicked worldlings' and 'the imbracements of unchaste desires'. If she has had a past, she doesn't much sound like the Dark Lady, although Dr Rowse (as he is entitled) thinks otherwise. What is pertinent is that these poems, which have gone unnoticed for three and a half centuries, have some character. An individual voice speaks, a feminist voice at that:

> Not that I Learning to my selfe assume,
> Or that I would compare with any man:
> But as they are Scholers, and by Art do write,
> So Nature yields my Soule a sad delight.[19]

Dr Rowse would persuade us that Emilia is the second female poet of the

Elizabethan age, after Sidney's sister, the Countess of Pembroke. Maybe so. Certainly the poems should find an editor. Thus we have looked for a Dark Lady, and instead we find a lady poet. We seek verifiable truth, and settle for the consolations of art. In a Keatsian sense we have perhaps not gone too far astray.[20]

NOTES

1 James Winney, *The Master Mistress: A Study of Shakespeare's Sonnets* (London, 1968), p. 27.
2 Charles Gildon, 'Remarks on the Poems of *Shakespear*', in William Shakespeare, *Works*, ed. Nicholas Rowe (London, 1709–10), vol. VII, p. 446. Hyder Edward Rollins puts Gildon and the legions of *Sonnets* editors and commentators in perspective in his New Variorum edition of the *Sonnets* (Philadelphia and New York, 1944). Rollins's own commentary is indispensable for any study of the textual and interpretative history of these poems, although of course much (from which I have profited) has appeared since 1944. I have previously considered the identification of the personages of the *Sonnets* in the context of the history of Shakespearian biography in *Shakespeare's Lives* (Oxford, 1970); for the historian it is an agreeable luxury to re-survey some of the terrain after an interval of years, and to bring the story (at least as regards the Dark Lady) up to date.
3 John Dover Wilson, Introduction to the New Cambridge Shakespeare edition of the *Sonnets* (Cambridge, 1967), p. xi.
4 Shakespeare, *Plays*, ed. Samuel Johnson and George Steevens (London, 1793), vol. I, Advertisement, pp. vii–viii.
5 George Chalmers, *An Apology for the Believers in the Shakspeare-Papers* (London, 1797), pp. 42–66; *A Supplemental Apology for the Believers in the Shakspeare-Papers* (London, 1799), pp. 21, 58–63.
6 Brainerd McKee, *Shakespeare in Limerick* (London, 1910), no. XXVI; cited by Rollins, *Sonnets*, vol. II, pp. 259–60n.
7 Bernard Shaw, *Misalliance, The Dark Lady of the Sonnets, and Fanny's First Play* (London, 1914), pp. 104–5.
8 Shakespeare, *Sonnets*, ed. Thomas Tyler (London, 1890), p. 80n.
9 Wilhelm Jordan, *Shakespeare's Gedichte* (Berlin, 1861), pp. 413–15; summarised (with translated extracts) by Rollins, *Sonnets*, vol. II, p. 243.
10 G. B. Harrison, *Shakespeare Under Elizabeth* (New York, 1933), p. 64.
11 Edgar I. Fripp, *Shakespeare: Man and Artist* (London, 1938), vol. I, p. 263. Rollins (*Sonnets*, vol. II, p. 272) disparagingly notes that Fripp makes no reference to Harrison; but the former, who died two years before Harrison's book was published, came up with the suggestion, somewhat laundered, on his own.
12 Anthony Burgess, *Shakespeare* (London, 1972), p. 146.
13 Leslie Hotson, *Mr W.H.* (London, 1964), pp. 244–55.
14 A. L. Rowse, *Simon Forman: Sex and Society in Shakespeare's Age* (London, 1974), p. 117. When, in 1973, *Shakespeare the Man* was 'Reprinted with alterations', Rowse corrected 'brave', and Emilia is now married to 'Alfonso Lanier'; but Sonnet 135 still 'plays upon the fact that there are two Wills: her husband and Will Shakespeare' (p. 94).
15 London, 1977.
16 Shakespeare, *Sonnets*, ed. Edward Dowden (London, 1881), p. 17.

17 J. W. Mackail, *Lectures on Poetry* (London, 1911), p. 188; cited by Rollins, *Sonnets*, vol. II, p. 251.

18 *Shakespeare's Sonnets*, ed. Stephen Booth (New Haven and London, 1977), p. 549.

19 Emilia Lanier, *Salve Deus Rex Judaeorum* (1611), sig. G1. The title-page describes her as 'Mistris *Aemilia Lanyer*, Wife to Captaine *Alfonso Lanyer*, Servant to the Kings Majestic'. Rowse gives an account of the poems in his *Simon Forman*, pp. 104–16.

20 I wish to thank I. A. Shapiro and am grateful to the late T. J. B. Spencer for helpful comments when this paper, in a somewhat different form, was given as a public lecture.

CHECKLIST OF WRITINGS BY KENNETH MUIR
1937–1979

(The following categories have been omitted: verse, fiction, articles later incorporated in books, articles on educational topics, articles on politics, pseudonymous and anonymous articles, and reviews.)

1 *The Voyage to Illyria: A New Study of Shakespeare,* by K.M. and Sean O'Loughlin (Methuen, London, 1937)
2 *English Poetry* (ed.) (Oxford University Press, 1938)
3 'The Imagery of *All for Love*' (*Proceedings of the Leeds Philosophical and Literary Society* [*PLPL*], 1940)
4 'The Chronology of Marlowe's Plays' (*PLPL*, 1943)
5 '*Locrine* and *Selimus*' (*Times Literary Supplement* [*TLS*], 1944)
6 'The Method of T. S. Eliot' (*Durham University Journal*, 1944)
7 'Swinburne on Middleton' (*TLS*, 1945)
8 'Shelley's Heirs' (*Penguin New Writing*, Harmondsworth, 1946)
9 'Matthew Arnold and the Victorian Dilemma' (*PNW*, 1947)
10 'Three Anglo-Jewish Poets' (*Metsudah*, 1947)
11 'Unpublished Poems in Add. MS. 17492' (*PLPL*, 1947)
12 *Collected Poems of Sir Thomas Wyatt* (ed.) (Routledge and Kegan Paul, London, 1949)
13 'Shakespeare and Dante' (*Notes and Queries* [*NQ*], 1949)
14 'Sonnets from the Hill MS' (*PLPL*, 1950)
15 'A Chapman Masque' (*TLS*, 1950)
16 'A Test for Shakespeare Variants' (*NQ*, 1950)
17 *Macbeth* (ed.) (Methuen, London, 1951; revised several times)
18 'Marvell and Virgil' (*NQ*, 1951)
19 'The Dramatic Function of Anachronism' (*PLPL*, 1951)
20 'The Jealousy of Iago (*English Miscellany*, 1951)
21 'Shakespeare Interpretation' (*Shakespeare Survey* [*SS*], 1951)
22 *King Lear* (ed.) (Methuen, London, 1952; revised several times)
23 *Elizabethan Lyrics* (ed.) (Harrap, London, 1952)
24 'Collier Fabrications' (*NQ*, 1952)
25 'Shakespeare and Rhetoric' (*Shakespeare-Jahrbuch* [*SJ*], 90, 1952)
26 *The Painful Adventures of Pericles* (ed.) (Liverpool University Press, 1953)
27 'Andrew Marvell' (*Leeds University Review*, 1953)
28 'The Order of Constable's Sonnets' (*NQ*, 1954)

29 'Kipling and Eliot' (*NQ*, 1954)
30 *John Milton* (Longmans, London, 1955)
31 'Changing Interpretations of Shakespeare', in *Pelican Guide to Literature*, vol. II (Harmondsworth, 1955)
32 *The Pelican Book of English Prose*, vol. I (ed.) (Harmondsworth, 1956)
33 *Shakespeare's Sources*, vol. I (Methuen, London, 1957) [cf. no. 93, below]
34 *The Life and Death of Jack Straw*, ed. K.M. and F. P. Wilson (Malone Society, Oxford, 1957)
35 *John Keats: A Reassessment* (ed.) (Liverpool University Press, 1958)
36 'Elizabethan Remainders' (*Library*, 1958)
37 'Wittes Fittes and Shakespeare' (*NQ*, 1958)
38 'An Unfinished Prompt Book' (*Shakespeare Quarterly*, 1958)
39 *Shakespeare and the Tragic Pattern* (Oxford University Press, 1959)
40 'Three Shakespeare Adaptations' (*PLPL*, 1959)
41 *Five Plays of Jean Racine* (trans.) (Hill and Wang, New York, and London, 1960)
42 *Sir Philip Sidney* (Longmans, London, 1960)
43 *Shakespeare as Collaborator* (Methuen, London, 1960)
44 'Shakespeare le Dramaturge', in *Œuvres Complètes*, ed. P. Leyris and H. Evans (Paris, 1960)
45 'Source Problems in the Histories' (*SJ*, 1960)
46 'Surrey Poems in the Blage Manuscript' (*NQ*, 1960)
47 *Unpublished Poems of Sir Thomas Wyatt and his Circle* (ed.) (Liverpool University Press, 1961)
48 *Last Periods of Shakespeare, Racine and Ibsen* (Liverpool University Press and Wayne State University Press, Detroit, 1961)
49 *Shakespeare: The Great Tragedies* (Longmans, London, 1961)
50 *Shakespeare the Dramatist*, by U. Ellis-Fermor (ed. K.M.) (Methuen, London, 1961)
51 '*Antony and Cleopatra*, III.xiii.77' (*NQ*, 1961)
52 'Bernard Shaw' (*Lexicon der Literatur der Gegenwart*, 1961)
53 'Prose and Verse' (*Stratford-upon-Avon Studies*, IV, 1962)
54 'Some Words in *Devoreux*' (*NQ*, 1962)
55 *Richard II* (ed.) (Signet, London, 1963)
56 *Shakespeare: 'Hamlet'* (Arnold,.London, 1963)
57 *Life and Letters of Sir Thomas Wyatt* (Liverpool University Press, 1963)
58 'Calderón's *A House with two Doors is Difficult to Guard*' (trans.) (*The Drama Review*, 1963)
59 'Shakespeare and Politics', in *Shakespeare in a Changing World*, ed. A. Kettle (London, 1964)
60 '*Hamlet*', in *William Shakespeare* (Moscow, 1964)
61 'Shakespeare's soliloquies' (*Occidente*, 1964)
62 'Shakespeare the Dramatist' (*Filološki Pregled*, 1964)
63 'Shakespeare the Man', in *A Garland for Shakespeare* (Jalpaiguri, India, 1964)
64 *Shakespeare: The Comedies* (ed.) (Prentice-Hall, Englewood Cliffs, N.J., 1965)
65 'Shakespeare's Imagery: Then and Now' (*SS*, 1965)
66 'The Duke's Soliloquies in *Measure for Measure*' (*NQ*, 1966)
67 'Image and Structure in *Our Mutual Friend*' (*Essays and Studies*, 1966)
68 'Socialist Realism and the Freedom of Art' (*Coexistence*, 1966)
69 *Le Cid* (trans.), in *Seventeenth-Century French Drama* (Random House, New York, 1967)

70 *Introduction to Elizabethan Literature* (Random House, New York, 1967)
71 *Othello* (ed.) (Penguin, Harmondsworth, 1968)
72 *'The Winter's Tale': A Casebook* (ed.) (Macmillan, London, 1968)
73 *Collected Poems of Sir Thomas Wyatt*, ed. K.M. and Patricia Thompson (Liverpool University Press, 1969)
74 'Shaw and Shakespeare', in *Festschrift Rudolf Stamm*, ed. K. Kolbe and J. Hasler (Francke Verlag, Bern and Munich, 1969)
75 *The Comedy of Manners* (Hutchinson, London, 1970)
76 *A New Companion to Shakespeare Studies*, ed. K.M. and S. Schoenbaum (Cambridge University Press, 1971)
77 'Blake in the Eighteenth Century' (*Literary Half-Yearly*, 1971)
78 'Plays', in *Drama and Theatre*, ed. J. R. Brown (Routledge and Kegan Paul, London, 1971)
79 *Shakespeare's Tragic Sequence* (Hutchinson, London, 1972)
80 'A Trick of Style' (*Shakespeare Studies*, 1972)
81 *Shakespeare the Professional* (Heinemann, London, 1973)
82 *Essays and Studies 1974* (ed.) (Murray, London, 1974)
83 *'King Lear'*, in *Shakespeare: Select Biographical Guides*, ed. Stanley Wells (Oxford University Press, 1974)
84 'Personal Involvement and Appropriate Form in Milton's Poetry' (*Etudes Anglaises*, 1974)
85 'Theophanies in the Last Plays', in *Shakespeare's Late Plays*, ed. P. C. Tobias and P. G. Zolbrod (Ohio University Press, Athens, Ohio, 1974)
86 *Three Plays of Thomas Middleton* (ed.) (Dent, London, 1975)
87 'The Critic, the Director and Liberty of Interpreting', in *The Triple Bond*, ed. J. G. Price (University of South Carolina Press, Columbia, 1975)
88 'The Case of John Ford' (*Sewanee Review*, 1976)
89 'American Critics of Shakespeare's Tragedies' (*Shakespeare Studies*, 1976)
90 *Aspects of 'Othello'*, ed. K.M. and Philip Edwards (Cambridge University Press, 1977)
91 *Aspects of 'Macbeth'*, ed. K.M. and Philip Edwards (Cambridge University Press, 1977)
92 *The Singularity of Shakespeare* (Liverpool University Press, 1977)
93 *The Sources of Shakespeare* (Methuen, London, 1977)
94 'Imagery in Prose Fiction' (*Káñina*, 1977)
95 'The Order of Shakespeare's Sonnets' (*College English*, 1977)
96 *'Hamlet'*, in *Notes on Literature*, ed. R. Adlam (Tokyo, 1977)
97 *Aspects of 'Hamlet'*, ed. K.M. and Stanley Wells (Cambridge University Press, 1979)
98 *Shakespeare's Comic Sequence* (Liverpool University Press, 1979)
99 *Shakespeare's Sonnets* (Allen and Unwin, London, 1979)
100 *'Sabrina and Ophelia'* (*NQ*, 1979)

INDEX

Akrigg, G.P.V., *Shakespeare and the Earl of Southampton*, 197
Alexander, Peter, 152
All's Well That Ends Well, 177, 183, 185, 19c
Anderson, Mary, 61
Antony and Cleopatra, 69–70, 77, 95–109, 187–8, 190
Aristotle's *Poetics*, 113, 125
Armitage, Charles, 60
As You Like It, 27, 123, 124, 141, 167–8, 184, 186, 202–3

Baldwin, T.W., 6, 200
Barish, Jonas, 66
Barton, Anne, 45, 46, 98
Beaumont, Francis, *Knight of the Burning Pestle*, 153
Bell, John, 57
Benson, Sir F., 60
Bethell, S.L., 136
Booth, Stephen, 237
Bowdler, Thomas, 61
Bradley, A.C., 70, 71, 76
Brand, Tita, 63–4
Brooke, Arthur, *Tragicall Historye of Romeus and Juliet*, 59–61, 64
Brooke, Nicholas, 52, 195, 201
Brown, John Russell, *Shakespeare's Dramatic Style*, 88, 93
Browning, Robert, *Caliban upon Setebos*, 218
Bullough, Geoffrey, 60
Burgess, Anthony, 231
Burton, D.M., *Shakespeare's Grammatical Style*, 22

Caliban *(The Tempest)*, 205–20 *passim*
Capell, Edward (editor), 57
Catullus, 105

Chalmers, George, 228
Charney, Maurice, *Style in Hamlet*, 93
Cibber, Theophilus (editor), 60
Clapham, John, *Narcissus*, 197–8, 199
Clemen, W.H., 209
Coleridge, S.T., 26, 53–4, 62, 95–6, 102
Comedy of Errors, 164, 186
Coriolanus, 108, 128, 186
Craig, Hardin, 2, 152
Cuningham, Henry, 79–80
Cymbeline, 113, 136, 138–48 *passim*

David, Richard, *The Janus of Poets*, 93
Day, John, *Isle of Gulls*, 154
Dowden, Edward, 236
Dryden, John, 151
Duthie, G.I., 54, 62

Edwards, Philip, 126
Eliot, T.S., 108
Empson, William, 80–1, 82, 92
Ervine, St John, 59–60
Evans, Edith, 59–60
Everett, Barbara, 66

Fiedler, Leslie A., *The Stranger in Shakespeare*, 218–19
Fitton, Mary, 229–31
Forbes-Robertson, Sir J., 61
Ford, Arthur, *The Life Beyond Death*, 215
Forman, Simon, 233–4, 235
Fripp, Edgar L., 231

Garrick, David, 57, 60
Gildon, Charles, 227
Gower, John, *Confessio Amantis*, 115, 116
Greene, Robert, 149, 151, 154, 199, 203

Hamlet, 7, 27, 65, 69, 84–5, 92, 128, 137, 141, 155–6, 160–1, 163, 184, 203
Harrison, G.B., 57, 231
Hart, Alfred, 187
Hazlitt, William, 214
1 Henry IV, 68, 86–9, 90, 92, 106, 134, 173–6, 186
2 Henry IV, 134, 148, 155, 176
Henry V, 5, 89–92, 134–5, 176, 187
1 Henry VI, 4, 9–24 *passim*, 13
2 Henry VI, 1, 3–4, 9–24 *passim*, 58
3 Henry VI, 9–24 *passim*, 58
Henry VIII, 189–90
Hotson, Leslie, 231–2
Hunter, G.K., 194

Irving, Sir H., 57, 61

Jaggard, William, *The Passionate Pilgrim*, 29, 31, 32
Johnson, Dr, 138, 145, 154, 159
Jonson, Ben, 34–5, 68, 104, 105, 153–4, 157, 161, 201
Jordan, Wilhelm, 231
Julius Caesar, 5, 99, 135, 156, 186

Keightley, Thomas (editor), 57
King John, 5, 6, 58, 101, 145–6, 185
King Lear, 44–6, 65, 113, 121, 122, 128, 159–61, 185
Kittredge, G.L., 187
Knight, G. Wilson, 69, 124
Knights, L.C., 71, 84
Kyd, Thomas, 194, 203

Lacy, T.H., 61
Lanier, Emilia, *née* Bassano, 233–6, 237–8
Latham, Agnes, 123
Leavis, F.R., 158, 159
Lever, J.W., 187
Longfellow, H.W., *Hiawatha*, 210, 218
Love's Labour's Lost, 2, 25–38, 145–6, 163–6
Lyly, John, 203

Macbeth, 4, 27, 67–77, 79–83, 85–6, 92, 97–9, 104, 128, 135, 143, 153, 157, 218
Mackail, J.W., 237
McLuhan, T.C., *Touch the Earth*, 211
Malone, Edmond (editor), 227
Marlowe, Christopher, 22, 153–4, 191–204
Marshall, Frank A. (editor), 57
Marston, John, 161
Measure for Measure, 5–6, 64, 123, 169, 178–80, 187

Merchant of Venice, 113–14, 168–9, 185, 191–4, 201, 213–14
Meres, Francis, 152
Merry Wives of Windsor, 144, 183–5
Midsummer Night's Dream, 208
Miriam Joseph, Sister, 6, 16
Montaigne, M. de, 181
Much Ado About Nothing, 122–3, 218
Muir, Kenneth, 4–5, 16–17, 58, 71, 72, 81, 129, 189, 199, 241–3
Murry, Middleton, 71, 97

Nashe, Thomas, 64
Nurse *(Romeo and Juliet)*, 51–66, 139

O'Loughlin, Sean, 199
Olson, Charles, 136
Othello, 7, 27–8, 69, 77, 84, 132–3, 135, 158–9, 186, 188–9
Otway, Thomas, 57

Padel, J.H., 229
Parkman, Francis, 210, 216
Passionate Pilgrim, The, 29, 31–32
Peele, George, *The Old Wives Tale*, 132
Pericles, 111–30, 137–8, 141–3
Pope, Alexander, 21, 227
Powys, J.C., 215
Prior, Roger, 237

Richard II, 6, 7, 27, 58, 68, 145, 181–3, 196, 198
Richard III, 3, 5, 69, 140, 169–71, 186, 195–6
Rollins, Hyder, 231
Romeo and Juliet, 39–43, 51–66 *passim*, 202
Rowse, A.L., 233–6, 237
Rylands, George, *Words and Poetry*, 93

Schmidt, A., *Shakespeare-Lexicon*, 40
Seltzer, Daniel, 114, 136
Sheridan, R.B., *The Critic*, 183
Siddons, Mrs, 72
Skillan, George, 187
Smith, Hallett, 136
Sonnets, 28, 120–1, 196, 198, 200–3, 221–39 *passim*
Spencer, Thomas, 61
Spenser, Edmund, 5
Staunton, H. (editor), 57
Steevens, George, 121, 189, 227–8
Stirling, Mrs, 61, 63
Stokes, Charlotte, C., 232
Stoll, E.E., 189
Sutherland, James, 136

Taming of the Shrew, 164
Tempest, 45, 127–8

Timon of Athens, 214
Titus Andronicus, 194–5, 198
Tree, Beerbohm, 218
Troilus and Cressida, 46–50, 83, 124, 134, 163
Twelfth Night, 125–6, 141, 167
Twine, Lawrence, *Patterne of Painefull Adventures*, 115, 116
Two Gentlemen of Verona, 166–7
Tyler, Thomas, 229–30, 231

Van Doren, Mark, 206

Venus and Adonis, 196–200 *passim*, 208
Vickers, Brian, 2, 5, 93

Walker, Alice, 3, 188
Wells, Stanley, 235
Willcock, Gladys, 3, 13
Williams, G. Walton, 57–8
Wilson, Dover, 57, 106
Winter's Tale, 5, 43–4, 114, 120, 131–49 *passim*, 183, 186